KU-653-538

Also by Melanie McGrath

NON-FICTION

Silvertown

The Long Exile

Hopping

FICTION

Motel Nirvana

The Boy in the Snow

White Heat

The Bone Seeker

Give Me the Child

The Guilty Party

Pie and Mash
down the Roman Road

100 years of love and life in one East End market

MELANIE MCGRATH

TWO
ROADS

www.tworoadsbooks.com

Some names, places and features have been changed to preserve anonymity.

First published in Great Britain in 2018 by Two Roads Books
An imprint of John Murray Press
An Hachette UK company

4

This paperback edition first published in 2019

A CIP catalogue record for this title is available from the British Library

Paperback ISBN 9781473641976
eBook ISBN 9781473641983

Typeset in Bembo MT by Hewer Text UK Ltd, Edinburgh
Printed and bound in Great Britain by Clays Ltd, Elcograf S.p.A.

Hodder & Stoughton policy is to use papers that are natural, renewable
and recyclable products and made from wood grown in sustainable
forests. The logging and manufacturing processes are expected to
conform to the environmental regulations of the country of origin.

Hodder & Stoughton Ltd
Carmelite House
50 Victoria Embankment
London EC4Y 0DZ

With gratitude to everyone who shared their stories and in memory of Alfie Burns, 1945–2016, and Ted Lewis, 1929–2017, true cockney gentlemen.

Everything needs to change so
everything can stay the same
Giuseppe Tomasi di Lampedusa, *The Leopard*

I

> I've had many a curry in a hurry,
> Many a rabbit out of habit.
> But the one thing that still makes me squeal
> Is a pie, some mash and a jellied eel.
>
> T. Rundall

A middle-aged man walks off a flight from Sydney, gets into a minicab and asks to be taken to Kelly's eel, pie and mash shop on the Roman Road in London's East End. He's lived in Australia for thirty years and thinks of himself as an Aussie now, but ever since the plane left Sydney he's been dreaming of his first taste of eel jelly, which, in spite of everything, remains the flavour of home.

On the other side of London, where the city borders Essex, a pregnant woman makes her way on to the Central Line, heading for Mile End station. From there she'll take the 339 bus to Ford Road then walk the couple of minutes down the Roman to Kelly's, where she will order a 'two and two', two pies and two helpings of mash, with liquor. Though she seldom eats pie and mash these days (there aren't many pie and mash shops in Essex), she's had cravings for a two and two throughout her pregnancy and thinks it might be something to do with wanting to connect the baby in her belly to a heritage she barely remembers but in some undefined way continues to live by.

A few miles to the south of the pregnant woman a man is released from Brixton prison in the clothes he was wearing when he came in ten years before, carrying a travel warrant and a £46 discharge grant. He's not sure where he'll spend the night but before he even thinks about that there's something else he must do. At Brixton Tube he gets on the Victoria Line, changes at Oxford Circus and heads east on the Central Line to Mile End station. From there it's ten minutes' walk to Kelly's in Bow. In the decade he's been inside, the district has changed so much it is almost unrecognisable. It's market day on the Roman Road. Among the traders are a few familiar faces – Rashid with the unpronounceable surname, Tracy and her mum – but it's mostly strangers from outside the area. The man recalls the time you could buy anything you could name here; meat, fruit, haberdashery, even eels. Now, it's almost entirely clothes, mostly cabbage* or overstock. On the Roman, where the old grocers used to be, a café selling fancy coffee and overpriced toasties disguised as paninis is crowded with beardy young men and skinny girls. The old printers, Arber & Sons, has closed and the ironmongers has become a cycle shop. Opposite the library, which is now called an 'ideas store', there's a Tesco Metro. A new market has set up in the car park beside Ace cars, selling things the man can't imagine ever needing. Here the toasties are £6.50 a pop. For an additional fifty pence the man can get double pie, mash and liquor, though it's not really about the price. The moment he enters Kelly's eel, pie and mash shop the man is reminded of everything he has lost, of everything he has, and of the things that might one day make their way back to him. The cost of a plate of pie and mash matters less to him than its value, or rather, *values*. It's the values represented by pie and mash that have drawn him here.

For a hundred years the Kelly family has been serving beef pies and mashed potato and parsley liquor, and jellied and hot stewed eels to the people of Bow, Mile End and Bethnal Green (and

---

Cabbage is the overstock or seconds from the tailoring trade. The word itself is derived from the French *carbage* or *garbage*, meaning the remnants left over when cutting cloth.

further afield). And for more than a century generations of East Enders (from all parts of the world) have grown up on what has come to be known as *the* Londoner's meal. As the fields east of the Old Gate (now Aldgate) were turned into market gardens and as huddled terraces divided by railway lines were built on those gardens and then sandwiched between factories; as the docks opened to the south and canals were dug and Victoria Park was carved from gravel pits and land too poor to grow on; as terraces crumbled or were bombed or slum-cleared and replaced by council estates and tower blocks; as the docks closed and tower blocks were pulled down and 'affordable' flats built in their place and the factories converted into artists' studios and some very unaffordable flats; as a velodrome and athletics track appeared alongside more unaffordable flats on the marshes, and houseboats collected on to the canals where once horses towed timber barges, and West Ham United Football Club moved its stadium to the old Olympic Park – during all this time Kelly's has continued to bake minced beef pies with rough puff pastry tops and a dough base and serve them with mashed potatoes and parsley liquor and with hot or jellied eels on the side.

But even Kelly's has changed. Today there are shops in Bethnal Green, Roman Road and Debden, all run independently by different branches of the Kelly family. At the Roman Road shop, managed by Sue Vening, née Kingdon, and her son Neil, chicken, ham and leek and vegetarian pies are now served alongside the more traditional beef. The provenance of the ingredients is listed on their website (beef from Aberdeen Angus Hereford crosses reared by Tim Johnson of Stokes Marsh Farm in Wiltshire and sold by Walter Rose & Son; free-range chicken breast in the chicken pies; potatoes from East Anglia; eels from Barneys of Billingsgate; vegan apple crumble using Kentish apples, served with dairy-free ice cream). There will be East Enders of all stripes eating at the Formica tables: octogenarian cockneys, market porters, builders and tradesmen, families from the Afro-Caribbean community, plus hipsters, Japanese tourists, artists and outsiders whose roots are in the East End and whose hearts have never left it.

I cannot claim to be an East Ender, though my mother certainly was, and her mother, and many generations before her. My parents met in East Ham and both had family deeply rooted in Bishopsgate, Bow, Bethnal Green, Mile End, Poplar and the outer suburbs of West and East Ham and Waltham Forest. By the time I arrived Mum and Dad, like so many East Enders after the war, had moved out to Essex, so I was born in Romford. Now I live in Hackney in east London, I think of myself as part of the cockney diaspora. London has been my home for more than thirty years and ever since my father's untimely death a quarter of a century ago sent me on a search for my roots, I have been drawn to the East End by the conviction that, for me, its history is by a long mile the richest and most textured in the capital. Nothing I've ever learned about any other part of London, which, of course, is bursting with the past, has caused me to waver from that view. For unlike Westminster, say, or the City, the East End's history is not about buildings or the great institutions of state. Unlike south, west and much of north London, it's not about urban development or suburbanisation. At its heart, the East End's history is about trade, and the dynamic flows of people, capital and goods which trade both demands and sustains. At its broadest, it is about how the great upheavals of industrial revolution, Empire, war, mass migration and now globalisation, themselves intimately connected to trade, have shaped a corner of the city and its inhabitants. At a micro level it's about the relationships, whether between newcomers and the long established, between classes, neighbours or within families, which trade in goods or labour either promotes or discourages. Nowhere is this more vividly true than in the Roman Road.

The great eighteenth-century economist Adam Smith observed that we are a nation of shopkeepers. This phrase is frequently repeated by politicians or diplomats, often disparagingly, to make a point or further an agenda, but to me it lies at the raw, life-giving heart of a great truth about us as Britons. In our water and in our bones we're traders, with all the good (dynamic, quick-thinking, relationship-orientated) and the sometimes not so good (transactional, opportunist, exploitative) this implies. I challenge anyone who has ever been to a Sunday morning car boot sale or a late opening night at a shopping centre, a livestock market in the West Country or the trading room in a City brokerage, a street market or Oxford Circus on Christmas Eve to doubt the truth of this.

This fact about us, the nugget of truth at the heart of our identity, is nowhere more on display than in the market stalls and shops of the East End, and in the ghostly remnants of its docks and warehouses. To get to the real meat of us as islanders, Britons, and Londoners, why not start there, with something as simple and as iconic as a shop selling the Londoner's meal of pie, mash and eels? It cannot tell the whole story, which is as complex and dynamic as trade itself, but just as an archaeologist in revealing a scrap of pottery or a fragment of mosaic in the rubble of a building site on which a skyscraper is about to be built can cast light on the history of the Roman Empire and its citizens, a light shone on a pie, mash and eel shop in what might at first seem to be an unremarkable road in east London can help illuminate more general truths about who we really are. Working on this book has been very much like undertaking an archaeological dig. By delving into pies and mash and eels, and the lives of people who made and ate them, who washed up the plates in the kitchen or served at the counter or passed by the shop on their way to work or to the market, the people who lived in the grid of streets around or worked in the nearby shops or played in the park up the road, or whose lives intersected in meaningful ways with others who did, I have tried to reveal parts of London's history through stories that are often obscured – and sometimes literally built over – by other, flashier narratives.

A set of established customs around the consumption of pie and mash marks out the eater as a Londoner. A Londoner will not eat their pie face up, but will turn it over and make a tear in the pastry base with a fork and spoon (never a knife) to let out the steam before beginning. Seasonings are kept to a minimum – ground white pepper and salt and vinegar will usually do. A chilli pepper might spice up the vinegar. The mash will be just that, potato, and the liquor will be a simple concoction of flour, water and dried or fresh parsley. Eels will be boiled with a bit of white pepper, salt and perhaps a chilli pepper or two, and either served hot or left to cool and jellify. Jellied eels are served in a separate little bowl. Few pie and mash shops sell hot eels now, but some, like Kelly's, still do. There are those who prefer a portion of hot stewed eels and mash without the pie. The occasional oddball, often on a nostalgia trip, will ask only for mash and liquor to remind them of their penniless childhood, or because they don't like pastry, or just because they can. Your preferred temperature for your meal, whether the pie crust is better browned or slightly burned, whether the liquor is poured on the plate first or on the potato, or else on the pie or pies, or just on top of everything; how much vinegar, salt and white pepper to add; and what, if anything, is good to drink before, during or after the meal, are all matters of personal taste. Ketchup, brown sauce, mustard, mayonnaise or any other kind of condiment is neither traditional nor, indeed, provided. You could bring your own. No one would ask you to leave, but there might be pointed looks or even laughter. Any variation on this basic theme would mark the eater out as someone who is not a Londoner. And in an eel, pie and mash shop in London most of the customers are Londoners, eager to come across as Londoners, or curious as to what it feels like to be a Londoner.

Like most Londoners, at least those of working-class origin, I've eaten my fair share of pie, mash and liquor, not least while research-ing this book. I have sat in the kitchen at Kelly's on the Roman as the morning's batch of pies has emerged from the oven, stirred cooking eels and watched mash turning in great vats. I've listened to the flow of conversation between customers as they announce births and deaths, dispute good naturedly over politics, laugh and grumble about the state of the world or the temperature of the liquor, because Kelly's is the sort of place where regulars come to share their lives with one another. I have taped interviews, but I have also sat at a corner table on my own nursing a mug of tea and felt both distant and impatient, keen to get back to my less intimate but more habitual world of Facebook and broadband. Then, as the morning has slipped towards lunchtime and the bustle has grown louder and the action has moved from the back of the shop to the front, I've found myself fully immersed in the liveliness, the rootedness, the toing and froing, the sheer pleasure that continuity and the sense of witnessing a ritual both ancient and everyday brings. And I've forgotten all about Facebook and the rest, because compared to this it's hard to see how they count.

This book isn't about me or my family – I've written on both these subjects elsewhere – except in so far as it deals with themes dear to my heart (namely home and a sense of belonging), along with a desire to discover in the layered history of east London something of my own, but it is perhaps a bid fully to comprehend how what we like to think of as new is often not new at all. With our smartphones and hot spots and general bustle, it can sometimes seem we have little in common with the people who inhabited London a hundred years ago or a thousand years before that. But I wonder whether that's something we tell ourselves in order to make living in a place as rich in history as London feel more spacious and less clamorous with the voices of the dead? Cities change all the time, their dynamism is part of their pull, but the reasons for those changes often don't change at all. The same is true of the people who inhabit them. Human desires, needs, aspirations, failures are the same wherever and whenever. Only the ways those needs, desires, aspirations and failures are pursued, expressed or else avoided really change.

On one level this book is about pie and mash. But it's also about those fundamental human impulses. If I've done my job well, you should be able to imagine yourself sitting at a table in Kelly's eel, pie and mash shop on the Roman over the course of a hundred years, watching the world go by and picking up the flavour of the place and the warp and weft of the lives of some of the people who are or were closely or loosely linked to it, either because they are related to the founder, or because they or their families were or are regulars, or because they hauled the potatoes or managed the counters, or bought pies to take away or ran market stalls down the same stretch of street, or worked in the family-run businesses that grew up along-side Kelly's, because they spent their schooldays at the Roman Road school opposite and ate pies at dinner time or else didn't eat pies but came in for a penn'orth of mash and liquor. By the end of this book, if I've done my job well, you will know more about what it means to be a Londoner and have a greater sense, specifically, of how it feels to be an East Ender whose head is in the twenty-first century but whose feet still walk the Roman Road.

Many of the customers in this book are Kelly's regulars, though there are a few who come in only once, never to return. Sometimes a whole life is revealed, other times only snippets; it may be some-one's everyday world or one or two incidents or events which, for the person involved, have overshadowed all the rest. Some of the stories here are family histories, encompassing generations of Kellys, Robertsons, Lucionis, Randolfis, Da Costas, Plentys, Arbers, Shratskys and Bakers, who worked variously as pie-makers and eel dealers, tram drivers, match-makers, looking-glass gilders, printers, ice-cream makers, café proprietors, costermongers, barrow builders, newspaper vendors, market traders and Billingsgate porters. Others are the tales of individuals whose lives intersect with the shop: people like Marian Old who manned (or womanned) the public toilets; Sylvia Pankhurst who based her East London Federation of Suffragettes just round the corner, and handed out suffragist pamphlets to the lunchtime queue; Ron Moss who as a kid filched sausages from the butcher's stall down the road; Ann Simmons who shopped with her mum down the Roman in what was then called the 'women's market'; Ray Gipson who rose to become a Tower Hamlets councillor; Christine Yeend who with her wild sister Georgia scoured the Roman on market day for hot pants and platform boots; Tel Willets who once painted Lady Di's loo, and ate eight Kelly's pies in a pie-eating competition with his mate; and Meg Bradley, Kelly's long-serving manageress whose working life could be measured out in pies and scoops of mash. All these people, and most others in the stories that follow, either knew one another directly or by one or two degrees of separation, because, wherever their lives took them, all roads on the Roman eventually led back to Kelly's.

The stories are true, and like all life stories they are based on recollections. In a couple of cases, people's names and identifying details have been altered at their request. Wherever it has been possible to check the facts that has been done, but sometimes the view through the window is obscured by time and memory and it isn't always possible to know what is fact and what is family lore or something that feels so true to the teller that it is indistinguishable from actuality. In one way it doesn't matter. We all create myths about our lives and those of our families to sustain us, to give us a sense of continuity in a world that transforms almost daily. A plate of eels, pie and mash with liquor is a kind of myth too, one understood by millions of ordinary men and women to represent a way of life which is always in the process of changing while, in some small but essential way, remaining forever the same.

2

On Mother Kelly's doorstep – down Paradise Row . . .

George Stevens, 'On Mother Kelly's Doorstep' (1925)

Samuel Robert Kelly and his wife Matilda opened the first Kelly's eel, pie and mash shop on 14 March 1915 on Bethnal Green Road near the junction with Paradise Row,* a couple of miles east of Shoreditch along the busy thoroughfare connecting Shoreditch and the City in the west to Bethnal Green in the east. To the north lay Haggerston and to the south Stepney and Mile End and beyond that, Shadwell, Poplar and the docks. The district was anything but a paradise, though like the rest of the East End, Bethnal Green had its patches of grandeur. The Green itself in 1915 was a public garden (a rarity in these parts), bordered on the north side by an imposing red-brick terrace of large Georgian houses and a red-brick museum, and to the south by the grand early nineteenth-century edifice of St John's Church, where Samuel (we'll call him Sam the Pie) and Matilda were married. Here the road crossed Cambridge Road,† with the Salmon and Ball pub on one side and the Bethnal Lunatic

---

* Paradise Row was and partly remains a pretty cobbled street of Georgian town houses. It is notable for being the home of 'Mother Kelly' or Nelly Moss, a Jewish Lithuanian immigrant whose son, Billy Martin, became Deputy Mayor of Finsbury in 1939, and also of Daniel Mendoza, aka 'Mendoza the Jew', aka 'The Human Windmill', a pugilist of Portuguese descent who became English prizefighting champion between 1792 and 1795.

† Cambridge Road was renamed Cambridge Heath Road in the interwar period, long after the heath itself had been built upon.

Asylum on the other, before narrowing into Green Street and then widening out once more to become the Roman Road.

The district was still surrounded by grand old Victorian factories. Here and there buildings had been added and subtracted or repurposed, the tram had arrived, and Victoria Park Cemetery had been converted into Meath Gardens. The old Bancroft's Hospital on the Mile End Road was by then the People's Palace community centre, and Mile End workhouse, at the northern end of the Jews' Burial Ground, had become more euphemistically known as the Guardians' Institution. Up and down the Roman Road numerous small patches of undeveloped ground had been recently filled with three-bedroom terraces, sawmills, chemical and fertiliser works and coal depots. The Regent's canal hemmed in the area to the east and on the border with Mile End Old Town to the south, trains rushed along the Great Eastern Railway en route to greener, leafier outlying suburbs. In 1915 Bethnal Green remained a district defined by water, rail and industry, with a population that could be described, for the most part, as falling somewhere between 'respectable' poverty and chronic want.

On the day of the pie shop's opening, the Kelly family had been living in England for nearly a century. The last Kelly family member to be born in Ireland, Robert Kelly, Sam the Pie's great-grandfather, had left Cork for London around 1820, fleeing the agricultural depression following the Napoleonic Wars. Instead of the promised city paved with gold, he found the brown murk east of the Aldgate pump. In 1820 London was in a period of rapid development. Moorfields, until the early nineteenth century just a patch of open marsh ground, had recently been built upon. The tenter grounds around Spitalfields had been filled in, and the area's original population of weavers was moving eastwards and building terraces of large-windowed houses most suited to their trade in Globe Town and Bethnal Green. In the twenty years since the start of the nineteenth century the population of Globe Town had more than doubled. In the decade after Robert arrived, it would triple.

Not long after he arrived in London, Robert Kelly married Mary Kicks in St Dunstan's Church in Stepney. Mary was a Kentish woman by birth but, like Robert himself, her family had moved to London to find work. The couple lived at first in Mile End Old Town then settled in Stratford, just over the River Lea from Bow, where their son Samuel, who we'll call Sam the Sailor, was born in 1833. Back then Stratford was a rapidly developing but still parochial backwater, its riverine margins lined with slaughterhouses, timber and coal yards, tanners and other noxious industries, as well as a famous porcelain works, and with its own dock and wharves. Away from the banks of the Lea the settlement was still green with market gardens and fields of potatoes. (It seems Londoners had an appetite for mash even then.)

Several more children were born before Mary died, aged forty-three, in 1844. Between 1845 and 1855 around 2 million Irish fled the Great Famine in their country, many arriving in east London attracted by the prospect of jobs in the docks and the new railways. With a few exceptions, the new arrivals lived in the poorest areas and had the worst jobs, often as casual labourers in the docks and coal yards. Not everyone found employment, and a significant number ended up on the streets at the mercy of charitable institutions. The great chronicler of the Victorian East End, Henry Mayhew, estimated that in the 1850s 10,000 Irish men and women were scraping a living on London's streets hawking and costermongering, among other things, meat and eel pies. The newcomers quickly found themselves the target of resentment not only among the English but also among more established Irish immigrants. Their poverty crept like a bad smell over their former countrymen, including families like the Kellys, who were now firmly settled in the capital.

The census of 1851 doesn't record what Robert Kelly thought about the 'famine Irish', though it does tell us that he was living back across the Lea in Bromley-by-Bow and working in the West India Docks. The London docks were expanding, with Victoria

Dock opening the same year Robert and Mary's eldest son, Sam the Sailor, married nineteen-year-old Martha Holt. The couple moved near to the new dock, to a location now occupied by a Holiday Inn Express, with Martha's mother Ellen and older brother Mark. There Martha gave birth to the couple's children Truman, Robert, twins Samuel (who we'll call Sam the Cabinetmaker) and Ellen, Sarah and Joseph. As a boy Sam the Cabinetmaker would have witnessed the transformation of the area from the tranquil little backwater of his parents' childhoods to the swamp of housing, railway lines and sidings, factories and industrial development which went up to support the docks. Despite his father's profession, and the area's deep dependence on marine trade, Sam the Cabinetmaker wasn't tempted to go to sea. Instead, at the age of nineteen, he married his sweetheart, Catherine Bales, and settled into life as a cabinetmaker, working in one of the furniture workshops serviced by the neighbouring timberyards. In due course they too had children, the eldest of whom, Samuel Robert, or Sam the Pie, Robert Kelly's great-grandson, would be responsible for changing the Kelly family's fortune.

After a spell in his father's line of work, Sam the Pie got a job driving the horses on the London tram system. By the outbreak of the First World War the system had been electrified and was now the largest electric tram system in Europe, and Sam the Pie was working as a driver. Since bus and tram driving was a reserved occupation, Sam the Pie wasn't in danger of being called up, and his two sons with Matilda, George and Sam Junior, were too young and therefore also exempt. Compared to foundry work, say, or mining or soldiering, tram driving wasn't a particularly dangerous occupation, but it wasn't entirely safe either. The new electric trams travelled at speed and ran away and derailed more frequently than the old horse-drawn vehicles. At some point in the lead up to the war Sam the Pie had an accident. It may be that the tram he was driving turned over or collided with another vehicle or with a horse, or that the brake failed and he was caught under a wheel.

The only major tram accident recorded around that time was in south London on 2 September 1911, when the London County Council number 110 tram derailed on Lewisham High Road, leaving one dead and thirty-five injured. It's possible that Samuel may have been involved in this; on the other hand, he may have got caught up in another accident at a different time no longer recorded. As to the nature of the injury, it's a bit of a mystery. There's a clue from Alfie Burns, though. Alfie was a schoolfriend of Sam the Pie's grandson and was a child in the thirties, and he recalls that one of the man's legs was longer than the other and that he walked with a limp. What we do know is that Sam the Pie was sufficiently badly injured to end his career on the trams, but that he successfully claimed some modest compensation from his employers at London County Council. And it was with this money that he was able, for the first time, to take full charge of his destiny. And so the accident, which could quite easily have killed him, in one way saved his life. No longer was he dependent on low wages and the grind of the nine-to-five. By the time he opened his first pie and mash shop in March 1915, Samuel Robert Kelly had become his own man.

As anyone who's ever eaten in a pie and mash shop in the capital knows, there is only one true London pie. It's oval in shape, about 6 inches in length and 4 inches at its widest. The base and sides are a pastry dough, similar to shortcrust but not quite so fatty, the top is a richer rough puff, made with white flour, water, margarine and a little salt, and rolled slightly thicker than the sides and base. The top crust simply rests on the remainder of the shell. There's no fluting or fancy pinchwork or scalloping. A pie is not a pasty. The filling is nothing more (or less) than seasoned minced beef, and not a very generous quantity of it. There's enough fat in the meat to keep it moist and produce a small amount of gravy. The gravy shouldn't gush from the crust once cut, but sit companionably with the meat awaiting the attentions of a fork.

Despite – or perhaps because of – its status as *the* London meal, the iconic food of the capital's working classes, the pie, like the Kellys – like most Londoners – is an immigrant. Eels, mashed potato and parsley are too, but we'll get to them later. Even the word *pie* is an import, derived from the old French word *pica* meaning 'magpie', presumably a reference to that bird's habit of stuffing its nest with found objects. Like so much we now think of as part of the British scene (apples, carrots, cats, heated baths, leeks, peas, police, rabbits and stinging nettles), pies were first introduced to Britain by the Romans, though they in turn almost certainly borrowed the idea of enclosing meat inside an envelope of pastry made with flour and olive oil from the Greeks, who may well have got it from the ancient Egyptians. We know that the Egyptians and the Greeks both enjoyed sweet cakes and pastries made with honey, dates and nuts and a version of what we now think of as filo pastry. Sweet pastries are mentioned by the Greek playwright, Aristophanes. In the Roman version the pastry is merely used as a cover to prevent meat from burning and keep it moist while it cooks over an open fire. Once the meat was cooked the pastry was peeled away and discarded.

As the Romans moved north they were forced to substitute olive oil for more readily available lard and butter, and a more palatable and mouldable shortcrust pastry was born. It's this version that the Romans most likely brought to the marshy terrain of what became the Roman settlement of Londinium over the River Lea at Old Ford, somewhere between the current Roman and Bow Roads, and only a few moments' walk from Samuel and Matilda Kelly's original eel, pie and mash shop.

The pie's portability made it particularly popular with those whose work took them far from home, such as shepherds, hunters and foresters, and it proved invaluable at sea, where space and stability are at a premium and a meal needs to be carried in the hand. Crusaders returned from the Middle East with the idea of adding spices and fruits to pies, in part to disguise spoiled meat.

The earliest English pie recipe is in the mid-fourteenth-century book *Forme of Cury*,* written on a velum scroll, the official record of recipes used in Richard II's court. In the book the pies are called 'chastletes', 'little castles' or 'coffins', and, translated into modern English, the recipe reads as follows:

> Roll out a sheet of good pastry so it's a foot long and the width of your forearm. Cut four little castles from the sides of the roll and another, bigger one, in the middle. In the middle castle put a mixture of pork and raw egg with salt and colour it with saffron. Into another put crème of almonds and another cream with egg. Colour them with sandalwood. Fasten the edges of the pastry at the top. Carve keyntlich [battlements] out of the pastry, and dry them in an oven or in the sun until they're hard. For an alternative filling use a mixture of figs, raisins, apples and pears or use meat prepared as you would for blanched fritters and colour it green. Bake the castles in the oven and serve with hot water.

The Doomsday Book of 1086 records eight mills on the banks of the Lea River and its tributaries, and in the thirteenth century bakehouses and flour mills lined the banks of the Lea on both sides, using waterwheels to generate the energy to grind wheat as well as to mix dough. By the fourteenth century the hamlets of Old Ford and Bow, then rural settlements not far from the city walls at Aldgate (Old Gate), were gaining a reputation as London's bakehouse. Early each morning carts of loaves trundled west through Aldgate bound for the markets in Cheapside and Bishopsgate.

Such was the rivalry between the bakers at Stratford, Bow, Old Ford and Bromley-by-Bow and those in the City that the 'Bromley' loaf was required to be heavier than the 'London' loaf, with the mayor himself supervising the weighing. City bakers were subject

---

* *Cury* is the Middle English term for cookery.

to tougher restrictions than those set by the bishop's court outside the city's walls, though, so while any Bow or Old Ford baker selling underweight loaves would be liable to a fine, a baker convicted of the same offence within the walls could be dragged on hurdles or flung into Newgate prison. Bow's bakers continued to undercut the city bakers and got round the rules for underweight loaves by sending out women to do the selling since women, considered feeble-minded, were not held personally liable for acts of blatant fraud. So dependent did London become on Bow's bakeries that William Langland in *Piers Plowman*, written around 1370, speaks of the alarm generated in London when, during a spring drought, the bread carts failed to arrive from the east.

All this says more about life in the hamlets lying to the east of the city walls than it does about the city itself. Survival in the hamlets demanded a particular canniness and mental agility. For centuries the inhabitants there found ways to get around laws imposed by a city establishment unwilling to share its privileges. Being outliers made them resourceful, bloody-minded and entrepreneurial. It still does.

There were times, though, when circumstances so conspired against the residents of the outlying hamlets that no amount of ingenuity was sufficient to overcome them. One such event took place at the start of the fourteenth century when the bridge spanning the Lea at Old Ford, where the Romans first entered London and which had become the main route from the east into the city, collapsed. A journeyman named Godfrey Pratt was tasked by the Abbot of Stratford with repairing it and keeping it open and free to travellers. For this service Pratt was paid in loaves baked in the abbot's own bakehouse. But Pratt grew greedy and started imposing an additional toll. The abbot responded by stopping his bread allowance, and Pratt gave up the job. From then on, bakers in Stratford were no longer guaranteed passage over the bridge, and although bread baked inside the city walls was more expensive, Londoners found they could rely more on local bakers, the medieval equivalent of shopping at the corner shop rather than driving to the out-of-town shopping centre. By 1500 city bakers had outpaced their eastern rivals and bread baking in Bow and Stratford was on the decline.

Over the next few centuries the settlements east of the Tower rose and fell and rose again, and by the end of the eighteenth century there were rows of grand houses and elegant terraces scattered all along Mile End Road and Commercial Road, inhabited by ship owners and wealthy merchants. By the time Robert Kelly arrived in around 1820, though, many of the district's wealthier inhabitants had moved elsewhere, or were about to, and speculators were busy building terraces of small, poorly built workers' cottages with no sewage systems to house migrants drawn away from the land to work in the docks and, later, on the railways. With the exception of a few main thoroughfares like Mile End Road and Cambridge Road, and one or two smart enclaves such as Tredegar Square, the area around Bow, Bethnal Green and Old Ford was on the way to becoming a slum.

With long working hours and the absence of decent kitchens and cool stores in the flop houses and lodgings, the need arose for plentiful supplies of cheap, nourishing hot food to feed the growing ranks of workers who supplied an expanding capital with furniture, leatherwork and clothes from the many thousands of tiny workshops and ateliers that had sprung up like weeds east of the Aldgate. And as the need arose, itinerant piemen arrived on the streets to meet it. 'The itinerant trade in pies is one of the most ancient of the street callings of London,' noted Henry Mayhew, who counted about forty itinerant piemen in London in the winter and about eighty in the summer. The pies were often made by bread bakers as a sideline – pastry doesn't require such high oven temperatures as bread, so pies are ideal for using up the heat in cooling bread ovens. They are humble inventions, both in the original sense of *umble*, a word for minced offal derived from the French for deer offal, *nomble*, and in the sense of being an ideal food for the poor (you can stick more or less anything in a pie and the chances are it will taste delicious).

In the early Victorian period eel pies were more common and cheaper than meat pies but eels are bony and fiddly to eat, and, as the prosperity of the city grew, minced beef gained in popularity over fish. The meat – 'stickings' or trimmings – would be bought in pieces and put through a mincer by the pieman or baker. Half an ounce (14 grams) per pie was the norm, about the size of a large walnut or small ping-pong ball. Rancid butter or lard would have been used for the pastry along with weevily flour. In 1869 the French chemist Hippolyte Mège-Mouriès invented a method of churning beef fat with milk to make margarine, which was both cheaper than butter and kept better, and from then on the pastry for the pies sold on the streets of London would almost always have been enriched with margarine. The manufacturing cost of five dozen pies in the mid nineteenth century was about 2s 6d, and the profit about the same. Each pieman carried a portioned metal can with two drawers, one at the top for cold pies one at the bottom for pies kept warm from a charcoal fire beneath. The pies were served with 'gravy of salt, browned flour and water' poured into a hole poked into the top of the pie with a finger until the crust rose. Despite the mark-up, it was hard to make a living selling pies in the street. Mayhew found one pieman catering to the porters in Billingsgate fish market who sold 240 pies in a day, but he was a rarity. Most sellers were boys or men unable to find more lucrative work.

According to Mayhew, 'The generality of customers are the boys of London', many of them costermongers, and 'The best times are during any grand sight or holiday-making', or from ten at night to one in the morning. Women seldom, if ever, bought pies in the streets. And so Victorian piemen would often wait outside pubs at closing time, in the hope of catching drunk and hungry men on their way home – the nineteenth-century equivalent of a burger van. It was common practice in Victorian London for a pieman and his customer to toss a coin. If the pieman won the toss, his customer had to give him a penny without getting anything in return. If he lost, the customer got the pie for nothing. For the customer it might well have been the only chance of a meal that day. For the pieman it might have been the only way to shift old stock before it went bad. Mayhew also reports that 'gentlemen out on the spree' would often toss for pies for the sport. If they won they would amuse themselves by throwing the pies at one another, or, if they were drunk enough, at the hapless pieman.

Parsley sauce, that bright green goop known as liquor, is synonymous with the London pie, but parsley too is an immigrant, having originated in the central Mediterranean, where, according to Greek mythology, it sprang from the blood of the infant Archemoros, after his nursemaid laid him in a patch of 'wild celery' and he was bitten by a snake. (The Latin name for parsley is *Carum petroselinum*, from the Greek words *petros*, meaning 'rock', and *selinon*, meaning 'celery'). The plant was considered a forerunner of death and was not eaten by people but, as Homer relates, given to chariot horses on their way to battle. The ancient Romans didn't eat parsley either, but they did wear wreaths of the herb around their heads to ward off evil spirits, and it may be that this is how, like pastry and pies themselves, the herb first reached Britain. It was initially paired with fish and appeared in a sauce served with eels and eel pie.

Potatoes are a more recent arrival in Britain than pies or parsley. They arrived from Peru, where they had been cultivated by the Incas since 5–8000BC, somewhere between 1588 and 1593, either by Sir Francis Drake or by Sir Walter Raleigh's employee, Thomas Harriot. In 1662 the Royal Society recommended their cultivation, though they were primarily grown as animal feed and did not become a staple part of the British diet until the late nineteenth century, when the French Revolutionary Wars brought about food shortages. The first recipe for mashed potatoes may have originated with the French pharmacist and obsessive potato promoter

Antoine Parmentier. Having been captured by the Germans in 1757 and fed a diet almost entirely of potatoes, on his return to France in 1763 he spent his life promoting the tuber, trial planting a potato bed in the Tuileries Palace, watched over by armed guards who were instructed to accept bribes to 'steal' the crop, and persuading Marie Antoinette to wear a posy of potato flowers. Another, more plausible candidate is the British food writer Hannah Glasse, who includes a recipe for mashed potatoes made with milk, butter and salt in her 1747 cookbook *The Art of Cookery made Plain and Easy*. The version of mashed potato at Kelly's calls for salt and pepper but no added dairy in the form either of butter or milk. Added flavour is provided by liquor, though this, too, differs from its original incarnation. Until the middle of the last century liquor was made with the fishy water left over from boiling eels (the word *liquor* meaning a broth made from meat or fish) thickened with flour and seasoned with salt, pepper and parsley, but by the 1950s, as eels became more expensive and less popular, traditional liquor morphed into what is now effectively a very simple parsley sauce of seasoned flour, water and herb.

We don't know who first had the brilliant idea of putting pie and mash together but it seems likely to have happened in the Victorian era, when shops began to take custom from itinerant sellers of pies and hot jacket potatoes. Baked potatoes take a great deal of oven heat, time and space, but mashed potatoes can be made in twenty minutes on a burner and kept hot by means of steam. The first recorded pie and mash shop in London was Henry Blanchard's at 101 Union Street SE1, which opened for business in 1844 selling meat pies, mash from floury potatoes – King Edward, say, or Désirée – served with liquor. The shop also sold jellied eels made from freshly killed fish chopped into chunks, cooked in seasoned water and left to cool and form a natural jelly; hot stewed eels; split-pea soup made with hambone stock; and fruit pies. The new shops could bake pies more cheaply and serve them hotter and fresher than the mobile piemen, and offered customers a warm spot to perch while they ate. By 1874, according to Kelly's Directory,* there were thirty-three pie shops across London, and by the time S. Kelly ('pies a specialty') opened for business in Bethnal Green Road in 1915 there were more than a hundred, most famously Cooke's, founded by Alfred Cooke in 1899, and Manze's, whose first branch was established by the ice-cream maker and Italian immigrant Michele Manze in 1902. And so the itinerant pieman, 'one of the most ancient street callings of London', as Mayhew described it, had all but disappeared.

What we think of now as the iconic Londoner's meal is, like us, a product of Roman conquest, New World exploration, colonialism and immigration. Pie and mash is yesterday's version of chicken tikka masala and, like that current national favourite, it has both nourished us individually and forged deep bonds between us. To create it, we took a series of foreign imports and reshaped them according to our needs and by doing that we made them our own. It's what we British have always done. Which is what makes pie and mash much more than a meal. It's what makes it our nation's history on a plate.

---

* A trade directory founded in the mid nineteenth century listing the trades and business people of cities and towns in the United Kingdom. There is no relationship to the pie shop owners.

3

Women have always stood up for themselves in this area.

Ted Lewis*

A short walk east from Samuel and Matilda Kelly's first pie and mash shop in Bethnal Green Road brought you to Harold Street. The street no longer exists, having long since been slum-cleared, but in the late nineteenth and early twentieth centuries it was typical of the many impoverished alleys, backwaters and turnings of the late Victorian East End. The houses were modest two-storey, three-bedroom early Victorian terraces, mostly divided for multiple occupancy. Opposite number 19 sat a carpentry shop. At the top of the road were a bakehouse and a pub, but in his late-nineteenth-century poverty maps the social reformer Charles Booth categorised the whole street as 'very poor, casual, chronic want'.

It's 1888 now. In June, Henry Mayhew dies and Sam the Pie turns seven. In August the body of Mary Ann Nicols, the first known victim of Jack the Ripper, is found in Whitechapel. Unemployment in the East End stands at 27 per cent. The workhouses are full to bursting. Hundreds of homeless people sleep in the streets. In October demonstrations are ruthlessly put down by the police.

* Unless otherwise stated, the chapter epigraph text throughout the book is taken from interviews with the author.

In two rooms at number 19 Harold Street lives six-year-old Martha Robertson and her five siblings (there will eventually be nine), along with their father George, a casual labourer, and their mother Jane, a matchbox maker at the Bryant & May match factory in Fairfield Road, Bow, a mile or so east. Also at number 19 are another couple with their son, plus a woman, Ann Cousins, also a matchbox maker, with her six children, the eldest of whom, another Jane, makes matchboxes too. That's nineteen people living in five rooms and a scullery.

Martha, Ann and the two Janes are typical in that almost all the women and girls in the turning are matchbox makers. In 1888 and for the next eighty years Bryant & May factory will be one of the largest employers of women – as both homeworkers and site workers – in the East End. Men too work in the factory, at either end of the manufacturing cycle, hauling timber and loading boxes of finished matches onto horse-drawn carts for distribution, but the match-makers are overwhelmingly female. In 1888 there are around 1,400 women and girls working at the Fairfield Road plant, dipping matches, filling boxes and packing and labelling. Hundreds more, like Martha and her mother, work from home, making up matchboxes from pressed balsawood sheets. It's fiddly piecework which, in the absence of any space, must be done on the tiny kitchen table in the scullery. Any broken boxes have to be paid for. Splintered fingers, raw and infected nail beds, arthritic joints, what we would now call repetitive strain injury, plus dermatitis from constant contact with animal-bone glue all come with the job. Pay is two and a half pence per gross, which is to say, per 144 boxes, and to earn one penny Martha and her mother have to make 58 matchboxes.*

It's Martha's job to haul the newly made boxes to the factory, a distance of a mile or so, and exchange them for more blanks. Sometimes, when her mother is ill or there's no space to work at

* Some of the information in this section comes from *Striking a Light: The Bryant and May Matchwomen and their Place in History* by Louise Raw (Bloomsbury, 2009).

Harold Street, she will stay at the factory for a few hours making up boxes. Otherwise, she'll carry a few new sheets of blanks back home, stopping off en route to pick up milk and bread for the family breakfast. Work comes first. School has to fit around it.

Making up boxes is boring and exacting at any age but when you are six it must be crucifying. At least, though, it isn't actively dangerous, like splint dipping. In 1888 children do that job too, creating match-heads by dunking the wood splints into a mix containing white phosphorus. The children are told not to touch the phosphorus mixture or put it in their mouths, but they're kids so they forget and lick their fingers after they've handled the splints. Every year children die of phosphorus poisoning. White phosphorus is no longer used in match-heads – today it's a weapon of war, used in conflicts in Vietnam, Iraq and Syria.

The chemical also affects the women and girls working at the factory, entering their bodies through contaminated food. They cannot see, smell nor taste it, but they can't get away from it. There is nowhere to eat except at their workbenches, and the midday break isn't long enough to leave the building. The symptoms of phosphorous poisoning or 'phossy jaw' start with fatigue and yellowing of the hair or alopecia. There is nausea and lavishly fluorescent vomit. Skin begins to separate from bone. Foul-smelling pus collects in fistulas under the chin and ears. Before long the women's jawbones begin to disintegrate. Death is never very far away.

In 1888, as Martha and her mother are making balsawood blanks at home in Harold Street, the reformer Annie Besant publishes her findings about working conditions at the Bryant & May factory in Fairfield Road. 'White Slavery in London' appears in Besant's newspaper *The Link*.

The hours are 6.30–6 in the summer and 8–6 in the winter, with half an hour for breakfast and an hour for lunch, which is always called dinner. For that a young girl earns an average 4s a week for piecework of which 2s immediately goes on rent. Older married women are paid by the day and might earn 10s [a week]. There are deductions for everything from lateness to dirty feet.

The article creates a stir. Bryant & May's management do their best to force the women workers to sign a document refuting Besant's findings. The women refuse. Management scurries about looking for the source of the leak and suppose they have found it in three young workers. They do not dismiss the women immediately, which might to the outside world signal guilt, but instead keep them short of work and thus on at starvation wages for a week before – they hope – quietly letting them go. They certainly don't bank on the female workforce coming out on strike. Yet that is what happens. Fourteen hundred women and girls who cannot afford to be without the money nonetheless walk out in protest. At first the management stands firm, but the publicity is too much. On 16 July, two weeks after the women first down tools, management at the factory abolishes unfair fines and deductions for the cost of materials, establishes proper grievance procedures and sets aside a dining area so that the women can eat their lunch without it killing them. The strike is famous now, and from the vantage point of the twenty-first century it is hard to fully comprehend how radical it was back then, and what courage it took. The striking women had no employment rights, no strike pay, no savings, and only the encouragement of activist outsiders like Annie Besant, but they were determined and resolute, and all the more so, perhaps, because they knew they were fighting for their lives.

Martha is too young to take any active part in the strike, but she knows many who do, and later recalls the courage of the strikers in coming out even though they were poor, had children to feed, and with no strike fund to help them. She will never forget the horror of phossy jaw – the gutters outside the factory are often aglow in toxic, necrotising vomit – and even if at age six she does not fully understand the cause, there must have been moments when Martha could not fail to wonder whether a similar fate awaited her. It was thanks to the strike that it did not, and Martha continued to work at Bryant & May's for the remainder of what passed for her childhood and for most of her adult life, as we shall see.

Nearly a hundred and thirty years later, her grandson, Ted Lewis, shows me a photograph of his nan as a young woman, taken at Griffith's studios at Armagh Road. The image, which must have been captured at the very start of the twentieth century, is of a small-framed woman of around twenty, clothed in a tight bodice with three parallel straps and a frilly collar, sitting beneath a short, layered cape. She is standing with her right arm behind her back and her left forearm leaning on what looks like an upholstered chair. Martha has widely spaced black beads for eyes, a pretty mouth and wide flat nose. Her dark hair is curled into horizontal ringlets and she wears that odd, static expression common in early photographic portraits where the sitters had to remain still for a long time. But Martha's most striking attribute is her left hand, which is pressed into a loose fist, a real clodhopper, huge as a ham bone, the fingers five swollen sausages. It's a worker's hand, calloused and arthritic-looking, sore in winter, most like, and prone to hang nails and chilblains, but there is something defiant and persistent in that fist. It seems to say 'bring it on' to life, even to a life as hard and full of loss as Martha's.

Ted loved his nan. She was a warm and generous-hearted woman whose chief loves, aside from her family, were flirting, singing and having a good time. She wasn't averse to a Guinness or two. Ted remembers helping his father load Martha into a wheelbarrow outside some pub or other and wheeling her home, three sheets to the wind and belting out old music hall numbers. Later, when she had a little money, she would buy cockles for Sunday tea from the seafood seller who'd come round with his barrow, and on a Saturday lunchtime would treat the family to pie and mash from Old Walleye Kelly down in Bethnal Green. Nearly a hundred and thirty years later, her grandson, Ted, is still a regular customer.

4

You had the posh women, but people like my grandmother
were the muscle, the ones who threw the bricks.

Gary Arber

It is 1901, and at number 125, Tredegar Road – not to be
confused with the much posher Tredegar Square – not far from
Martha Robertson's home, in the shadow of St Stephen's
Church and the Tredegar Works, Emily Fosh tends to her baby
son. The baby's father is Walter Francis Arber, but at the time
of the birth Emily is a boarder in the house owned by Walter's
mother and father – Charles Arber, paper bag printer, and Lucy,
dressmaker – and she and Walter Arber are not married. The
Arber family are fixtures in the Roman Road, having a print
and toy shop just around the corner from where, in 1939, a new
branch of Kelly's pie and mash will open. The Arbers are also
Unitarians, generous spirited, remarkably unjudgemental for
the times, and willing to give shelter to Emily until such time
as a wedding can be arranged.

This act of generosity was not the first. Born four years earlier
than Martha Robertson, in 1877, but in no less difficult circumstances, Emily Fosh lost three sisters in childhood, and at twelve
found herself orphaned. She was sent to live with her elder sister
and brother-in-law, Eliza and Henry Bailey, in Stainsbury Street, a
comfortable turning according to Booth's, running perpendicular to
Cyprus Street, where the Kellys were then living. Neighbourhoods

28

being tightly knit in those days, it's possible that the two families knew one another.

At the age of thirteen Emily was already working with her sister, Eliza, making paper bags. It must be through their work that Emily met Charles Arber, who printed the bags for local shopkeepers. Charles must have taken to Emily or else taken pity on her, for some time in the 1890s he and his wife Lucy invited her to be their lodger. A few years after this, in 1900, Emily becomes pregnant by Walter, her landlord's son, and Walter junior is born.

In the East End at the turn of the twentieth century illegitimacy is both common and commonly frowned upon. Pregnant, unmarried women are often left to the mercy of nuns, lunatic asylums or the workhouse, as we shall see. But this is not Emily's fate. In September 1901 she and Walter are married at St Mark's in Victoria Park. They will go on to have another three sons and a daughter, all of whom will follow their father into the family business.

Like most women living in and around the Roman Road at this time, Emily Arber will do her shopping in the Roman Road market, or the women's market as it is often known. The men have their pubs, sports clubs, pigeon sheds, dog and horse tracks, where women are tolerated but by and large the talk is masculine. The market is where women go to shop and exchange pleasantries, ask after one another's children, find out where there might be paid work going, flirt with the stallholders and catch up on local gossip. In Emily Arber's day, 250 stalls cover over a mile, selling fruit, vegetables, haberdashery, chinaware and silverware, rags sized both for polishing and for weaving into rugs, stockings, flowers, cat's meat, pigs ears and trotters, sheep heads and hearts, stove blackening, gas light mantles, furniture polish, eels and shellfish, pies and muffins; and, above all, cabbage, of both the green and fabric kind.

Unlike Smithfield or Billingsgate, the Roman has no medieval charter. Nor is it, like the Caledonian (subsequently Bermondsey),

a market overt.* This may be why there has always been an infor-
mality about the Roman, and a kind of carnival atmosphere, a sense
not only that if you played your cards right you might come away
with a bargain and the satisfaction of knowing that, for the next few
days your children would be fed, but also that, in a small way, you
had turned the tables on your own poverty and outwitted a system
which in every other way worked against you. Being poor mattered
less down the Roman than almost anywhere else. In the East End
of the time a woman with children and few resources was only ever
a short slide from destitution. Her employer could sack her without
notice, her landlord could turf her out, she and her family could be
stalked by sickness, her husband could abandon her, her babies
might die, but in this one small corner of her life, in this daily act
of bargaining and provisioning, she could beat the cheese seller
down, pick up some bruised apples on the cheap, or persuade the
butcher to throw in a lamb's heart with a half-pound of sausages
and do it all playfully and with humour and without having to
demean herself or beg or be humiliated. The market was one of
life's few level playing grounds, perhaps the only one, and to wander
among the stalls a shopper could, at least for a few moments or a
few hours, feel what it was to be queen of her own destiny.

People have been trading in the Roman Road since, well, the
Romans. It was they who built the ford across the River Lea and
the road connecting London, then Londinium, to the fertile agricultural land beyond. In what is now Hertfordshire they founded
Verulamium, or St Albans, and in Essex, Colchester or Camulo-
dunum, populating both settlements with demobbed Roman
soldiers. En route they would have hunted birds, boar and deer in

---

* Charter and overt markets are both governed and regulated by medieval laws.
Overt market or *marché ouvert* laws stipulated that any buyer purchasing an item from
the market in daylight hours was entitled to keep it, even if the object subsequently
turned out to have been stolen. The last overt market in London, Bermondsey,
became notorious for dealing in stolen antiques and had its overt market status
revoked in 1994.

the forests and fished for bream, roach and eels in the River Lea, and there would no doubt have been some pillage and looting, but there must have been trade too. In AD 60 or 61, when the Roman settlement of Londinium was only twenty years old, Boudicca, Queen of the Iceni, led an army of 100,000 Iceni and Trinovantes from Colchester to London along the enemy highway,* destroying Colchester and St Albans as they went, and though the rationale for the two journeys differed – the Romans were on a colonising mission, whereas Boudicca was out for revenge, for her lost independence, for the whipping the Romans had given her, and, perhaps most vividly of all, for the Romans' rape of her two daughters – the logistics of moving so many warriors and equipment must have been essentially the same. Word of the Iceni's arrival preceded them, and finding the Roman city largely abandoned they set about destroying it and killing anyone still left inside the fortifications. In all, around seventy to eighty thousand Romans and British were slaughtered as Boudicca's army swept through the three towns, and although the queen was subsequently defeated elsewhere, buried deep in the marshlands of east London, there remains some slow-burning cinder, some spark still of her victory.

For a thousand years after Boudicca left, the area around Bow, Old Ford, Mile End and Bethnal Green returned to its former life as a quiet backwater, a terrain of marshy meadows, market gardens and rural coach houses. As late as the 1830s the area remained not much altered since Roman times, the old road now reduced to a cart track or drift-way known as Green Street. Cattle were probably traded here, and, gradually, the slaughterhouses, glue manufacturers and tanneries that are generally associated with raising cattle came to be erected along the banks of the Lea. In the

---

* The original Roman road almost certainly ran east between what is now Old Ford Road and Mile End Road across the Lea at Old Ford, from where it headed north through Stratford to Colchester. Today's Roman Road was built parallel to the route of the old road. Roman remains including tiles have been found beside the Lea at Old Ford, suggesting that the Roman bridge was originally located there.

1840s the drift-way was upgraded to a proper road known as Green Street. Soon afterwards the railway arrived and with it houses, shops and factories. The market expanded to service the ballooning population, and in 1888, that momentous year for the East End, there is so much bustle and congestion in the area that the police move to close the market down. A meeting is convened at the Hand and Flower pub, and 950 costermongers and traders sign a petition against the threat of closure. The meeting is a success. There is never again a move to close what is fast becoming the most important London market after Petticoat Lane.

On Emily's trips to the market she can hardly fail to run into a suffragette. The Women's Social and Political Union (WSPU), established by Emmeline Pankhurst in Manchester, has had a presence in the East End of London since 1906, but only really gains visibility and traction in the district after Emmeline's daughter, Sylvia Pankhurst, takes over the rent on a baker's shop at 198 Bow Road in 1912, paints 'Votes for Women' over the entrance, and officially opens the East London Branch, from where she holds meetings, makes rousing speeches and organises rallies.

A year later, on the tenth anniversary of the start of the suffragist movement in 1903, WSPU meetings have become so well attended that Sylvia has to move them to the roomier surrounds of Bow Baths at 555–559 Roman Road, a stone's throw from Alfred Arnold's café, which, many years later, will become a branch of Kelly's pie and mash. In February 1913, to be nearer to the meeting rooms, Sylvia also exchanges the old bakers at Bow Road for a clapped-out, bug-ridden former second-hand clothes shop at 321 Roman Road, a few doors down from W. F. Arber Printers and the future G. Kelly's pie and mash. The shop rent is 14s 6d a week, and Sylvia writes, 'The shop window was broken right across and was only held together by putty.'* Despite this,

* This and subsequent extracts from Sylvia Pankhurst, *The Suffragette Movement: An Intimate Account of Persons and Ideals* (1931; reissued Chatto & Windus, 1984).

the place was a centre of joyous enthusiasm. Plenty of friends at once rallied round us. Women who had joined the union in the last few weeks came in and scrubbed floors and cleaned windows. Mrs Wise, at the sweet shop next door, brought in a trestle table for a counter and helped us to hoist the purple, white and green. Her boy volunteered to put up and take down the shutters night and morning; her girl came in to sweep.

Sylvia continues,

The sun was like a red ball in the misty, whitey-grey sky. Market stalls, covered with cheerful pink and yellow rhubarb, cabbages and oranges . . . lined both sides of the narrow Roman Road. The Roman . . . was crowded with busy, kindly people. I had always liked Bow. That morning my heart warmed to it forever.

As a result of Sylvia's grassroots activism, the suffragist cause takes root here, in Bow, where Boudicca once came to exact her revenge on Roman London. One of the principal recruiting grounds for the Union is the Roman Road market, where, on Saturdays, the East London branch of the WSPU hands out flyers. The MP for Poplar, George Lansbury, resigns in order better to fight for women's suffrage. And women earning pitiful wages in horrible conditions – at Bryant & May match-makers, at Cundle & Eve box manufacturers, at Barrett & Elers and Wersmann's Eyeglasses, at Locke & Thomas and at Compton's machinists and sweatshops throughout the district – and paying taxes with no say in who governs them, begin to answer the suffragists' call to action. On Monday, 17 February, a few days after her move to 321 Roman Road, at an outdoor meeting held at the junction of Devons Road in Bow (where George Kelly will also one day open a pie and mash shop), Sylvia, her friend Zelie Emerson and Willie Lansbury, son of George Lansbury, are arrested along with three others, for throwing stones, and sentenced to a month's hard labour.* The women of Bow and the surrounding area, many of whom have been sentenced to hard labour all their lives, nonetheless take it upon themselves to march to Holloway Prison in solidarity with the toiling prisoners. During the spring and summer of 1913 nearly 1,000 women in north Bow and Old Ford join the Federation. One of them is Emily Arber.

* This detail is taken from Sarah Jackson and Rosemary Taylor, *East London Suffragettes: Voices from History* (History Press, 2014).

5

In 1913 the Arbers and their children are living in the flat above the
family's print shop on the Roman Road, only a few doors down
from Sylvia Pankhurst. Emily rarely spoke about her life and we
don't know how she and Sylvia met and became friends, but
friends they were. Emily cared enough about Sylvia or the suffragist cause or both to persuade her husband to print the suffragettes'
handbills on the family's Golding printer for free.

In May 1913 Sylvia has Arbers print a handbill calling for all
suffragettes and their sympathisers to join a march from the gates
of the East India Dock through Bow to Victoria Park on the 25th
of that month, in support of giving women the vote. The march
becomes the largest demonstration ever to take place in east
London. Sylvia and George Lansbury speak in front of an audience
of women and men numbering thousands, many dressed in the
green, purple and white suffragist colours, and the women wearing red caps of liberty. We don't know if Emily was among the
demonstrators, but it seems likely, and although police break up
the protest and arrest Sylvia, as they have done so often before,
it is clear that from this moment on the suffragist movement is
unstoppable. Sylvia writes:

On the night of my arrest Zelie Emerson had pressed into my hand an address: 'Mr and Mrs Payne, 28 Ford Rd, Bow.' Thither I was now driven in a taxi with two wardresses. As the cab slowed down perforce among the marketing throngs in the Roman Road, friends recognised me, and rushed to the roadway, cheering and waving their hands. Mrs Payne was waiting for me on the doorstep. It was a typical little East End house in a typical little street, the front door opening directly from the pavement, with not an inch of ground to withdraw its windows from the passers-by. I was welcomed by the kindest of kind people, shoemaking home-workers, who carried me in with the utmost tenderness. They had put their double bed for me in the little front parlour on the ground floor next the street, and had tied up the door knocker. For three days they stopped their work that I might not be disturbed by the noise of their tools. Yet there was no quiet. The detectives, notified of my release, had arrived before me. A hostile crowd collected. A woman flung one of the clogs she wore at the wash-tub at a detective's head.

The 'Cats', as a hundred angry voices called them, retired to the nearby public-houses, there were several of these havens within a stone's throw, as there usually are in the East End. Yet, even though the detectives were out of sight, people were constantly stopping before the house to discuss the Movement and my imprison-ment . . . My hosts carried me upstairs to their own bedroom, at the back of the house, hastily prepared, a small room, longer but scarcely wider than a prison cell – my home when out of prison for many months to come.

On 13 June 1913 Emily Davison was killed in a collision with King George V's horse, Anmer, at the Epsom Derby, when she walked on to the track. Six months later Sylvia was summoned from her headquarters in Bow to Paris, from where her sister Christabel was running the WSPU. To Christabel and Emmeline, the violence and turbulence which had come to characterise the movement over the past year were bad for business. Sylvia and her sister Adela disagreed. It was clear that something or someone would have to give.

Adela was the first to go. Emmeline furnished her daughter with a letter of introduction and a one-way ticket to Australia, but Sylvia was not about to be banished. She had given up too much and had too many women counting on her to allow her mother to dissuade her from her present course. Back home in Bow, Sylvia formally split from the WSPU and set up the East London Federation of Suffragettes. It was to be a grassroots organisation, mobilising women from the bottom up, dedicated to women's suffrage but also to socialism and with an increasingly pacifist outlook. From her digs in the back room at 28 Ford Road Sylvia began to outline her vision in a newspaper she called *The Women's Dreadnought*.

In that little room I slept, wrote, interviewed the Press and personalities of all sorts, and presently edited a weekly paper. Its walls were covered with a cheap, drab paper, with an etching of a ship in full sail, and two old-fashioned colour prints of a little girl at her morning and evening prayers. From the window by my bed, I could see the steeple of St Stephen's Church and the belfry of its school, a jumble of red-tiled roofs, darkened by smoke and age, the dull brick of the walls and the new whitewash of some of the backyards in the next street.

Our colours were nailed to the wall behind my bed, and a flag of purple, white and green was displayed from an opposite dwelling, where pots of scarlet geraniums hung on the whitewashed wall of the yard below, and a beautiful girl with smooth, dark hair and a white bodice would come out to delight my eyes in helping her mother at the wash-tub. The next yard was a fish curers'. An old lady with a chenille net on her grey hair would be passing in and out of the smoke-house, preparing the sawdust fires. A man with his shirt sleeves rolled up would be splitting herrings, and another hooking them on to rods balanced on boards and packing-cases, till the yard was filled, and gleamed with them like a coat of mail. Close by, tall sunflowers were growing, and garments of many colours hung out to dry.

Next door to us they bred pigeons and cocks and hens, which cooed and crowed and clucked in the early hours. Two doors away a woman supported a paralysed husband and a number of young children by making shirts at 8d a dozen. Opposite, on the other side of Ford St, was a poor widow with a family of little ones. The detectives endeavoured to hire a room from her, that they might watch me unobserved. 'It will be a small fortune to you while it lasts!' they told her. Bravely she refused with disdain, 'Money wouldn't do me any good if I was to hurt that young woman!' The same proposal was made and rejected at every house in Ford Rd.

Flowers and presents of all kinds were showered on me by kindly neighbours. One woman wrote to say that she did not see why I should ever go back to prison when every woman could buy a rolling pin for a penny.

The first edition of *The Women's Dreadnought* was published on 8 March 1914. Sylvia and her supporters sold copies from their stall in the Roman. From the Arber family print shop, Emily's husband, Francis, continued to print suffragist waybills and flyers without charge. We can only speculate on what Francis thought about this. What we do know, though, is that Emily Arber had an unanswerable persuasive technique. 'She was deaf all my lifetime,' her grandson, Gary Arber, says now, 'and that gave her the advantage – she was a good lip reader but if she wanted to win an argument she would just turn away and refuse to look at you. That's how she ruled.'

This was not how Boudicca ruled or how Sylvia operated, but the three women undoubtedly shared a fierce determination and a gift for recruiting others to their cause. Whether leading an army or a political revolution, or overcoming a childhood of terrible deprivation and the stigma of unwed pregnancy, they succeeded against almost unimaginably difficult odds. Even today, their achievements feel almost miraculous. It is as if Boudicca left something of herself on the Roman Road which, in the quiet of the night, when the barrows were sitting in the yard, the trams were garaged, the horses stabled and the factory gates padlocked, rose from the layered world beneath the Roman to offer solace and courage to Sylvia and Emily and the women of Old Ford and Bow who, in those heady years of the suffragist activism, took to the streets to march for the rights of all the East End's wronged daughters.

There's another suffragist march in May 1914. Once again it is halted by police, and once again the leaders, including Sylvia, are arrested. But by now there's a palpable change in the atmosphere, in the build up to war. The assassination on 28 June 1914 of Archduke Franz Ferdinand of Austria, heir presumptive to the Austro-Hungarian throne, and his wife Sophie, Duchess of Hohenberg, by Gavrilo Princip sets the ball rolling. On 4 August Great Britain declares war against Germany. Votes for women will have to wait. The world's focus is on a war to end all wars.

6

When you get sentimental and think there's someone looking
over you, Martha would be the one I'd like to think was there.

Ted Lewis

To understand Martha Robertson's war you have to go back to
the turn of the century, when the Robertson family is living at
22 Cambridge Road in the former lodgings of a baker of bread
and pies. On his poverty map Booth labels the road 'mixed'. It's a
busy, dirty, noisy thoroughfare. The tram, driven now by Samuel
Kelly, rattles by the front door.

Martha is eighteen, still working as a matchbox maker, but with
an eye to a family of her own. A sociable young woman, fond of a
drink and a sing-song. Martha's grandson, Ted Lewis, will say that
his nan 'got about a bit'. There's a childhood sweetheart by the
name of William Leary in the background, but the couple won't
go on to marry. Or not yet, anyway.

In the summer of 1901, at the age of nineteen, Martha meets
the man who will become her first husband, James Lakin of
Walter Street, off Green Street (now Roman Road). James's
mother, Mary, is a matchbox maker, so he and Martha almost
certainly meet through Mary. James labours in the docks, as does
his father, William. In the era before cinema, the young couple's
courtship is most likely conducted in pubs – Martha and James
are both fond of a Guinness – and cemented on walks along
the Greenway at Hackney Wick or picnics in Vicky Park, with,

perhaps, an outing or two on the boating lake. Home is too crowded, and everywhere but the pubs and the park too pricey. It's unlikely that Martha and James travel as far as the West End during their courtship, and why would they? The East End is where they belong.

The newly-weds rent two rooms in the airy* at 50 Libra Road just off the Roman. The place is airy all right. Drafts howl through and whatever air remains quickly grows stale and damp. The floor is stone with a covering of rice sacks. There's a shared kitchen on the ground floor with a copper in one corner and a meat safe in another. The privy is a shed in the yard surrounded by chickens, ducks and rabbits. Martha grows dahlias. In time they will move to rooms on the upper storey, but this building, 50 Libra Road, will remain James and Martha Lakin's home for the remainder of their lives together.

Children quickly arrive. (The census for 1911 lists three categories of offspring: those 'born alive' but now dead; 'those which are dead', presumably from birth; and those still living.) Two – Martha and George – die in infancy, but James, Harry, Clara and Bet survive, so there are now four more mouths to feed and not much money. James's work is casual and depends on how many ships are in and whether you have the right connections and have greased the palms of the gangmasters. Martha is still sitting at the kitchen table making up matchboxes. Conditions have improved for Bryant & May workers, and women are no longer puking up fluorescent vomit and dying of phossy jaw, but pay remains scandalous. To make ends meet, Martha has diversified into egg-box manufacture and pickling onions for a local factory. Both jobs require repetitive fine motor movements and probably contribute to the back problems that will plague Martha later in life.

For now, though, she's young and has her James and her growing brood, and is thrifty enough to keep everyone at Libra Road

---

* Cockney name for Victorian houses with basement accommodation.

clothed and fed. Faggot stew is on the menu. Plus the chickens, ducks and rabbits in the yard. She's 'artful' about money, Ted says, remembering how, as a boy, he is sent to the butcher for bones with instructions to inspect them first for scraps of meat so that Martha can boil them into a nice soup.

In the autumn of 1914, at the start of the Great War, James volunteers for service and is put to work as a driver in the Royal Engineers. The promise of a steady wage may be a motivator, as it is for many men of working-class origin. There's not much under-standing of the war yet. The prevailing wisdom seems to be that everything will have blown over by Christmas. While James is gone, Martha heads down to Pluckley in Kent with the kids, to earn a few bob picking hops.

In October, with the hopping done, the family returns to Bow to discover that things have changed. Sylvia Pankhurst is opening up a cut-price restaurant at 400 Old Ford Road, selling cheap hot food to the wives and children of soldiers whose allowances haven't yet reached home, a situation the bureaucrats and politicians, none of them East Enders, haven't anticipated. Sylvia has also set up an airy house at 45 Norman Grove, Bow, as a toy factory and nursery where women can mind their children while earning a living. (Later, Gary Arber will say the toys made at Norman Grove were of poor quality compared to those sold by his grandmother, Emily Arber, in the print shop, but that may just be family loyalty talk-ing.) The factory is followed a few months later, in April 1915, by a nursery, milk depot and clinic for destitute women in a former pub, the Gunmakers' Arms, at 438 Old Ford Road. Pankhurst renames the pub the Mothers' Arms. A day's childcare, from 8 a.m. to 7 p.m. (reflecting long factory hours), and including meals, costs 3d. Bessie Lansbury, wife of George, becomes the centre's director. Later, Sylvia will reorganise the nursery around Montessori prin-ciples, among which is that there will be no physical punishment – revolutionary for the time and context. When the East End poet, Israel Zangwill, sometimes dubbed the 'Jewish Dickens', opened a women's exposition near Victoria in 1915, he declared that 'The future of the world lies in the transformation of the gunmakers' arms to mothers' arms.'

Among the babies at the Mothers' Arms will most likely be some delivered by Martha, midwifery and undertaking being just two of her sidelines, along with pickling onions and making up egg boxes. In the era before free healthcare, each turning or group of turnings appoints a well-liked and trusted 'wise woman' to assist at births and in the laying out of bodies. Around Libra Road, Martha Robertson is that woman, a sort of honorary matriarch. Women will go to her with their problems and crises and trust her to advise them and even, on occasion, to intervene. Martha sees her neighbours at their most vulnerable, in the act of giving birth or of grieving for a loved one. She's paid for her trouble and though it's never very much, Martha is glad of the money. Very soon, she'll be gladder still.

The year slides by and the war does not end as promised. Jim Lakin – Private Lakin as he now is – continues to soldier out on the Western Front, appearing sporadically for a few days' leave. By January 1915 over one million men have enlisted, encouraged, in part, by Kitchener's famous poster declaring 'Your Country Needs You'. Casualties are already horrendous, though conscription is still a year away. In the spring of 1915, just as the Kellys are opening their first eel, pie and mash shop near Paradise Row with the compensation money from Samuel's accident on the trams, a lone message-boy will make his way down Libra Road towards the Robertsons' house bearing a telegram.

7

I've swallowed all my tears and brought them up in handfuls.

Marian Old

As 1915 folds into 1916 all Martha knows about her husband is what was written on the telegram, which, being illiterate, she had to have read to her. Private James Lakin is missing in action. This not knowing is the cruellest thing, and in the absence of any confirmation of his whereabouts or fate, there can be no widow's pension and it's hard to get by. There's nothing for it but to step up the laying out and bringing in, the gluing of matchboxes and the pickling of onions, but without Jim it must feel that life itself has come unstuck. The endless waiting and uncertainty is a kind of torture.

Conscription begins on 2 March 1916, initially for all single men between the ages of eighteen and forty-one, unless widowed with kids or a man of the cloth. On 25 May it's extended to include married men. One of the first to be sent out is Bill Lucioni, Ted Lewis's grandfather. He's twenty-four, married to Mary Hall, with children Teddy, George, Wally and Mary. When he's called up, Bill is working as a porter in Billingsgate and running a sideline as a bantamweight boxer, fighting under the name of Bill Lewis. After cursory basic training he joins the 9th Battalion, Rifle Brigade as a rifleman, and is swiftly dispatched to the horror that is the Somme. Between 1 and 13 July the village of Montauban is taken after fierce fighting by the 9th Scottish Division. During the fighting

44

the British forces make use of the cover provided by a pear-shaped stretch of woodland to the east of the village, the Bois de Bernafay, to set up a dressing station, which quickly becomes a cemetery. With Montauban and Bernafay now in British hands, a plan is hatched for the 41st and 42nd Brigades of the 5th Battalion King's Shropshire Light Infantry to launch an offensive to clear the last of the enemy from nearby Delville Wood on 24 August. In preparation, the brigades will swap positions. On the night of 22 August, relieved of its position, 9th Battalion, Rifle Brigade marches to Montauban. Somewhere along the way, after only a few months as a soldier, Rifleman Lucioni loses his life. There will be no grave; instead, the name Rifleman William Lucioni will be carved on the Thiepval Memorial to the Missing.

Soldiers from the Western Front are returning almost daily to makeshift military hospitals set up across the East End, some crazed, others so burned and blasted as to be virtually unrecognisable. Martha walks among them, giving comfort to the wounded and the dying when she can, and laying out the bodies when she can't. Maybe this is her way of keeping the memory of Jim close. Maybe there is always the hope that among the wounded, in the rows of camp beds filled with the recovering and the dying, there will be someone who knows what happened to him.

On her rounds one day she passes a man, his face obscured by bandages and, it seems, completely mute, shot through the cheek, the bullet shattering the jawbone. She stops and, we imagine, offers some words of comfort, noticing that from two tiny openings in the bandages tears are welling up. She's about to move on when something in the man's eyes stops her, some small inflection, a reflection of the light, that seems familiar.

Is that you, Jim?

The eyes narrow then flare. There are more tears.

It is, it is you!

Alive, alive, oh! James Lakin, husband, father of her children. After months of no news and not knowing. Here in this hospital, lying in this bed. Here he is! Jim Lakin, the very same. She takes another look. It's Jim, all right, though not quite. The man on the bed is a barely recognisable version, a Jim with half a face and with terrible shrapnel wounds on his arms and body. A ruined Jim. A dreadful, broken Jim.

As soon as he is well enough, Martha takes Jim home to Libra Road. But the Jim who is finally discharged as no longer fit for war service in June 1917 is not a Jim she understands. He's a man on whom the war will forever sit like a giant immovable rock. And Martha is now a not quite widow, a woman with eight children, a pickler of onions and maker of matchboxes, a bringer out and a layer in, living with a not quite husband so disabled by the trenches that the only job he can find is as a pot man in a pub, clearing away empty glasses.

Not far from Martha and Jim's house, in Stratfield Road, Bromley-by-Bow, the Davies family anxiously awaits news of Herbert Henry Davies of the Royal Garrison Artillery, wounded in the leg and on his way back to a former insane asylum now serving as a makeshift military hospital. Herbert is a small man – he's only 5 feet 6 inches – and a proud one. The story goes that his family has money – his mother, Alice, owns a house at 48 Monier Road on Fish Island – but Herbert is cut out of whatever inheritance there might once have been for tarnishing the family's reputation by getting Margaret Salter in the family way, even though he does the right thing by Margaret and weds her. He's not been long married to Margaret when he's shipped out to the front to endure the mud and gas and terror. Not long after his call-up, Herbert finds himself back home and in the military hospital with a mangled leg and no chance of being fit to fight again. There's the prospect of a very modest pension at least, but upon discovering he's convalescing in what was, until very recently, an insane asylum, he cannot stomach the stigma, discharges himself and in doing so unwittingly gives up his entitlement. A man can afford to lose his leg before he loses his pride, apparently. And Herbert does seem to be very good at giving up money. By war's end he and his family are lodging with his mother in Monier Road, and staring down a hard road into an uncertain future.

On the night of 31 May 1915, only a couple of months after the opening of Samuel Kelly's shop in Paradise Row, the zeppelin menace begins. The Kellys will hear the bombs fall over Stepney, Shoreditch and Whitechapel. That night there are seven killed and many more injured, but the real horror begins with daylight bombing raids on the morning of 13 June 1917 in fine if hazy weather, when a phalanx of Gothas begins dropping bombs on East Ham and the Royal Albert Dock. Between 11.40 and 11.42 a.m. seventy-two bombs are dropped within a mile's radius of Liverpool Street, before the bombers split into two groups, the northern phalanx attacking Saffron Hill then moving east into Bethnal Green and north along Cambridge Road to Dalston. The Kellys will have found themselves in the midst of the bombing. Their future is only two months old, and already in doubt.

Not for long, though, as it turns out. Perhaps it's because everyone left in the East End is working crazy hours for the war effort, and is in need of the comforting, warm familiarity. Perhaps it's just that those returning from the front on leave crave a taste of home. In any case, Kelly's is busy. In the mornings workers stop by on their way to work to buy freshly cooked pies to eat cold at midday. By mid morning the porters at Billingsgate, Spitalfields and Smithfields, who have been at work since 4 a.m., are ready for their dinners. Children whose mothers are busy with war work pop in during their school dinner-time for a penny's worth of mash and liquor to keep them full till teatime. Women working long hours for the war effort will buy pies to take home and reheat on the kitchener. Samuel and Matilda Kelly are kept busy from the moment they open the shop at 8 a.m. to closing time at 5 p.m. and very often beyond.

Pretty soon there's a need for bigger and better premises. A shop is rented further down Bethnal Green Road at the junction with

Vallance Road. Samuel sets white tiles around the walls and builds a long counter at the front, where steel vats of parsley liquor, pea soup and hot stewed eels are kept warm over burners. The pies are baked in a coke-fired oven at the back while in a shallow tank by the front window, live eels wiggle and gape, advertising their freshness. The family moves into the flat above. It's cramped and damp and painted, so it is said, 'nigger brown',* but it's an easy commute downstairs and while the hours are long, Matilda can work at the counter and keep an eye on the children.

By virtue of his injury Samuel is exempt from conscription, the children are all too young to be vulnerable and business is booming. If anyone can be said to be having a good war, it must be the pie and mash branch of the Kelly family.

---

* This is how the flat was described to me by an interviewee in the parlance of the time. I have chosen to keep the quote anonymous.

8

A huge cockney chuckle of delight . . .

Mollie Panter-Downes, *London War Notes*

It's 11 a.m. on Monday, 12 November 1918 and a blast of maroon
rockets rips through the East End. Moments later church bells,
factory sirens and the whistles of ships in the docks join in the
hubbub. Young boys in red, more accustomed to sounding the all
clear, blow their bugles to signal the end of the war, and bit by bit
the alleys and turnings of Bow and Bethnal Green begin to billow
and heave as machinists, munitions girls, dockers, costermongers,
soldiers, matchwomen, coal heavers, tailors and factory workers
take to the streets to celebrate.

What now? The war has strewn its human wreckage across the
East End. There is grieving to be done for fathers missing in
French fields and sons drowned in Belgian mud, for husbands not
gone exactly, but, like Jim Lakin and Herbert Davies, somehow
absent. There's sorrowing for widows and fatherless children. And
there's reconstruction to be done after the bombings, and newly
demobbed civilians to be catered for. There are holes to be darned
in the fabric of life, remnants to be picked up and stitched together,
patching to be done. There is life to be lived. There are dreams
to cultivate. There is hope.

Goods pour in and out of the docks. Factories long diverted to
war production turn their attention back to civilian manufacture.
In 1921 the King George V Dock opens at Silvertown, bringing

jobs, mostly for dockers and stevedores, all men, mostly from London and the outlying regions, but including many Irish too. More surprisingly, by the end of the war there are 5 million working women. On 18 August 1918 women bus and tram drivers go on strike to demand the same 5 shilling a week war bonus as their male colleagues, and on 30 August, in the dying days of the war, the Committee on Production extends the bonus to women in munitions factories. On 6 February 1918 women over age thirty on the Local Government Register or married to a man who is, or who own property or have a university degree, are given the vote, and in 1919 the Housing Act is introduced to provide 'homes for heroes'. As the 1920s start to get underway, it's as if a new sun is coming up on a better world.

It doesn't last. As the decade progresses, the economy begins to falter and stall. In the East End, dark clouds of poverty and unemployment once more dim the sky. Life narrows and hardens, work becomes harder to find. All over the East End, the husks of men huddling on street corners begging for money, a cigarette or food are a common sight. Others stumble blind-eyed from the pubs at closing time, eaten alive by what they saw and did in the four years of the war, or by what they failed to do. Soup kitchens open and the lines of men, women and children never seem to shorten. It all comes to a head in 1926, during the general strike, when the docks are virtually closed down by striking dockers and cyclists block the approach roads to stop troops taking over. Cars are set on fire or dumped into the River Lea.

Ultimately not much changes. Whole families are routinely left to manage on whatever the women can scrape together from hawking or taking in laundry or making matchboxes or drawing brushes or fabricating silk flowers to go on wealthier women's hats, or by pickling onions like Martha Robertson, or taking coats and linen to the pawnbroker. In the face of such privation it becomes all the more important to be respectable. But how? First, keep up appearances. Blacken the kitchener, scrub the front step, beat the rug, boil a ham knuckle or a sheep's head for Sunday dinner, accept the goldfish the ragman gives you for your broken bits, and when his back is turned give it to the cat. Take up religion, or, like the Arbers, keep churching; join a savings club, marry if you can, lean on family. Above all, don't take charity.

At 39 Auckland Road on Fish Island, Rebecca Austin is trying to support herself, her mother Old Becs (a woman so behind the times she does the household chores by oil lamp and won't light the gas mantles for fear of an explosion), daughter Little Becs and a son. Rebecca's husband, Nicholson, had an ironworks opposite the Royal London hospital in Whitechapel and died young, leaving Rebecca to manage on what she can earn as a cleaner at Chisenhale School and by renting out rooms in the house to couples (though only on presentation of their marriage certificate – Rebecca is a respectable widow running a respectable boarding house).

In the dying days of the war, and to Rebecca's undoubted surprise (she's in her early forties by now, virtually an old crone), a Royal Marine by the name of Turner* begins paying court. Rebecca won't remarry until the fighting is over because she can't risk being widowed all over again, particularly if the union brings more children, though she's hoping that, at her advanced age, it won't. Evidently none of that puts Turner off. By Christmas 1920 he has found a job with a boiler maker, and much to the chagrin of Little Becs, who is disgusted by the prospect of her mother marrying and, more to the point, sharing her bed, Rebecca and Turner are wed. The couple set up home in Rebecca's house. Within months, Rebecca finds herself pregnant. A daughter, Elsie, arrives auburn haired and ringletted, followed fifteen months later by Doris. Nicholson's father comes to see the child and says, 'Oh look at that scrawny little thing', which is all the more hurtful for

---

* I have been unable to find his full name.

its being true. So that's three girls and a boy now, not so many by early twentieth-century East End standards but more than enough for Rebecca. It's not that she doesn't love the new arrivals. It's just that having kids in her forties is not what she ever had in mind.

As the twenties grind on, Turner is let go from the boiler maker's workshop, and after a frightening period of unemployment, finds work as a stoker and then finally as anything going. Having lodgers helps – one or two couples in the two large rooms at the top of the house and another in the front room downstairs bring in a few shillings – but it's tight. In the midst of a rare argument with her husband one evening, Elsie recalls her mother bursting out, 'I'd never have married you if I'd known you'd fill my arms up with children.'

It's not always possible to remain respectable. Take Herbert Henry, the man invalided out of the war with a gammy leg. He and his wife Margaret have nine offspring and they've had to move in with Herbert's mother, Alice, in Monier Road. Herbert has a job cleaning bricks, but he's unable to do anything more strenuous – or lucrative – on account of his war wound. On a Monday he can't work anyway because he's always so hung over from the weekend. And what with walking out on his pension, and all those kids to worry about . . . there's never enough money. So Herbert is eventually forced to hatch a Plan B. He'll take a docker's hook up onto the open top of the number 8 bus and, as it lurches down the Roman Road, he'll swing over the side and scoop up joints of meat hanging outside the butcher's and sometimes other things – gas mantles and baskets and rag rugs and household items – like the fairground game with ducks but for real, because a man must provide for his family even if it makes him a thief.

In the midst of all the economic hardship of the late twenties, it takes a man with superhuman reserves of courage to give up a wage in pursuit of a dream in Bow. Or else a man with a great deal to prove. Len Baker may be one such man. Len's two brothers are in horse-drawn haulage, but Len doesn't get along with Alf, so he finds work driving horse trams, and by 1914 he's working alongside Samuel Kelly on the new electric trams out of the Bow garage. Since it's a reserved occupation, Len, like Samuel, avoids conscription, but by the end of the war he's had enough of working for someone else. It's 1918 and his future stretches out clearly before him. He's keen to become his own man. All Len Baker needs is a plan.

A friend comes up with an idea. Why not start a hand-barrow business and offer out his services for house removals? Most people in Bethnal Green and Bow rent from private landlords, and they are always being evicted or having to move. It sounds good on paper, but, given the economic situation, Len's wife Ginny remains unconvinced. What does Len want with barrows when he has a steady job on the trams paying a steady wage? Len isn't about to be dissuaded. He is a man on a mission. He can make a barrow himself – he has wood to carve out the wheels, iron strip for the tyres and a couple of springs, planking for the barrow's bed.

For the next few months he throws himself into the work, converting the basement at his 38 Medway Road home – a turning of small Victorian houses just off the Roman – into a makeshift workshop. He discovers he has a knack for the work. The wheels balance, the handgrips are evenly weighted, the thing rolls well when empty and even better when loaded. With his new barrow he begins doing a few general removals. Soon he's adding another barrow to the first, then another, and not long after that he has stopped pushing the barrows himself and is making his money renting them out and spending his time in the workshop making more. A few of the traders down the Roman want barrows for rent on market days, and before long Len's made half a dozen, proper costers, three by six, with spoked wooden wheels and iron tyres. His business expands so much that he soon takes rent of a little yard in the mews round the back of the house. He's still on the trams, though, and it's while driving a tram through Aldgate one day that he makes a life-defining decision. Finding himself ten minutes behind schedule with the inspector barking at him for his tardiness, something inside snaps. Clambering from the tram, Len says 'You take the ruddy thing back yourself, then', and that's it, he's walking away, leaving the vehicle in the middle of the road. Enough of low pay and snot-nosed bosses and working bank holidays and Sundays. As he makes his way back home, Len Baker feels like a free man, the boss of himself. On the barrows. One day he'll own a fleet of them.

Len's former colleague on the trams, Samuel Kelly, is in a similarly expansive mood. By the end of the decade the eel, pie and mash shop on the Bethnal Green road is flourishing, despite the economy. People have to eat, and in troubled times, as in good ones, what they continue to want to eat is pie, mash and eels. His children Sam junior, George, Joe and young Matilda are keen to help out with their parents' business. Sam junior has taken over the shop at 284 Bethnal Green Road. George, the second son, has gone into eels. He's running an eel yard in Viaduct Street, supplying the family shop, among others, and he's taken over a pie, mash and eel shop from the Harisses a little to the north in Broadway Market. Before long he'll open up at 414 Bethnal Green Road, further east from Sam's shop. George will be the big family success story, and so it's to him we'll turn.

There's a black and white photograph of George Kelly, taken in the fifties or sixties, clutching an eel that's at least three foot long. He's wearing a hand-knitted fisherman's sweater and an apron smeared with what looks like slime but may also be blood. He's holding the fish upright and with a firm but gentle grip. The eel, which is still alive though, perhaps, sensing its fate, is giving George a beady eye. George is eyeing the eel in return. There appears to be a connection between man and eel, a grudging respect. His grandniece, Sue Vening, will one day claim that her uncle was 'obsessed with them'.

It's fair to say that George's obsessions do not extend to romance, as we'll see, though in 1930, at the age of twenty-six, he does manage to catch himself a local beauty, Theresa Kingdon. Everybody loves Theresa, and not only for her tall, dark good looks, her creamy Irish skin and Greta Garbo cheekbones, but also because she is kind, thoughtful and likes to think well of people. What she sees in George we don't know. Perhaps it's his flash and confidence, or the size of his ambition. Of these there can be no doubt. By the mid thirties George has opened shops in Bethnal Green Road, Broadway Market in Hackney and Devons Road in Bow, but he doesn't stop at pie and mash. George has his sights on an empire. And pretty soon he gets it. By the time the thirties are over, he and Theresa are living in the leafy suburb of Walthamstow and George is managing his eel and pie shops and supplying live and jellied eels to pubs along the 'beano route' out of the East End as far as Southend and Margate. He'll be driving a van and a fancy car. And he and Theresa will be sleeping in different beds.

9

That old story, that old lady that lived in a shoe, had so many
children she didn't know what to do. That was how we was.

Ron Moss

To the kids growing up in the thirties in Bow, the Roman is an
Aladdin's cave – its shops bursting with treasures, its turnings path-
ways to adventure, its picture houses boxes full of dreams, and at
the centre of it all, its market a marvel of sounds and smells and
everyday miracles. Above all, it is an escape from the cramped,
overcrowded, bug-ridden, damp collection of rooms most of the
kids in Bow and Bethnal Green count as home.

It's 1929 and in Summerford Street, Bethnal Green Marian
Stratford, aged six and one of eight siblings, is making a few
pennies fetching cats in baskets to the cats' home to be looked
after while their owners are away. She's a pretty girl, sweet and
funny, though born rheumatic and with a cyst the size of a potato
on her head, which she covers with her auburn hair. The other
kids tease her so she avoids the bus, preferring to walk to the
Catholic school at St Patrick's on Cambridge Road. From time
to time she'll meet up with Sister Aiden at St Anne's in Brook
Lane, and help the nun carry her shopping. The school 'didn't
have to learn you to read and write', and so it didn't. 'It was all
religion, everywhere you went, it was all rosary beads,' Marian
says. 'You learned your prayers. It's an automatic thing for me
to say a prayer.'

Marian's father, William Stratford, brings home 10 shillings a day for unloading lorries in the docks. He keeps a pipe between his lips. It's empty because there's no money for tobacco, but you chew it for the comfort as much as anything. His wife, of the Irish Donaghues, stays at home. She has enough on her hands with eight kids, and she's a good cook and thrifty and can rustle up some cracking dumplings, stew and bread pudding out of almost nothing. The couple are fond of a Guinness, but they say it's good for you.

Summerford Street is an 'old-fashioned area', a street mostly of Victorian tenements, along which live the Rubins, Mrs Pearman, the Whites and the Savoys. 'I was brought up with Jewish people,' Marian says, 'we'd sit on the pavement and play marbles.' Marian is sporty, a fan of netball and swimming, and grows up loyal, sociable, teased for her rheumatism, the potato on her head, not a reader as such, or a writer, but a good talker. A 'right old bunny rabbit', and her mother's favourite. 'Marbles, skipping, bike riding and skates,' says Marian of her childhood. Georgie Turner has the grocer's at the end of turning. The Gommeses have the fish and a chip shop. Everyone knows everyone.

Elsie Hobart, hair the colour of embers, is living at 39 Auckland Road along with her parents and her sister and two half-siblings, and a pile of lodgers.

> We used to have a big rope . . . and the mums would come out and
> turn the rope for the children . . . one boy found out that, if you
> got a rope, you could tie it up and climb the lamp post, and you put
> the rope through the loop and it made a swing.[*]

The children play on that swing until the lamplight man comes round to light the gas lamps. And a milkman comes round with 'a

---

[*] Elsie Hobart in an interview conducted by Carolyn Clark in 2010 and used with kind permission.

horse and a huge brass churn and little metal measuring jugs . . . and there was a kind of roundabout on a trolley. They would come round, the children would give them a halfpenny to ride on the roundabout.' Their world is the street and the entertainment to be found in it.

> There was one that you didn't speak about . . . That was the Nancy-
> boys, they used to come round dressed up as women and they
> would dance in the street. My mother used to make us come in. I
> don't know what she thought was going to happen to our morals
> out there.

School is a delight. Elsie's at Chisenhale where her mother is employed as a cleaner. Her sister Dora hates it. But at fourteen Elsie is pleased to move up to secondary school, leaving at sixteen for the Royal School of Needlework in Exhibition Road, South Kensington, where she learns the art of hand embroidery and prepares for a life making clothes she will never be able to afford, clothes to stock shops she will never visit, to be bought by women living up West with more comfortable lives than her own.

The Roman of Ron Moss's childhood is a place of risk and opportunity, somewhere a fast-footed boy with a rumbling stomach can nick a link of sausages or a pot of jellied eel. Ron grows up on the banks of the Regent with canal water running in his veins. His granddad on his mother's side, Joseph Hart, a bargee and a slow wanderer, had been born in the Midlands, though by 1886 he'd drifted down the Grand Union as far as Hertford; six years later he'd made his way east to Sandridge near St Albans, then kept going south along the Lea navigation until he reached Stratford. By the turn of the century, it seems, his meandering days were over and he settled with his daughter Melinda in a house in Ripporth Road on Fish Island, with a garden that sloped right down to the banks of the Hertford Union.

It's here that Ron was born, in August 1927, the youngest of
seventeen. There's never any money in his household for marbles
or swings, but it's no matter to Ron, for whom the canal is a year-
round playpen and the marshes and market a pantry. Ron is a
water baby who spends his summers diving off the bridge into
water heated by outflow from the Carliss, Capel & Company
chemical factory, or else building rafts or fishing for roach, bream
and eels, or spearing pike from the canal-side to salt overnight and
cook for tea. 'I was a lovely swimmer. I'd swim everywhere.
Underwater. On top. I'd dive off anything . . . I was mad, I was! I
was absolutely mad.'

This is Ron's kingdom, his little patch of heaven. No matter to
him that the place is heavily industrialised: the Clarnico sweet
factory is down the road, Gliksten's timberyard is at the far end,
then there's Cooks the dry-cleaners – it's his manor; the slow,
heavy horses and the factories, the barges, the bridge over the Lea
at Victoria Lock, the warehouse for Queen Victoria's toys,* the
railway yard littered with rabbits; the watercress beds, the sour
Jewish chicken slaughterhouse aflutter with so many feathers you'd
think it was snowing all year round near there, the bright stripe of
the Greenway drift-way following the Northern Outfall Sewer,
and beyond it the glory of the marshes.

It's a poor kingdom, is Ron's. No one pays a boy to take the
Moss household linen to the pawn shop to save face. Ron and his
mother do it themselves. Every Monday, get it out on a Friday.
Three shillings to spend on food, Ron dressed in hand-me-downs
from his brothers, boots far too big, their leaky soles patched pieces
of cardboard cadged from the box factory down the road. Outdoor
privy, one sink and a kitchener with a copper in the corner which

---

* Ron Moss spoke about this in an interview for Mapping the Change, an oral
history project hosted by Hackney Museum as part of the 2012 Cultural Olympiad,
and also mentioned it in an interview for this book. The Royal Archives at Windsor
have no records of any such toy store. It's possible that what Ron was seeing was
actually the store for one of the toy shops or market stalls on the Roman.

is used for boiling up clothes and dinner and – with the addition of a drop of Kawl detergent – for bathing babies. Ron's mother has had a great many of these, though five of the seventeen are 'brown bread'. Those of her offspring still living and still at home are crammed into the front parlour, which is serving as a bedroom. Seven, as Ron remembers it.

Rumour has it that old Joseph Hart has money, but if he has, neither his daughter nor his grandchildren see any of it. Ron reckons it might be buried somewhere, but who knows. His dad, Frederick, a stoker on a fishing trawler, is a patchy provider. Away for months at a time, he'll occasionally turn up with fruit and a few treats, other times he'll leave money for Linda in a pub and none of the family will even see him. You can't rely on it, on him. Nor on Linda either. They both like a drink. The children learn to be canny or pushy or both. There is never enough of anything. 'The first at the table was . . . lucky. 'Cos if you was last you got nothing. And me being little small squirt, like I couldn't even reach the stuff, could I? I had to get up on the chair.'

Teafing (cockney: 'tea leaf'/'thief') and foraging become a way of life because there is no other. From a very young age Ron, known as the Artful Dodger, learns to steal coal from the yard and take swans' eggs from their nests, bring home snared rabbits and fish scooped from the river and the bodies of pigeons that fanciers on the marshes deem too weak or confused or incompetent to race. By the time he's seven or eight he knows all the angles. For example, round the back of Clarnico's you can sometimes find a few sweets, the odd forgotten bar of chocolate, a bit of rejected fudge hidden among the boxes. You have to be on the lookout, though.

I had to run for me life sometimes, 'cos they was on me, like . . . and I'd dive off the bridge and swim down the River Lea, you know? And I always used to swim underneath, all amongst the mud, it didn't deter me one bit. I had nerves of steel.

But the best pickings are to be had down the Roman. No question. On market days Ron crosses over the Lea at Old Ford – for so long now the link between the hustle of the city and the older, feral place of the marshes – bowls down St Stephen's Road and into another world. On market days you can teaf most anything if you put your mind to it.

I used to go up the market and I used to nick the fruit and stuff under the stalls. And I had a big coat with the long pockets and one of them had no pocket in the end and I used to put me arm right through and take what I wanted and pull it back up the coat. Touch wood, I never got caught and I used to do that week in and week out, to feed the [family].*

It's Ron's mother Linda who encourages his expeditions, especially when they result in a bit of meat for the family tea. There's never enough cash to stretch to a nice roast, a leg of lamb, say, or a lovely joint of pork, or even some bangers. It's easiest in winter, he finds, when he can put on his long coat with the ripped lining and not attract attention. Small joints can be pulled into the coat with surprising ease, but you have to watch with bangers that you don't pull on a long set of links that you can't stash away fast enough. It happens to him one time. His only recourse is to flee, dragging the string behind him. The sausages pick up a bit of street grime on their journey but, once his mother has brushed that off, they're fine.

Another thing: Ron wraps pennies in silver paper and passes them off as sixpences. As long as the stallholder is distracted he doesn't notice. It's all a matter of timing, knowing when to make yourself visible and when to disappear, something Ron has down to a fine art. Which is why they call him the Artful D. And though Ron is in no doubt that teafing is wrong in the traditional sense

* Ron Moss, Mapping the Change.

and, if caught, he's likely to be punished, shame and pride inhabit his interior world in equal measure. He knows what he does is wrong, but he also knows he's very good at it. If he weren't, his family would go hungry. Wouldn't that be wrong too? In any case, it's not like he has any choice. His mother will bash him if he admits to stealing, but she'll bash him if he returns empty-pocketed.

Linda Moss considers herself a pious woman and won't have swearing or blaspheming around the house. Oddly, given what the Bible says about suffering little children, though, she appears to have no qualms about using her fists and worse on her offspring. One time, an iron pan lands on Ron's head with a loud bong. 'It was like Big Ben . . . And I had a bump there big as a chicken's egg. And I think that done me brain in.'*

It's hard keeping up with what adults expect of a boy. Ron's father isn't around enough to bother with him much, his grand-father is a skinflint and a tyrant and his mother is permanently angry. School's no better. The teachers are always at him for his failings. The general gist is that he'll never amount to anything. There's one teacher in particular who's always giving him grief and, worse, the cane. A mean old bastard. One day Ron finds out where he lives, lifts the foil lids from the milk bottles on his door-step, gobs in them, and carefully seals them back down. Ha! A lesson for the teacher. Seven decades later Ron still gets a kick out of that. Inevitably, given how little encouragement he's offered, he gradually stops bothering to go to school. He never learns to read or write. The life makes you resourceful.

I was dodging here, there and everywhere . . . I was up to every-thing that went . . . I never went on the thieve no more when there was no need for it. But . . . when we was kids there was a need for everything . . . I always used to go in Lash and Cookes to get a suit,

* Ron Moss, Mapping the Change.

you know, to thieve or sell. And I come out the door and the watchman's chasing me. And he's went to grab me, like, and I had the bags behind, that I dropped, he fell over them bags and he fell out the bloody door . . . And I was off. Well, I was like a bullet . . . I went round the lock, quick, and along the fence and I was home and gone.

One time – he's about thirteen – Ron and a friend walk into a Navy Cadet office in Mile End and ask to join. They have no intention of becoming cadets – Ron's seen all he needs of the seagoing life from his dad – but they've set their sights on the uniforms. A nice new pair of trousers, some boots that actually fit.

What Ron doesn't know is that he's been spotted by the next-door neighbour, a policeman who has a sideline in barbering.

And he said to me one day I was having me hair cut . . . 'If I didn't know your mother I would of put you away.' I said, 'Well you wouldn't of got my bleeding hair cut then, would you?' . . . It wasn't much . . . about thruppence, something like that . . . and he never did shop me, you know? I used to learn his son to swim.

For all this, Ron's is not an unhappy childhood, though it could so easily have been. The reason for this is Ron himself who, at a young age, comes to the profound understanding, that, in the world into which he has been born there is more freedom, more excitement, more happiness to be found in trees and birds, marshes, railway yards, dogs, canals and fish, and, indeed, *inside his own head*, than ever there was or probably ever will be in the company of adults.

IO

We was Italian but there was no one more British.

Ted Lewis

How much time must elapse before a family stops being thought of, or thinking of itself, as immigrant? A generation? Two? Twelve perhaps? In the East End it's so hard to say because almost everyone's family is from somewhere else if you go far back enough. Marian's originated in Ireland, Ron's in the Midlands; Ted Lucioni's family is from Italy and Harry Da Costa's from Portugal. But they are all, equally, East Enders. All their many roads have led here. So it's not surprising that East Enders have a sense of being in it together. All for one and one for all. On any East End street in the thirties you'll see Jewish kids kicking balls with Catholic kids, hopscotching with Unitarians. Go down the Lido at Vicky Park on a summer's day in the 1930s and you'll see children from all corners of the world. Or, rather you won't: what you will actually see are kids mucking about in the water.

One of these kids may well be Ted Lucioni. Unlike Ron, Ted cannot recall a time in his 1930s childhood when he doesn't have enough to eat. It's more that he has to eat his mum Lizzie's food. Ted's mother Lizzie, Elizabeth Helen, is the daughter of Martha Robertson, the match-girl, and her husband James Lakin, the man who lost half of himself in the Great War. Whatever skills Martha might have passed down to daughter Lizzie, cooking isn't one of them. Her food is horrible. Lucky for Ted, he's at school in the Roman, right opposite Kelly's pie and mash, where he goes most days to fetch his lunch of mash and liquor. He grows up strong too, skinny to look at but with a punch powerful enough to stop any boy in his tracks. 'Lucy' the boys call him at school, after his surname. That's where the punch comes in handy.

The real cook in the family is Ted's dad, Teddy senior, who can and does whip up the kind of Sunday roast you'll spend all week thinking about. Teddy's a whiz at puddings too, the Italian blood maybe. Not that Teddy has ever been to Italy or thinks of himself as anything other than British. He's big on the ties of blood, though, as we'll see.

By the time Ted is born in 1929, the Lucioni family hasn't lived in Italy for around a hundred years. The young Ted's great-great-grandfather, Aquilino Lucioni, was the last to be born in the old country, around 1802, to a fifty-three-year-old father and a forty-two-year-old mother, in the village of Mozzate in the flatlands south of Como in northern Italy. The age of the parents suggests a happy accident, but if that's the case then it didn't stay happy for long. By the age of three Aquilino was an orphan with two adult siblings and Lombardy was under French control.* In 1812 the Prussians invaded and two years later, when Aquilino was twelve, the territory was signed over to the Austrian Empire. Aquilino may have fled then, or perhaps later in order to evade conscription into the Prussian Army. We know he was granted a passport in Lugano, Switzerland, in 1822, and was listed as a resident of that city. He must have acquired the passport because he was intending to travel. In any case, not long afterwards he was living in Eyre Street in Clerkenwell, London, in what was then a thriving Italian enclave of skilled carvers, gilders, glass-blowers and barometer

---

* Much of this information comes from 'Lake Como to London and Beyond' by Jean Hood, www.jeanhood.co.uk (accessed August 2017).

makers.* Aquilino found work as a boot- and shoemaker and settled first at 12 Ray Street, round the back of St Peter's, the Italian church, then, after the lower end of the street was demolished to make way for the new Farringdon railway line, at number 36, where he lodged with a young woman, Mary Chapman, and a boy, Peter Flynn.

On Valentine's Day 1835 he married Mary, who was, by then, six months pregnant with their first child. In 1851 records show him living with her and their two sons, Giuseppe and Giovanni, at 36 Ray Street and working as a master looking-glass maker. It was during this time that he applied to be naturalised as a British citizen. Two years later, in 1853, Mary died, and by the following year only Giuseppe, who was now known as Joe, was still living in the house in Ray Street. In 1856 Ray Street was once again partly demolished, but Aquilino was then living in West Malling, Kent. Five years after Mary's death, in 1858, Aquilino Lucioni followed his wife to the grave. The death was reported by Elizabeth Hodge, who might or might not have been his lover.

A year after his father's death, Joe Lucioni, married Jane Carter and was, like his father, working as a looking-glass maker and living at 8 Granby Terrace, Bethnal Green. His younger brother, John, married Sarah Pimm, and the couple had a son, William, that same year, followed in rapid succession by another four sons and a daughter. They were living in Shoreditch and in Ramsey Street, Bethnal Green. Willliam grew up to be a walking-stick maker and married a woman in the same line of business, Sarah Rowe, and the couple had six children, two of whom, George and Julia, died in infancy. The couple's eldest son, William Lucioni, came along in 1881. The family suffered a series of setbacks, moving from one address in the Haggerston area to another, presumably as the money ran low. At one point they were homeless and living

* I'm grateful to Ted Lewis's family for some of this information, and in particular to Ted's cousin Barry for compiling a history of Bill 'Lewis' Luciano's boxing career.

under the railway arches in Wheeler Street, and were for a while in Bethnal Green Workhouse. So William Lucioni grew up with a full understanding of the phrase 'on the ropes'. By his late teens, at 5 foot 1 inch and weighing under 7 stone, William, now Bill, was already boxing at bantamweight under the name 'Bill Lewis'. By day he was portering at Billingsgate and by night he was delivering knockouts for money at Premierland.

On Christmas Day 1903 Bill married Mary Hall and three years later the marriage produced a son, William, who went on, as 'Young Bill Lewis', to become as successful a pugilist as his father, winning the Southern Area bantamweight title in 1931. Young Bill Lewis's brothers Teddy and George joined the rest of the family at Billingsgate and also went into the ring. But we're running ahead of ourselves. In August 1916, at the age of thirty-five, William Lucioni died on the battlefields of the Somme leaving behind five children – William, Mary, Wally, Teddy and George. Left with five mouths to feed, Mary Lucioni née Hall, quickly remarried Henry Whybrow. The couple went on to have another two children.

In the mid 1920s the son William Lucioni left behind, Teddy, met Martha Robertson and Jim Lakin's daughter Lizzie at a dance at the Roman Road Baths. The couple married in 1929 and moved to 5 Ordell Road, a turning off the Roman. The Lucionis are on the first floor. They have a kitchen but no running water, a bedroom and a 'best' room. It's not an ideal place from which to begin raising a family, but plenty of others are worse off. Like his father, Bill, before him, Teddy makes a half-decent wage working as a licensed fish porter at Billingsgate market, carrying up to three hundredweight (about 152 kg) of fish perched on his thick leather porters' hat. The work, it's said, 'turns the brain'* – the foreman keeps a 'loony book' in which he writes down the porters' many

---

* This phrase comes from a BBC Radio actuality recording of Billingsgate market porters made in 1935, and can be found at www.londonsoundsurvey.org.uk (accessed 5 May 2017).

oddities – it's one of those exclusive, self-contained worlds the East End seemed to specialise in back then, a world conjured, simply, by the word 'mate'.

The work also makes for the kind of strong back and sturdy neck it takes to be a boxer. And the Lucioni family now has three young brothers in the game, William 'Young Bill Lewis', Teddy and George. By the time he's in his twenties Teddy has 200 fights under his belt, though that's still fifty fewer than his dad, Bill Lewis, and not quite in the same league as his brother Young Bill Lewis, who has now risen to become Southern Area bantamweight champion.

It's 24 August 1929, a weekend, and lovely weather. Normally, Teddy would either be off to the pub, at one of his political meetings or at the flapper tracks at Hackney Marshes with his whippets, Fair Lizzie and Good Lizzie (both named after his wife) and, in the evening, at Mile End boxing arena. Today he's awaiting the birth of his first child, so he's most likely down the pub. The men aren't around, generally, when babies come into the world. It's very probable that Lizzie's mother, Martha, the matchbox maker, acts as midwife, or 'bringer-in' to her grandson, since that's what she does anyway. Ted thinks it was probably a Sunday since he's been told that he entered this world to the sound of the Sally Army singing outside the pub opposite.*

On the ground floor below the Lucionis lives Mr Gray, the landlord. On the third floor are the Pleasants. While Lizzie is going through her labours the men of the house will go out to the pub or otherwise tactfully disappear. There's no privacy to speak of. The outdoor privy has to serve all three families, though only the Lucionis and the Pleasants use the outdoor tap because the Grays have one in their kitchen. Still, at a time like this what matters is dignity. No one in the house feels poor and they aren't, at least, not like Ron. In some places, several families are living in a single

---

* 24 August 1929 was actually a Saturday.

room. At Ordell Road there is a small backyard with a tree and a columbine weed snaking up the fence, an outdoor privy and the tin bath and mangle, and what once might have been a chicken shed in which Teddy Lucioni now kennels the two Lizzies.

A few years later, after the birth of Ted's siblings, Norma and William, the Lucionis move to more spacious digs in McCullum Road, a turning of Victorian terraces running between Old Ford Road and the Roman.* At the end of McCullum Road is a tin-box factory beside which is a pub, the Eleanor Arms. Opposite are stables being used for storage. As soon as they move, Lizzie sees to it that there are clean net curtains at the windows, the rag rugs are shaken out, the floor is mopped, the sheets laundered, the woodwork polished and a half-moon is scrubbed on the pavement outside, working until all is spic and span and orderly. Still, in the council records, the place is designated a slum and slated for clearance.

Ted junior grows up fast in McCullum Road and, like many eldest children, takes on responsibilities not expected of the others. He's quiet and happiest in his own world. 'Dozy little sod' his father says, though the opposite is true. Two incidents in his early life stand out. In the first, he's about four and his mother, Lizzie, sends him to the shop to pick up something she's forgotten and needs for tea. It's young to be sent out on your own, but things are different then and the shop's only at the end of the road. Ted isn't fazed by the walk, only by the shopkeeper who, when he tells him what he's come for, throws back his head and laughs like a drain. What can four-year-old Ted have said to cause such hilarity? He has no idea and no one is about to explain it. Sensing the laughter is *at* him not with him, little Ted is soon running home empty-handed and in tears. His mother is incensed. Marching her son

* Renowned photographer Nigel Henderson's image of McCullum Road, 1949, is now in the Tate's national collection. The photograph shows a peeling, blank wall with a murky cityscape just visible behind.

back to the shop, she demands to know what's so funny about a little boy asking for a packet of dried mixed herbs? Well, nothing, the shopkeeper explains, but what little Ted *actually* asked for, very politely, was a packet of dried mixed turds.

The second incident occurs some while later. Ted is adept at shopping now and because he's the oldest child he's often asked to do it. This time his parents want Nelson cakes, one each for themselves and one for Ted. So off goes Ted to the bakery. 'So as I'm coming back, a bigger boy has come up to me and said, "What have you got in the bag?" and I've opened the bag to show him.' And the boy removes one of the cakes, takes a bite out of it and puts it back in the bag. So Ted goes back home and relays what's happened, and Teddy senior says, 'Well, all right, that's your one', and now Ted is crying again and protesting, 'No, no, I can't eat that, [the boy] had a snotty nose!'

Unsurprisingly, Ted's friends are the quirky kids, the ones everyone else has rejected. There's 'Eggy', a boy with an oversized head and some kind of mental incapacity, and 'Soppy Ada', who, at about thirty, isn't strictly a kid but has the mind of one. Mostly, and at school particularly, though, Ted keeps himself to himself. He's small and skinny and sick of being nicknamed Lucy. So, no school friends as such. He's close to his nan, Martha, but his best pal is his mother's youngest sister, who is only a couple of years older than Ted, and walks with him to Roman Road school, except on those days Ted hitches a ride with Uncle Fred (who is not a real uncle) the Coal Man.

In the way of all imaginative kids, Ted grows up awash with odd notions and half-baked ideas concocted from fragments of information gleaned from adults. One of these is that Itchy Williams's boy, who works in the fish and chip shop opposite the house, acquired his freckles from hot fat spitting from the chip pans. Another, gleaned from visits to nan Martha in Libra Road, where a moneylending neighbour keeps a large aspidistra in the window of her front room, is the conviction that a moneylender can be found wherever there is an aspidistra, just as a pawnbroker can be found at the sign of three gold balls.

From a young age Ted learns to graft because he likes the money. He finds work collecting clothes and household items from his neighbours and transporting them in an old pram to the nearest pawnshop on the Roman. For the neighbours it's worth a few coppers to avoid the shame of being seen. On market days he helps the Baker family wheel out their trolleys early in the morning and wheel them back to the yard late at night. He grows up like his father and his father before him, small and wiry and very, very strong. For Ted it's tickets to the Saturday morning tuppenny rush at the Ritz on St Stephen's Road* and an ice cream at Randolfi's on the Roman, then in the afternoon perhaps a long wallow in hot suds at the Bow Baths for thruppence, or sixpence if you want soap and a towel. He's partial to the hot potato or portion of batter bits that he gets from Arnold's, which in the not too distant future will become Kelly's pie and mash shop, and from the fish and chip shop down the road. On a Sunday he might head up to Vicky Park or to the bank beside the Regent's Canal, from where he will watch the draught horses on the towpath, heaving timber barges along the murky water, so quiet and peaceful 'you wouldn't think you was anywhere near a city or anything'.

At the centre of Ted's world is the Roman. In the mid 1930s the market is humming, as big as any in London, Petticoat Lane excepted. The whole raucous carnival of it. Two hundred and fifty stalls and barrows, rented from Len Baker's yard on Old Ford Road and stocked with everything from hairnets to doormats. Ted grows up with the clatter of calling out and auctioneering, with shouts of feigned outrage at prices demanded and offered, sharp intakes of breath at juicy tidbits of gossip, barking at errant children and belly

---

* Also known as the Bughouse. So bad are the infestations that an usherette comes round with Flit spray before each day's first performance.

laughs at *risqué* jokes. He remembers stalls laden with artfully stacked goods, illuminated long after dark in the smoky, smelly light of naphtha lamps; turkeys hanging over the butcher's at Christmas; pretend indignation of stallholders and buyers; satisfied grins at bargains bought and deals done; and sudden bursts of drama as a kid makes off with an orange or an unlicensed vendor opens a suitcase of something that's lately fallen off the back of a van.

At home in McCullum Road life is a little more ordered. A bust of Edward VIII sits on the mantelpiece, marking Teddy Lucioni out as a patriot and a royalist. A proud Tory. Looking back, Ted reckons his father 'thought that the Tories, or only the people that had been to universities or Eton or wherever, were the only people wise enough to govern the country'. But by the middle of the decade there's a shift in Teddy's thinking. 'My father was a gentleman, everybody loved him, but he was a Blackshirt,' a member of the fiercely anti-immigrant and anti-Semitic British Union of Fascists (BUF). His motivation is a mystery. Ted, who in later years will become a union man, insists that 'Some of his [father's] best friends were Jews.' Perhaps Teddy is drawn to the cause by the abdication of his hero, Edward VIII, in December 1936. This shook him hard. He may also have been swept up in one of the recruiting drives held regularly by the BUF in East End gyms, or, possibly, he feels some kind of atavistic admiration for Mussolini and the Italian-style fascism adopted by the BUF at this time. It might just be that he's anti-communist. The East End in the 1930s is a turmoil of extremist politics on both sides, and Teddy is by no means alone in his affiliations – the BUF has 40,000 members and an East London headquarters at 222 Green Street, now Roman Road.

According to one source,* Teddy Lucioni quickly moves up the ranks and is appointed the BUF's candidate in Whitechapel, which is something of a surprise, and perhaps says something about the

---

* Nigel Farndale, *Haw-Haw: The Tragedy of William and Margaret Joyce* (Palgrave Macmillan, 2005).

scarcity of other candidates, since, if this same source is to be believed, Teddy was illiterate and, having memorised a speech, would deliver it verbatim throughout the East End. Unsympathetic locals would follow him around and do their best to put him off his stride by jokily reciting it back to him. Despite this, or perhaps because of it, Teddy takes his political work seriously. Soon, he has recruited his seven-year-old son to deliver the fascist newspaper, *Action*, a chore particularly troublesome to Ted since it often involves sparking the anger of their many Jewish neighbours, which means having to hotfoot it down the road with an irate adult in pursuit.

II

From the time we came from Portugal in the 1600s, seven
Gomez Da Costa brothers, we were in the markets. So you see,
I was born to be a market trader.

Harry Da Costa

While Ted Lucioni is delivering *Action*, his contemporary Harry
Da Costa is in the market, working at his dad's stall. The two
boys are about the same age and both small, dark and beady,
given to drifting on their own choppy inner seas. Like Ted,
Harry is the descendent of immigrants, though the Da Costas
are earlier arrivals than the Lucionis, having been living, hawking and trading in the East End more than a century before
Aquilino Lucioni arrives in Clerkenwell. And, unlike the
Lucionis, they are Jewish.

There have been Jews in London since William the Conqueror
invited them in. A Jewish community settled around the
Tower, only to be expelled by Edward I in 1290, and for 200
years London was a city without a noticeable Jewish population. After their expulsion from Spain in 1492 and Portugal
in 1497, a few families were allowed under special permits
to take refuge in London, the most notable of whom was
Rodrigo López, physician to Elizabeth I. For the next century
and a half Marranos, or 'secret Jews', continued to arrive in
London from the Iberian Peninsula, until in 1657 Oliver
Cromwell officially reopened Britain's doors to them once

more.* The Da Costas probably arrived in the first wave not long afterwards. A house in Creechurch Lane in the City of London was converted into a synagogue, but there wouldn't be an official place of worship until half a century later, in 1701, when London's first dedicated synagogue, Qahal Kadosh Sha'ar ha-Shamayim, opened its doors in Bevis Marks near Aldgate.

By the middle of the nineteenth century a thriving Dutch Jewish community is living around Cobb, Leyden and Toynbee Streets in Spitalfields and working as cigar and cigarette makers,† and in 1857 a Jewish soup kitchen is opened in Brick Lane. By 1858 the kitchen is feeding more than a thousand people, and by 1878 the Board of Guardians of the Jewish Poor is taking out advertisements in the Russian and Romanian Jewish press trying to dissuade Jews from coming to London by warning them that conditions are tough. But the East European pogroms continue, and the warnings prove to be no deterrent. Between 1901 and 1914 the Jewish population in the East End rises to 126,082, the vast majority Polish and Russian Jews, the remainder from Germany, Austria, Holland and Romania.

Suddenly there are synagogues popping up all over the East End, but it's at Bevis Marks that Harry's father Hyam and his mother Kate are married. Harry follows, then a sister, Jean, and finally Joel. At the time of Harry's birth the Da Costas have been trading in the East End's markets for more than two and a half centuries and operate twenty stalls, about a dozen of those in the Roman. Family life is dominated by the business. Harry's granddad, old man Hyam, runs a stall specialising in quality hardware, overstocks mostly, often from Selfridges, his nan and great-aunt sell babywear and smalls, another aunt deals in glassware. Harry's dad, another

---

* In 1649, anxious to fulfil an ancient prophecy suggesting that the Second Coming would only happen when Jews were scattered across the globe, two English Puritans living in Amsterdam petitioned Cromwell to allow Jews back into England.
† In 1858 these workers lead the first Jewish workers' strike in the UK for better pay and conditions.

Hyam, deals in job lots, whatever he can get his hands on cheap and sell fast. Beside them sit the long-established shops: Abbott's, Dennington's, Arber's print and toys, Arnold's pie and mash (the shop that will soon become G. Kelly), Percy Ingles the baker, Randolfi's ice-cream parlour run by Lou and Francesca, the diary round the back of Arber's printers where Welshman Davies keeps his cows, Cohens the tailor, Shorts oil and paint – selling paraffin, 'the Bug blinder' – and Yetta Morris, formerly Mogolovksy, who runs the beigel* shop with her brother Jackie and, as Gary Arber remembers from his boyhood, swears like a sailor. Beside Yetta is Sid Shaw, Jewish and auburn-haired, a quiet grocer whose wife Sylvie (a bit uppity, a bit too grand for the shop, according to Gary) has an affair with Petrovksy the chemist around the corner. Sid will go on to earn the Military Medal for bravery in the Second World War but will never boast about it; and that, says Gary, is a measure of the man.

Harry's father Hyam Da Costa is a bit of a comedian, a bit of a singer and a bit of a drinker. When he's in his cups he can be found belting out duets with Kate. Rest of the time, he and Kate are working. Tuesdays and Thursdays they'll be out of the house at 6 a.m. and setting out the stall in the Roman by half past. Fridays they'll be trading till midnight and Saturdays they'll be in the Roman twelve, thirteen hours. At the time – this is the thirties – the market stallholders are predominantly Jewish, though there are plenty who are not. One of Hyam's market pals is Prince Monolulu, who styles himself Prince of Abyssinia but was born Ras Peter Carl Mackay to a horse-breeding family from St Croix in the Danish West Indies. Monolulu made his name in the East End as a roving tipster, having won £8,000 by picking Spion Kop in the 1920 Epsom Derby at odds of 100 to 6. He became synonymous with the catchphrases 'I've got a horse' and 'Black man for luck'. Harry junior remembers Monolulu because, at 6

---

* East Enders pronounce beigel with a long 'i' as in 'bygel'.

foot 6 and black, he was hard to forget. He'd stop by Hyam's stall, which from the age of seven Harry junior would sometimes run, taking the money and shouting out, while his dad nipped off to the pub for a quick one. Harry's early experience makes him as quick a study in mental arithmetic as it does in human nature, and there are always lessons to be learned. One time, Hyam has a consignment of cheese. He's laid out half on the stall with the extra tucked underneath, but when they go to fetch it there are six kids underneath the stall and no cheese. It can be like that down the Roman: you've got to watch your back, but you've also got to watch your cheese.

Unless he's helping out on the stall, Harry doesn't see that much of his parents. Kate works all hours and Hyam will sometimes be away for a week or more picking up stock. Hyam never does learn to drive, however. Instead he hires a pantechnicon and a driver. The day before he's due to return from his travels he'll send a telegram. The next day the pantechnicon will reappear carrying Hyam and a load of overstock and job lots, plus a packet of wine gums for Harry. Always wine gums.

The Da Costas employ a live-in maid, Elsie, at their house in Benworth Street, Mile End, to help keep house and look after Jean, who has Down's syndrome. While his parents work, Elsie takes the kids out for adventures. One time, Harry must be about six, they go on a tour of HMS *Hood* and from then on Harry decides he'd rather be a sailor than a trader. Until such time as he's able to start his seafaring, though, the Roman isn't a bad home port. There's Elsie plus the three old maid aunts – Rosie, Hetty and Julie, living in Merchant Street with their father – who dote on Harry and whisk him off on day trips to Bournemouth and Dovercourt. Every year he gets to join the annual Roman Road traders' beano to Dreamland in Margate. A fleet of coaches leaves Morgan Street in Mile End at 8 a.m., and they're in Margate by eleven. Then it's fish and chips or cockles and winkles and jellied eels and pie and mash for lunch, a paddle in the sea or a go on the fairground carousel, and finally ice cream. They are back home in the East End full in stomach and heart by 8 p.m.

But this is the East End in the 1930s, so it's rare for a kid to get through childhood without some disaster, small or large, and Harry is no exception. In 1935, as storm clouds are gathering over Europe, his sister, Jean, contracts pleurisy and dies. Two years later, when Harry's just turned ten, his mother notices his nose twitching and something odd happening to his mouth. A visit to the doctor confirms St Vitus Dance.* No cure. The only thing to do is rest. A spell in the Royal London Hospital is followed by an extended eleven-month stay at Rowan House in Brentwood in a ward with a dozen other kids, stuck in bed all day at first, then gradually allowed up. Hyam and Kate visit on Sundays when they can. It's no fun; when you're ten, a year may as well be forever.

By the time Harry is discharged from Rowan House, Hyam and Kate have moved from Mile End to Barkingside and young Harry finds himself in another new world, one away from the doting aunts and the loving uncles and all the rush and tumble of the Roman. Out of school hours he's mostly in the company of his younger brother and the new maid, Annie, from County Cork. On Saturday mornings, 'the only mornings we were home', all three tumble into bed together and 'have a cuddle'. By the age of twelve Harry has learned to do more than cuddle. 'She [Annie] was young but not very pretty or very small,' says Harry, though he's not about to let any of that stop him. 'By the time I was thirteen there wasn't much I didn't know.'

In the history books the East End's Jewish population is often spoken about as if it were a single community rather than a number of distinct populations separated if not by geography, then by history, culture, even language. The Shratsky family, who will

---

* More commonly known today as Sydenham's chorea. A disorder associated with streptococcus infection and characterised by involuntary muscle movements, it disproportionately affects children and these days is treated both with penicillin and with the antipsychotic drug haloperidol.

come to play a role in the life of Kelly's, are probably more typical of the Jewish arrivals to the East End than the Da Costas, both in their origin and in the pace of their assimilation. By the time Isaac Shratsky arrived by steam packet from Hamburg at Irongate Wharf, beside Tower Bridge, with little more than a spare set of clothes, the Da Costas had been settled in the East End for eight generations. Born in 1851 in what is now Poland but was then part of Russia, Isaac would have had almost nothing in common with the Da Costas save for a passing knowledge of Hebrew and the insecurity of being both an exile and a Jew.

The details of Isaac Shratsky's life are very sketchy, not least because, as was often the case with immigrants, his family name is spelled variously in the records, making it harder to track him. Most likely he came to London with the first wave of arrivals in 1881. Ten years later he and his wife Annie were living with their children at 213 Cable Street, a long straight road of three-storey early Victorian terrace houses running parallel to The Highway just east of the Tower of London. Back then most of the houses had shops on the ground floor and flats or rooms on the two floors above. On Booth's map the street is marked as mixed poor and comfortable, just another turning, heavily populated by Jewish immigrants, among whom was the young Isaac Rosenberg, the celebrated war poet and artist, who, from 1897, lived at number 47. It's likely the Shratskys knew Isaac Rosenberg as an infant, though by the time of the poet's death, on 1 April 1918 at Fampoux near Arras, they had moved.

Like many East End Jews, the Shratskys were working in the tailoring trade, living from hand to mouth, toiling all hours and only just getting by. Their son Jack grew up in an East End still dominated by tales of another, more sinister Jack. In 1894, a young adult now, Jack married Minnie and the couple moved to 20 Alexandra Buildings, formerly known as the Jewish and East London Model Lodgings, at 45–55 Commercial Street in Whitechapel – the building had been opened by the Chief Rabbi on 18 August 1863, only five years after Jews were given full political rights, with money donated by the scions of two famous Jewish banking families, Sir Francis Goldsmid and Sir Anthony de Rothschild. At that time around 65 per cent of East London's population of just under 1 million were living below the poverty line – of these, around 120,000 teetered on the edge of starvation – and the Lodgings provided modest homes for thirty Jewish families. Rent was cheap and the tiny flats were crowded, particularly as children, first Solomon, then others, began to arrive, but where else was there? Private accommodation was buggier and damper and even more expensive.

As soon as he could, Jack quit his job as a tailor's presser and with his brothers set up a business selling newspapers, among them Yiddish and Jewish English-language papers like the *Jewish Chronicle* and the *Jewish Daily News* in which Isaac Rosenberg's death would have been reported. The couple moved to Coventry Road, only five minutes' walk from Samuel and Matilda Kelly's pie and mash shop, though it's unlikely, given the Jewish proscription on eel,* that they ever visited. Not long after the Battle of Cable Street, as Ted Lucioni is dropping off copies of *Action* and Harry Da Costa is doing the St Vitus dance, Jack and Minnie's son Solomon will leave home and take the big and very possibly shocking step of marrying outside the faith. His bride will be a Welsh woman, Ruth Price, a recent arrival from the Rhondda Valley, attracted to London, as are so many, by the prospect of work. The couple will set up home in Brady Street Dwellings, a couple of roads from Jack and Minnie and not far from Kelly's pie and mash shop, where, a few decades later, their son, Phil, will fetch his lunchtime pie and mash.

---

* The Torah forbids eating of fish without scales, which are defined as being detachable from the skin without breaking it. Eels do have scales, but these are not removable without damaging the skin, and the creature is therefore not kosher.

12

Homes fit for heroes
Lloyd George, 1919[*]

By the outbreak of the Second World War the East End is crammed and roaring with lives, its population sardines crammed into ill-fashioned tins. The war will empty out the whole of London, and most particularly the East End, and it will take more than seven decades for the capital to return to its pre-war population. The housing crisis of today is all the more shocking for being nothing new. All it took then is all it takes now: an illness, a patch of bad luck, an accident, an unforeseen pregnancy, a cruel or greedy landlord, or a rift in the family for a person to find themselves homeless.

After the Great War, Lloyd George promised 'homes fit for heroes', and in 1921 building began on the largest council estate in the world, near Dagenham, a few miles to the East of the Roman. The plans were for three-bedroom houses with a parlour and an internal bathroom and WC, and large front and back gardens with a privet hedge out front and an apple tree in the back. Heaven with the gate open. But as the 1920s proceeded the UK economy stagnated, and by 1934 the estate was still not fully built, rents were too high for the East End's poorest, and the plans had been scaled

---

[*] What Lloyd George actually said was 'Habitations fit for the heroes who have won the war', in an article in *The Times*, 15 November 1918.

down. Newer houses are being built with smaller, poorer-quality fittings and no parlours. A generation after the start of the Great War, the vast majority of East Enders are still living in the same overcrowded, bug-ridden, damp, multi-occupancy private rentals they were before it started.

By the 1930s the focus in the East End had moved to slum clearance. Slum officers were appointed to identify turnings ripe for redevelopment, and dozens of terraces around the Roman, such as the one at McCullum Street, where the Lucionis were living, were scheduled for demolition. In 1931, having been slum cleared from McCullum Street, the Lucionis are relocated to a three-bedroom semi on the new estate. It's a longer commute for Teddy to and from Billingsgate, but by and large the move is a success. Teddy and Lizzie share one bedroom, Ted and his brother the other, with their sister Norma getting her own. There is room to dream and space to breathe. Ted knows that the Lucionis are lucky to be there. All the same he misses the market and how easy it is to make a penny or two taking neighbours' linen down to the pawn. He misses being able to fetch mash and liquor from school for his lunch. He is used to being able to walk out of his front door, skip down the turning and be at his nan's – despite all her roaring and drinking, despite having to barrow her home to bed drunk from pub, Ted misses her. It is quiet out in Becontree. Sometimes as quiet as the tomb.

Meanwhile, private rents go up. In 1936 the Stepney Tenants' Defence League, led by Jewish communist Michael Shapiro, organise a series of rent strikes across the East End. These grow more political and fractious as the months go on. In June 1937 tenants throw bricks at police and bailiffs in Mile End. Just around the corner from the Lucionis' old home in McCullum Street, at the BUF's local headquarters in Green Street, Mick Clare, the Leader of the 8th London Area of the British Union of Fascists, is organising rallies and marches of his own.

The fight between opposing political forces comes to a head at the Battle of Cable Street in the late afternoon of 4 October 1936, when local residents, many of them Jewish, dockers, communists and other activists head off a group of Blackshirts marching west towards the Tower. Cable Street is only one of several BUF gatherings across the East End that day, including at Chester Street, Shoreditch, at Salmon Lane in Limehouse and at Stafford Road, Bow, and it has become symbolic of a particular brand of East End inclusiveness and pluck. But the story plays both ways. As Whitechapel candidate for the BUF, Teddy Lucioni is almost certainly at one of these meetings, albeit on the wrong side of history. All the evidence suggests he was a better boxer than a politician. I could only find one mention of his political career.*

Poverty is indiscriminate. Jews, communists, fascists, Italians, Irish and the rest are destined to return to the same inadequate homes, to warm themselves in front of the same meagre fires before sinking finally into their saggy beds. They get up each morning and see their kids off to the same schools, trudge to work in the same docks, the same factories, the same sweatshops, and when the weekend comes they will eke out their meagre wages in the same markets, sit in the same fleapits, cheer at the same football grounds and dog tracks, sit at the same eel, pie and mash shops and eat the same Londoner's meal.

---

* In Nigel Ferndale, *Haw-Haw: The Tragedy of William and Margaret Joyce*, (Macmillan, 2005).

13

> We had nothing, nothing at all. If . . . [Hitler] hadn't gone into
> Russia, we'd a lost that war.
>
> Ron Moss, Mapping the Change

A small plane flies low over the East End. The day is warm and humid. Thunder is forecast though there's no sign of it yet. It's a Sunday, not far off dinner-time, and on the outskirts of the city there are already long lines of traffic heading towards the countryside.

From the garden of his home on London's Essex border, Gary Arber watches the aircraft as it moves through the blue sky, following the black crosses on the underside of its wings. Inside the house his parents, printer Walter Francis Arber and his wife Florence, remain close to the radio. The Arber family print shop on the Roman Road is closed and locked up for the day. Florence is probably stringing late summer runner beans or peeling potatoes in preparation for the Sunday roast, though dinner will almost certainly be late today. In any case, food is the last thing on Gary's mind. He is too young to understand fully the solemn weight of the radio announcement (can anyone?), but is old enough to know that his life is about to change in ways neither he nor his parents can predict.

By the time Gary spots the plane it has passed over more than ten thousand years of history – over Neolithic timber piles where the Effra River, long since forced underground, meets the

Thames at Vauxhall; over remnants of a Bronze Age bridge and so many tarry lighters moored up on jetties along the river that you can hardly see the brown tidal murk beneath. On its journey eastwards it has soared over the medieval muddle of streets of the Square Mile and passed the ribbed dome of St Paul's and the sooty-black expanse of the Tower and carried on, the pilot perhaps registering the ancient crossroads in Shoreditch where the old Roman road to Chelmsford and Colchester transects Ermine Street on its way north to Lincoln. At Aldgate the plane will have entered the East End where the air, even on a Sunday, is hot with steam and thick with the outspill from factories. From there it will sail over the decks of numberless ships quayside at the West and East India Docks until at Blackwall it reaches the Thames meander, where Sir Walter Raleigh kept a house and from where in 1576 Martin Frobisher set out for the Northwest Passage and, thirty years later, three small ships left to found Jamestown in the Americas. There, along the skein of the Lea at Bow Creek, its banks clotted with abattoirs and factories, the pilot may have been momentarily dazzled by the sun bouncing off the silvery ox-bow where the Vikings steered their longboats north and where, if you are clever with your traps, eels are to be found.

A little way up river and to the west, in Bethnal Green, Samuel and Matilda Kelly's pie, mash and eel shop will be shuttered and closed. On any ordinary Sunday morning, Sam the Pie, Old Mutton Eye to his friends, might be in the pub while Matilda cooks the Sunday dinner. Their son George is likely to be with his eels at the yard in Viaduct Street, or else polishing his car or perhaps checking there are enough potatoes at his new shop in Broadway market for the lunchtime rush on Monday. George is thirty-five by now, long married to Theresa Kingdon and making the most of his money from trading eels. There are no children from the marriage, a fact that saddens Theresa, who will spend her Sunday either reading (a favourite pastime), playing with other people's children, or visiting her parents Theresa and Tom Kingdon in their flat above Kelly's at number 310 on the Roman, or her brother and sister-in-law, Bill and Bea Kingdon, in their flat above Kelly's at number 236 on the same road.

The Kellys' pie and mash empire has expanded considerably in the twenty-four years since Sam the Pie and Matilda opened their first shop on Bethnal Green Road. Some of that is down to George, whose ambition and gift for both hard work and the hustle has brought him shops at Broadway Market in Hackney and at 55 Devons Road, Bow, and, most recently, two more in the Roman. But although George's name is above the door on all these shops, his empire is as much the achievement of his wife's family, the Kingdons, as it is his own. While his parents-in-law manage the shop at 310, Theresa oversees business at 236 with her brother and sister-in-law, leaving George free to manage the other two shops and, more importantly, the eel supply business.

The shop at number 236 has only been open a month or so when the plane flies over. The place had been a pie and mash shop before George purchased it from Mr Lloyd, who had in turn bought it from Alfred Arnold in the late thirties. It is slap bang in the middle of the Roman, only a few steps from the Arber family print shop, and is perfectly positioned to take full advantage of the footfall on market days. In the few weeks since he bought it, George and Theresa have already given the old place a do-over. Up has gone a new fascia-board in shiny black Vitriolite with *G. Kelly Noted Eel & Pie Shop* in chromium lettering. The shop windows are also framed in chromium, and have a lower sash of plain glass which can be raised to counter level on the inside, from where take-away orders can be met. The left and right glass panels on the clerestory as you go in are etched *Stewed Eels, Jellied Eels* and *Meat Pies, Mashed Potatoes*. The shop's exterior is dressed in white faience, with chromium ventilation panels above the glazing. A smart striped shop awning can be pulled over the frontage to protect people standing in line from the rain, and there are two elegant milk glass and chromium lights that have been letter-painted *Kelly's* and *Eel Shop* respectively. Step inside and you will see to the left a marble countertop and beneath it a counter lined with pies. At the window vast stainless vats sit on stainless heaters. The walls are tiled white to match long marble tables. To one side stands a large screen of glass etched in the art deco style with a scene of eels floating in a kelp forest.

The kitchen is at the back. In a giant coke-fuelled oven pie crusts crisp, potatoes are peeled and mashed and eels are killed and chopped and stewed in huge vats. Pastry is rolled and cut on a grand old table, and there are butler's sinks for the washing up. At the counter, looking at a mirror etched with eels, a chromium clock and a sign reading *Kelly's for Jelly*, you'll see a picture of cleanliness and order, for it's here that George's wife, Theresa – beautiful, bookish, a bit of an intellectual and much loved by customers – serves pies and scoops mash and ladles liquor and eels with the help of Vera Leach, a washer-up, a few kitchen staff and a couple of Saturday girls.

George has a yard ten minutes' walk away, in Old Ford Road, where he swims his eels. To George Kelly an eel is as silver as a coin. Most of his money, and by the time the shop at 236 the Roman opens there is quite a lot of it, has come from the slippery snakelike fish. He'll buy them cheap from fishermen out on the Kent and Essex marshes or at Billingsgate at the end of the day, then swim them in tanks of moving water in the eel yard until it's time for them to meet their destiny. On market days at the Roman a large and handsome stall is wheeled out on to the pavement outside the shop for the purpose. From here, Vera's husband Dick Leach relieves live eels of their heads, guts and washes them, then wraps them in newspaper for waiting customers. On the other side of the stall Vera dispenses cold jellied eels in paper cones.

Because today is a Sunday the shops are closed. But even if they were open and the pilot of the small plane could see inside the etched-glass shop fronts to the smart marble countertops, the white-tiled walls, the neat tables with their white pepper pots, tubs of cutlery and bottles of malt vinegar, what he would see would be nothing more than a couple of modest shops serving cheap and humdrum fare to the working class of East London. The pilot, not being an East Ender, could hardly know or comprehend that some small but potent fragment of London's soul is on show daily here; nor could he know or comprehend that the people over whose airspace his little plane now bounces are about to prove tougher and more resilient than the hand-carved market barrows in Len Baker's yard, the elegant milk glass lights over Kelly's eel, pie and mash shops, and the grimy turnings of rackapaulty houses might suggest. East Enders themselves don't know this yet.

A few yards further east, only three and a quarter miles from St Paul's, near the spot where in 1110 Matilda, wife of Henry I, ordered a bridge built to ease her passage across the River Lea, at 43 Ripporth Road, the Moss family, Melinda, her father Joe and some of Melinda's surviving twelve children, are perched on the immaculate stoop of their cramped home with their neighbours, the Batlins. They have been listening to Alvar Lidell on the old crystal set (a wireless is too expensive), the men smoking and the women snorting snuff from the backs of their hands and looking forward to the off-licence opening, a beer being just the thing to calm jittery nerves right now. Later, Melinda might send her youngest, Ron – the Artful D – along to fetch a jug of beer. It was market day in the Roman only yesterday, but there's unlikely to be enough to eat. There wasn't enough for breakfast and there probably won't be enough for tea, unless the Artful D manages to snare a rabbit out on the marshes or come across some watercress. Once he's fetched the beer he'll most likely head along the Greenway. There might be some entertainment to be had at the Sunday afternoon flapper tracks. Who knows, Teddy Lucioni might be there with his whippets, Good Lizzie and Fair Lizzie. The Artful D is fond of a dog. On the other hand, he might go swimming in the canal or for a mooch in the railway yard.

The news will mean there's less money around. Not that there's much now. Fred Moss is in the fishing fleet and always away at sea. What he does with his leave is a mystery to Ron and maybe to Melinda too. He often makes an appearance only long enough to seed another baby. He'll be away for longer now.

There will be a few pennies to be made rowing men and women across the canal to the Lea Tavern opposite Clarnico's sweet factory, then rowing them back again after last orders. There will be a lot of drinking tonight. People will be wanting to drown their sorrows.

The pilot of the little plane will sense the warp in the air as he navigates the tidy, outer suburbs with their spacious streets of semis and countrified gardens, beyond Gants Hill where Harry Da Costa's father is preparing for drill practice, and Romford where the Arber household is still gathered around the wireless and Gary is about to run into the garden. Gaining height now, he'll fly the plane parallel to the Thames as it widens at Tilbury, past ships bringing in the bounty of Empire, while far below at Erith and on the Muckin Sands fishermen will be setting their eel traps – the fishermen go as far east as London Stone, just shy of Southend, where day-trippers will be spreading themselves on deckchairs in the sun and unwrapping packages of fish and chips or little paper cones of cockles and winkles and shrimp with vinegar and white pepper, or pots of jellied eels.

The plane is a speck in the sky now, the pilot and his passenger unable to make out the row of tiny hopper's huts at Toler's Farm in Staplehurst on the Kent weald, or to spot Ann Simmons at play beside the family's hut while her grandmother tends to their lunch on the open fire. In any other year Ann's mother would be with them, taking a 'Londoner's holiday' picking hops. It's a break from the cramped house on Lydia Street in Stepney, which she shares with her husband, his parents and his sister, and the money always comes in handy. But this year she's heavily pregnant. When he arrives, the little boy will quickly succumb to pneumonia and die before his eighth week, but as yet Ann's mother doesn't know this, or that she will never get over her son's death.

A few miles to the east of Ann and her grandmother, in Pluckley on the edge of the Kentish weald, Ted Lucioni will be anticipating Sunday lunch. His grandmother, Martha Robertson, is keeping an eye on him while his mother Lizzie carries their Sunday meat and potatoes in a cloth-covered pan to the local baker, who will put the pan to cook in his large bread oven. Later, Martha and Lizzie might walk to the pub. Ted might well come with them, and pass the time playing outside with the other kids. At some point Lizzie will bring out a glass of lemonade and an arrowroot biscuit.

Back on Fish Island, around midday, long after the plane has disappeared in the muggy summer sky, the proprietor of the off-licence near Ripporth Road is clearing up the mess of glass left by a stampede of panicked customers responding to what turns out to be a false alarm. The threat is not what everyone thinks it is. That is yet to come. But in the scrum bottles of beer and lemonade go flying, leaving a smashed heap on the floor and outside on the pavement. So much is broken and spilled that, as Ron remembers it, there's hardly any stock left. What a laugh Ron will have. Those ridiculous adults and their stupid notions! Scared of what? A voice on the radio?

And so the plane which began its journey on a Sunday morning will move out across the Channel towards a darkening continent and the day will continue to evening and the light will falter and a deep, unfamiliar pall will envelope the capital, and eight-year-old Gary Arber will go to bed that night with that plane so etched in in his memory that seventy-seven years later, relating the story on a warm day in the summer from the very same garden, it will seem as if it were only yesterday that a plane flew over the house, not long after the declaration of war, and he will recall discovering later that it was carrying Herbert von Dirksen, the Ambassador of Germany, hurrying back to Berlin. And though Gary's version does not *quite* fit the facts, because Ambassador von Dirksen left

Britain on holiday on 10 August 1939, to him there can only be one version of the story, the one lodged deep in his memory in which an eight-year-old boy spots a Nazi plane flying over the garden of his suburban home on the first day of the war. Three-quarters of a century later, he will remember the moment as if all the time between had been nothing more than the blink of an eye.

14

You will eat, by and by,
In the glorious land above the sky;
Work and pray, live on hay,
You'll get pie in the sky when you die
    Joe Hill, 'The Preacher and the Slave' (1910)

In the months since the Munich Agreement of September 1938 London has been preparing for a cataclysm. Gas masks are handed out, postboxes painted with gas-sensitive paint, floodgates installed in Tube tunnels under the Thames, deep shelters identified, trees, lampposts and kerbs marked with white paint. Machine guns installed on the roofs of power stations, zigzagging trenches cut in parks, public buildings sandbagged and their windows criss-crossed with tape, barrage balloons launched, Auxiliary Fire Service, Womens' Volunteer Service and Air Raid Precaution volunteers recruited, overground public shelters built, Anderson shelters dug for those with access to gardens or yards, and Morrison shelters distributed for those without.

In the build-up, the Committee of Imperial Defence secretly calculates that in the first twenty-four hours of the war 3,500 high-explosive and incendiary bombs are likely to be dropped on the capital, leaving 58,000 Londoners dead, the majority in the East End around the docks. Unless they are evacuated from the city, a good many of those casualties will be children. With the bombardment of the docks by fourteen Gothas on 13 June

1917 – in which, among others, fourteen schoolchildren were killed – still vivid in the minds of inhabitants, the committee concludes that if Londoners have to witness their children dying then the public will concede to the Germans in days. The East End's children and the mothers of those too young to be left alone will have to be evacuated. The committee recommends this be done within four days.

Anyone who can leave on their own account does so. During that first weekend of the war lines of traffic on the trunk roads leading out of London stretch for miles, as the better heeled move out to boarding houses, hastily rented cottages, holiday homes or relatives' accommodation. No vehicles are allowed into the city. In Romford, Gary Arber's family makes preparations to move to Gary's Aunt Ada and Uncle Arthur in Wembley, where Arthur, being a navvie, has already dug out an air-raid shelter, while Walter Francis installs his own in the garden of the family home. The shelter is damp and horribly cramped, and Uncle Arthur has to sleep with his head wedged against a bucket to catch the leaks. By November the Arber family is back in Romford. That first Christmas they'll stay with Uncle Wills in Chadwell Heath. Aunt Ada and Uncle Arthur will not be invited. They have served their purpose and Uncle Arthur is common. There may be a war on, but the family still has standards.

Among the other families whose stories appear in these pages as past, present or future customers of Kelly's pie and mash, whose lives revolve around the Roman and who too will emerge from the war forever altered, are the Lucionis, the Chorleys, the Mosses, the Simmons, the Shratskys, the Da Costas, the Gipsons and the Randolfis.

Ten-year-old Ted Lucioni is hop-picking with his mother Lizzie and nan Martha down in Pluckley when war is declared. A few miles away, in Staplehurst, four-year-old Ann Simmons is with her nan too. Anticipating a ferocious bombing campaign around the docks, neither family will come back to London immediately. It seems safer to remain in Kent. The infant Phil Shratsky and his brother will be packed off at the start of the Blitz to stay with their mother's sister in Merthyr Tydfil for the duration. They are all the lucky ones, sent to live with people to whom they are already bound by the ties of family.

For those who have no relatives outside London, evacuation is an unpredictable business. The country has been divided into danger, neutral and reception zones, according to a calculation of risk. The evacuation begins in earnest on 1 September, two days before the official declaration of war. No one knows where they are to be sent until they arrive at the terminus station. They are most often shipped off in school groups. After what might be a long journey, the evacuated children are lined up like soldiers and picked out by strangers for rehoming, like so many stray dogs. Harry Da Costa is thirteen, just too young to start work. He and his younger brother Joel are dispatched to Felixstowe where they remain until the German occupation of the Low Countries in May 1940, when they're sent westwards to an old lady in the Welsh Rhondda Valley. Bet Chorley, who will one day marry Ted Lucioni, and her older sister Edna find themselves in Paulton, Somerset. A teacher takes them in but she's only the lodger. The elderly couple who own the cottage soon decide Edna is a handful. They're happy to keep Bet but they don't want her sister. For their part, Bet and Edna won't be parted. Eventually an old lady with an ear trumpet, who won't be bothered by Edna's rambunctiousness, is located, and the two girls are dispatched to her cottage. She's the old-fashioned sort. From time to time Bet's mother Edith, a machinist, sends her daughters home-made clothes, but the old lady always says they're too good to wear and stashes them away in a box.

Despite the many deprivations of being an evacuee, the Artful D longs to be sent away. Not that he's ever *been* away, but he imagines the countryside to be full of long vistas, birds' eggs and rabbits. Instead, his mother Melinda insists he remain in London, more specifically, on Fish Island. Looking back, Ron thinks Melinda had become dependent on him and in particular on his dodging skills, and wanted him with her. It was a self-serving decision, he thinks. He doesn't consider the possibility that, having already lost five children, Melinda couldn't bear to be parted from her youngest.

In any case, the decision spells the end of the Artful D's education. Pretty soon the school closes, most of the other children leave for the countryside and Ron is left to roam across his solitary kingdom, where he is never short of entertainment. One particular highlight, early on in the war, happens when the German grocer and his son are interned, leaving their respective shops in Ripporth Road and Whyke Road unguarded. It's a bonanza for an artful dodger: sugar, flour, bread. 'I even finished up taking up the floorboards and finding all the coins, like the farthings and the pennies and the half-pennies, and oh, it was marvellous.'

There's a great deal else that's marvellous in the Artful D's world. Watching the Home Guard training with broomsticks for rifles in Vicky Park ('Oh, that was a big laugh!') and the tanks rolling along the railway line at the end of the road and the rabbits in the goods yard waiting to be snared and swapped with the neighbours for eggs and chickens. He will never now learn how to read or write, but what he discovers in his reign as the prince of Fish Island will arguably turn out to be of more value to him than anything he can learn in a book: an implacable if lonely self-reliance, a permanently watchful unease.

The absence of children, some women and a growing number of young men lends the normally bustling East End an air of unreality. No one quite knows what to expect or when to expect it. The cinemas, theatres and dance halls are forced to close, along with the dog tracks at Walthamstow, Clapton and Hackney and the speedway track out on the marshes. Not far from Gary Arber's aunt and uncle, volunteers paint Wembley Stadium's glass roof black, but it closes anyway. In shopping streets across London, including the Roman, with the exception of tobacconists, confectioners and newsagents, stores are required to shutter up at 6 p.m., thereby missing trade from the factory workers returning from work in the evenings. The market runs only during daylight hours, and stallholders are increasingly women and old men. Bacon and butter are rationed, but the hike in prices makes them unaffordable for many East Enders anyway. No politician or mandarin dares close the pubs. In the East End in particular there would be a riot. Beer has not been rationed, and won't be for the duration of the war, but grain will get harder to come by and the price will rise, and some landlords will choose to close for a couple of days mid-week and reserve their best for regulars. But that hasn't happened yet, and so for now, every night after work, those who are left in the East End cram into their local to gossip, drink and, for a few moments, forget.

Up and down the Roman small businesses grow fearful for their livelihoods as well as their lives. Randolfi's, which before the war did a roaring trade in lemon ice cream, is threatened with having its freezers requisitioned for use as blood banks. No matter. In a little while there won't be any cream or sugar or lemons with which to make ice cream. A couple of doors down at Kelly's, Bill Kingdon prepares to petition the War Ministry to keep meat pies off the ration, arguing that East Enders need the comfort of famil-iar, cheap and convenient hot food. To his and George Kelly's delight, the ministry agrees. Though supplies of meat will be rationed to Kelly's, customers will never have to use their coupons to buy pies.

Out in the countryside the Londoner-in-exile's passion for pies is not forgotten. As part of a new Rural Pie Scheme, women of the WVS go about at midday in vans or on bicycles distributing pies to land girls, field workers and children picking potatoes and even, eventually, to POWs also labouring on the nation's farmland.

All over the East End factories close or are diverted to war production. Women, who form the majority of workers, are first put out of work, then diverted into war production. In Bow and the surrounding area this often means sewing uniforms. So many uniforms. Marian Stratford, aged sixteen, who until now has been working as the assistant to a delivery driver, is dispatched to Schneider's in Whitechapel, where she will spend much of the war pressing army uniforms and machining trousers. Also sent to the machines is Gary Arber's mother Florence, who is appointed forewoman overseeing the production of army uniforms and hospital nightshirts at Compton's, where she will learn to turn a blind eye to machinists slipping notes inside sleeves, linings and pockets for soldiers on some godforsaken front to find and be comforted by.

The first air-raid warning, twenty minutes after the declaration, brings a rush to the shelters. It's followed by another in the early hours of the following morning. Then, not much, and as the days stretch into weeks, London braces for a cataclysm which doesn't arrive, or at any event, not yet. And as each new warning fails to produce the much anticipated carpet bombing, the response becomes more routine and, if not exactly relaxed, then muted. No one wants to tempt fate by wishing for an end to the impasse, but all the waiting lends an air of unreality to day-to-day life. The tiredness brought on by long days at work, difficult commutes, fire-watching, ARP and WVS service, and nights disrupted by air-raid warnings only serves to heighten the sense of being on notice without knowing quite what you are on notice for.

A new kind of normal sets in. Denial plays a healthy part in it. The population can only go on waiting for so long without breaking. Ordinary desires and needs must be serviced. And so, on 16 September, after only two weeks of darkness, cinemas and dance halls reopen their doors. Kids being to trickle back from the countryside, and by January 1940 200,000 children, half of them returned evacuees, are living in London and requiring education, though the schools are slower to open than the picture houses.

In May 1940 Ted, Billie and Norma Lucioni return from Kent to a London 'changed completely', a city wrapped and barraged and sandbagged, its homes barricaded and mysterious. Their mornings are nominally taken up with school, which has become little more than gas-mask and air-raid drill, and their afternoons are spent planting and weeding and on other war work deemed suitable for children. In the deep dark of the blackout, it is almost possible to imagine yourself back in the countryside.

The war creeps closer. That same month the Luftwaffe carpet-bombs Rotterdam and Holland falls to the Nazis. In June Gary Arber's older brother Stanley is among the 338,000 Allied soldiers evacuated from Dunkirk. To make his escape he has to wade neck deep into the sea and in the process loses his trousers. He turns up at the print shop unexpectedly one day in dungarees, a train driver at Dover having given him his spare pair, and has to wait it out at home until a new pair of army trousers arrives, run up, perhaps, by his mother in Compton's off the Roman.

The first daylight raids on Britain begin in early July 1940. On the first of the month fifteen people are killed in Wick; on 9 July twenty-seven are killed in Norwich. Liverpool, Wrexham, Bradford, Birmingham and Coventry are attacked, and there are intermittent raids on London. Towards the end of the month the Luftwaffe targets the Channel ports and their defences as part of Operation Sea Lion, causing damage and casualties in many of the southern coastal towns.

A month earlier, and just one month after their arrival back home, Ted, Billie and Norma, three cousins and the rest of Roman Road school are once more evacuated out of London. It's a lovely day, Ted recalls, and he is obliged to wear most of his clothes so he won't have to carry them in the pillowcase with the rest of his belongings, including a tin of corned beef and some biscuits for the family, as yet unspecified, who will take him in. So he's hot, and lugging his gas mask in its cardboard box and his pillowcase, though what he remembers most is not the heat or the struggle with his belongings but the thrill of the journey and the boiled sweet he's given to counter the travel sickness. The train stops twice on the journey, and the Red Cross hands up drinks through the windows of the train. When they arrive at Tiverton, in Devon,

Ted, his siblings and cousins are loaded on to a charabanc and driven the four miles to Uplowman, where a crowd of adults has assembled in the local school. 'To us they were foreigners, we couldn't understand a word they were saying,' Ted recalls. The adults begin to pick out children to take home. Ted's two male cousins are among the first to go, then his sister and a female cousin, leaving Ted and Billie among the last. 'We're standing there and he's holding my hand and shaking and you could hear people saying "What are we going to do with them?"' A local teacher finally comes to the rescue, and they walk with her in deep darkness along a country lane to a farmhouse with an oil lamp on the table and a cauldron perched in an inglenook fireplace. Sitting at the table beside the lamp is an old lady in black, quite possibly a witch, by the name of Mrs Cleave. Two daughters and a son hover nearby. The newcomers are offered a meal of bread and cheese while the spare room is prepared. The single bed is dressed with sheets, a jug filled with water and placed on the marble tabletop beside a china bowl. Exhausted from their journey and unused to the coldness of the countryside even now, in June, the two boys cuddle together and fall into a dreamless sleep. They are woken early by an unfamiliar sound and, heading to the window, see passing beneath a miraculous sight: what seems like a stream of cows heading to the fields.

Before long a decision is made that the two boys can stay so long as they put themselves to work. Country work, the kind of labour they've been doing in the hop gardens of Kent every summer of their lives. They step in eagerly, picking crops, scything thistles, mashing apples for cider, even pumping the organ at church, for which they are paid small sums to put towards train tickets for visits home. 'We hadn't seen anything like this before, and I think it changed me entirely. I knew I was in another world then, and I loved it,' Ted remembers. By the time summer 1940 is over, old witch Cleave has become Granny, and her children are Aunts Florrie and Ivy and Uncle Frank.

15

Jesus is with you, don't be afraid
He will protect you, all through the raid
When bombs are falling and danger is near
He will be with you, till the all clear
Len Smith, 'The Way We Were'*

The Third Reich's Lightning War begins on the afternoon of
7 September 1940.† It's a beautiful late summer Saturday and
West Ham is playing at Upton Park. On the Roman the market
is beginning to pack up and people are queuing to buy their
teatime pie and mash at Kelly's to take home before the blackout begins.

Just after 5 p.m. the sky darkens as a phalanx of 348 bombers
and 617 fighters tracks above the barrage in stacked layers, the sun
catching on chrome and glass and filling the air with sinister
sparkles, undeterred by heavy flak and tracer bullets. There is no
mistaking this new attack for the fitful forays of the spring and
summer. This is the event for which Londoners have been steeling
themselves.

In Kent and Sussex and on London's borders Hurricanes and
Spitfires engage the enemy, and through the oily smoke and

---

* Unpublished manuscript, Newham Archives and Local Studies Library.
† I am indebted to Philip Ziegler's *London at War* (Sinclair-Stevenson, 1995) for some
of the details used in this chapter.

contrails and the flaming bodies of downed planes can be seen the swoops and spins of dogfights, but many inevitably get through, descending finally on the capital, an implacable flock of predatory birds. At 5.15 p.m. an incendiary lands in Shetland Road, damaging Marner School. Thirty-eight minutes later another caves in a roof at Malmesbury Road near Ted's old school. At 5.59 an incendiary breaks a roof in Arnold Road. Addington Road is hit at 6.07, Bow Road three minutes later, Mornington Grove two minutes after that. At 6.19 an incendiary bomb sets fire to the coal yard on Mile End Road. Not long after that the enemy is heading back east, leaving Woolwich Arsenal, the gas works at Beckton, the Anglo-American oil works at Purfleet and the East and West India, Surrey and Milwall docks in flames. Two miles to the south and east of Bow, Silvertown is an inferno, melted sugar from the Tate & Lyle factory covering the river in bitter, burning caramel.

Operation Loge, the Nazi codename for London, has begun. At 8 p.m. 247 bombers of the Luftflotte arrive, guided by the flames. The bombing goes on most of the night. By dawn 843 separate incidents have been recorded. In Bow there have been hits on Clarnico's sweet factory, the Southside Wharf Timber and Railway Yards, Sun Flour Mills at St Leonard's Wharf and a starch manufacturer on Grace Street. Berger Hall Church and Medical Mission, Marner School, St Andrew's and St Clement's hospitals have all been badly damaged. Incendiaries destroy homes and factories in Talwin, Furze, Merchant, Franklin, Empson, Otis, Alfred and Colin Streets, and in Devons, Burdett, Arnold, Longfellow, Addington, Cantrell, Clinton, Mornington and Turners Roads, St Paul's Way, Three Mills Lane and Drivers and Wellington Way Buildings. A high explosive rips out Bow Baths, depriving residents of the small comforts of a place to do their laundry and wash themselves; another lands on the Needle Gun pub, a block or so away, and blows out the beautiful milk glass lights and painted frontage of Kelly's pie and mash shop.

By the time the all-clear wails, around 400 souls have lost their lives and another 1,200 or so are injured. The following day Churchill pays a visit, but so does the Luftwaffe. By the dawn of 9 September, another 412 Londoners, most in the east and south-east, are dead, and a further 747 have been injured. Those who can, flee the city. Those who cannot are subjected to a waking nightmare. As if the bombs weren't enough, the city's infrastructure rapidly begins to break apart. Roads are blocked with debris, broken drains and spitting electric cables are left unrepaired. Civil society grinds to a halt. Births and deaths go unregistered. Opportunists loot bombsites and take advantage of the blackout to operate illegal gambling rings or thieve from bombed buildings, or even to commit street robberies. Food supplies fail to reach the shops and in some places people resort to looting.

Up on Fish Island, itself a target, Ron Moss hears the bombs fall from his Anderson shelter at the bottom of the garden. When the all-clear sounds he sits by the railway watching trains laden with tanks and personnel heading for England's seaports, and thinks of his father, Fred, out at sea on the little fishing trawler, the *Lady Love*, and of what an adventure all this is turning out to be.

The raids continue for 57 days and nights. On 7 October the Germans switch to night attacks. In the East End to sleep in one's own bed now is nightly to risk annihilation. On 14 October 380 Luftflotte bombers leave 200 dead and 2,000 injured, and they're back the next day. Overground shelters prove hopelessly inadequate. A group of panicked Londoners hides out in the Blackwall Tunnel and refuses to move. Bombed-out families are crammed into dormitories hastily laid out in converted schools. The city authorities begin to fear that nightly stampedes to the Tube will cause more casualties than the bombs.

But there rises from the chaos and terror of the East End a spirit, now legendary, of camaraderie and can do. People open their houses to strangers, old men trudge the streets on ARP duty, women sign up for fire-watching or to drive ambulances or be part of clearance teams. The blackout provides the ideal cover for knee tremblers and last-minute goodbyes. In what little spare time people have, they troop to the dance halls and cinemas and pubs and do their best to forget the desperate situation. A baker posts a sign outside his premises:

> Though bombs and blast come thick and fast
> We'll carry on quite gaily
> While we're still here, we'll persevere
> To bake out Hovis daily*

If nothing else, the war brings back into sharp relief the knowledge that East Enders have daily lived with during peacetime, and have grown used to pushing to the back of their minds – that life is random, chancy and unreliable, and death is never far away.

Children who had been brought back from the countryside during the Phoney War are once again dispatched to unknown destinations in the countryside, their mothers left for days with no notice of their whereabouts. Among the first to be sent away, along with their children, are the East End's pregnant mothers. On 19 November Ray Gipson's mother is sent to Northampton to give birth to him. (Ray will spend his life living and working around the Roman, fighting for the community as a councillor and at an advanced age co-founding the Bow Geezers, among whose members will be Ted Lewis.) Ray's father, Charlie, being too old to fight, remains on the streets of Bow with his rattle, shouting at residents to shut their windows and, once the all-clear has sounded, dealing with the damage: in the evenings he drowns his sorrows in the pub, even though beer is now both expensive and watery. Every day he spends dragging bodies out of the debris, the sorrows are a little deeper, and it takes more pale ale to drown them out.

* Len Smith, 'The Way We Were,' part of the BBC's People's War project www.bbc.co.uk/history/ww2peopleswar/stories (accessed 16 August 2016).

Four months after Ray is born, in nearby Dunstable Elsie Baker gives birth to Brian while his father is away in Darlington servicing the guns of the Royal Electrical Engineers. (Like Ray, the days and years of Brian's life will be marked out in pie and mash dinners, his work woven into the fabric of the Roman Road market. His heritage, his legacy, will all begin there, in E3.) Meanwhile not far from Dunstable, at Severalls asylum in Colchester, unwed mother Beatrice Bundock once again finds herself pregnant. Her first child, Ann, is at a Barnardo's home, Beatrice's mother having refused to have her in the house. The father having been killed in a motorcycle accident at Whipps Cross, and Beatrice not being right in the head, the baby, Robert, is sent into care while Beatrice spends her days mending the nurses' laddered tights and polishing silver for the local bigwigs, Colonel and Mrs Morris. Ann, meanwhile, is selected for adoption by a Mr and Mrs English, who are unable to have children of their own. The adoption appears to be progressing swimmingly until one day Mr and Mrs English fail to turn up for their regular meeting with the little girl and it is discovered that they have been killed in the bombing, after which Ann, then two, is dispatched back to the Barnardo's home where, for the next ten years, she will stay. Not long after the war Beatrice will marry and give birth to Christine, who will spend the seventies creating mayhem with her sister Georgia in the pubs and clubs around the Roman, before settling down to life as a single mother herself, scratching a living from cleaning what is still the Bryant & May match factory in Fairfield Road, Bow (in the nineties, when Christine still works there, it will become the Bow Quarter, a gated community of so-called luxury apartments).

Those youngsters who remain in London, kids like Ron, have to bear the nightly blasts. Since the schools have all closed, in the day they are put to work either harvesting potatoes in Vicky Park or filling out names and addresses in ration books, their formal education all but forgotten, or else they run wild amongst the fragments of what used to be familiar territory, clambering over pyramids of broken bricks and sifting through the dust and debris for buried treasure. As the Blitz goes on, all anyone left in the East End can do is listen for the air-raid warning and seek a place of shelter, mostly in dismal places, the Andersons soaked and mouldy, those above ground unreliable and frightening and the Tube shelters rat-infested, smelly and crowded. One minute 'you're warm in bed and then the siren sounds', remembers Ron, and the next you're underground and ankle deep in mud, poking spikes into the soil to drain away the water and competing for a space on a damp bunk. The Moss family are more like moles than people. Melinda, normally a brave if irascible woman, is driven 'scatty' from fear.

All the same, the shelters are better than nothing. When an oil bomb, then an incendiary device, both explode in the backyard at Arber's the printers, they take out the privy and the neighbouring dairy run for years by Welshman Dave Evans, his sister Mrs Jones and her daughters Anne and Blodwyn. The Arbers themselves are safely in their Andie. It's a lucky escape.

In Norman Grove, the site of Sylvia Pankhurst's toy factory and crèche in the Great War, an Anderson shelter is also responsible for saving Jono Smith and his nine siblings from a direct hit. They emerge on the all-clear to a pile of rubble for a house, and are added to the growing list of the bombed out. Jono, fifteen, is dispatched to stay with his grandmother Tilly in the two upstairs rooms at 12 Gaynes Place, where he'll spend the few months he has left before being called up.

Ruth Shratsky is living in a flat on the top floor of Brady Street Dwellings with her young son David and infant Phillip. Their father, Solomon, is over in Europe, fighting. In order to get her children to the safety of the nearest shelter at Charrington's Brewery on Mile End Road, Ruth has to carry Phillip and their sleep bundles and lead David by the hand down three flights of stairs, then along Brady Street to its junction with Mile End Road and right to the brewery. David may have had to be shaken awake, and, like most children, is likely to be ornery. Phillip is heavy. The whole journey takes ten minutes, by which time the bombs are already falling. As if this were not trial enough, opportunists lurk in the darkened corners of the East End, waiting to take advantage of the situation. One time, after the all-clear Ruth, David and Phillip arrive back at their flat to discover that, while they were taking shelter, a thief has broken in and taken everything. Not that there was much, but the radio, in particular, is a prize item and will be terribly missed. For Ruth Shratsky the break-in is a line in the sand. Not long afterwards she packs up a few things in a cardboard suitcase and takes David and Phillip on a train to her sister's house in Merthyr. It's one thing being aggressed by Hitler, quite another being exploited by your own kind. She'll miss her children terribly (war work keeps her in London), but the boys love it – 'all the fields and mountains to run up and down' – and there'll be no bombs.

By Christmas 1940 terror fatigue has begun to set in. You just can't live in a state of constant flight or fight. In the East End the old and the young in particular begin to tire of the shelters, though for different reasons. Among the former is Jono Smith's grand-mother, Tilly. She's old and perhaps figures that Hitler's not going to bring Death much closer to her than it already is. Her legs are stiff and it's too much to keep going up and down the stairs and running for the shelter. What will be will be. From now on, when the air-raid warning starts up, Tilly heads under the kitchen table and takes out her deck of cards.

Over on Fish Island the Artful Dodger's sister, Violet, twenty-one, is similarly blasé. She is young enough to convince herself that death can only be far away, at least until the night a bomb falls nearby blowing out the doors and windows and sending the ceiling of her bedroom crashing down on top of the bed. During the course of the war the door on to the street blows out so many times the Moss family runs out of hinges and has to wedge it with the sole of a boot.

By the time the Blitz is over, on 10 May 1941, London has lost 1.2 million homes, the great majority in the East End. Nearly 40 per cent of the houses in Stepney, put up on the cheap by speculators, have crumbled. And the deaths. Not the 56,000 forecast, but 28,556 killed and another 25,578 seriously wounded. Among the casualties is Albert Arber, Gary's uncle, who has been working by day in the print shop composing and printing the government handouts and information sheets which will keep the Arber family business flourishing, and spending nights in the Auxiliary Fire Service. During the night of 19 March 1941, Albert is manning a water pump and on hearing a bomb whistling, ducks by a wall, which collapses in the explosion, killing him. Left behind is wife Delia, pregnant with a child who will never see her father. Another casualty is the Artful Dodger's dad, who is on the fishing trawler *Lady Love* steaming 110 miles south of Iceland on 27 August 1941 when U-boat 202, captained by Hans-Heinz Linder, fires one G7e torpedo hitting the starboard side, sinking the ship within fifteen seconds with the loss of all fourteen on board. Fireman Frederick Moss, aged forty-two, is casualty number 2790832. Ron is twelve and later says of his father that 'The crabs probably ate him.' His name lives on, carved in marble on a memorial beside Tower Bridge, but it's moot if Ron has ever visited.

In Paulton, Somerset, evacuee Bet Chorley is six and at school when the telegram arrives with the news that her father, James, has died of tuberculosis at age forty-one. She does not go to the funeral. Only one memory of him will remain in her mind, of being out with relations and coming home late on her father's shoulders. 'I missed him more as I got older.'

The war will leave behind shortages of fruit and meat and cloth and all manner of things. Of missing people there will never be any shortfall. In the summer of 1941, as if he weren't already missing his parents and his nan Martha, Ted Lucioni will have to add another to the list, the woman who has been a substitute nan to him, Granny Cleave, who dies at home in Uplowman. Ted makes a wreath of moss and twigs, primroses and violets, and ties it around a cross of wood; he is 'glad to have been able to do that for Granny Cleave'. Even in the still and timeless landscape of Devon, people seem temporary. When summer comes dozens of Australians will arrive to help with the sheep-shearing, and Ted will wind the ratchet driving the clippers and for his troubles get a glass of cider. He will sit and drink it, and try to wrap his ear around the Aussie accents. Then, before very long, the Australians, too, will be gone.

Even in the midst of all this terrible loss, though, what you'll hear Elsie and most other East Enders say is that life goes on and you have to make the most of it, a sentiment which from anyone more fortunate might sound like a truism but here in the East End where stoicism has long been necessary for survival is a principle by which to live. Love affairs, proposals, marriages and new lives interleave with all the dead and dying. Take Elsie Hobart, who in 1941 stands before her Alf, a window cleaner by trade though currently serving in the Royal Artillery, in the aisle at St Barnabas's on the corner of Roman and Grove Roads, preparing to say her vows when the sirens go off. What to do? The head says run for the shelter but the heart says no. The heart says air-raid warnings are an affront, a vulgar and spiteful interruption. 'I don't want to be half done,' says Elsie. And so the ceremony carries on, through the warning and the bombing, because sometimes there are things you *do* just have to get on with and chief among those things is love. Afterwards there won't be anything as extravagant as a reception, but Elsie's mother does somehow manage to get her hands on a piece of salt beef to make sandwiches to mark the occasion. The following morning Alf gets up early and makes his new bride a cup of tea. In a day or two he'll return to his regiment.

Elsie continues to live with her mother, Rebecca, in the house in which she was born, 49 Auckland Road, Bow, and where she will spend the rest of her days. She's the product of her mother's second marriage. Widowed young, Rebecca survived the loss of her first husband by working as a cleaner in Chisenhale School and renting out rooms at Auckland Road. Times were often hard. 'If one woman had a few shillings, she'd loan it out: sometimes, my mother was a bit short, and she'd say take this envelope to Mrs Piercey, that was the lady who lived at the top of the same turning, and you'd come back with the envelope and it would have a few coppers in it,' says Elsie. Her mother met her second husband when he was in the Royal Marines, but wouldn't marry him until, at forty-two, she imagined she could have no more children. Then Elsie and her sister Rebecca came along, and this in itself was faintly scandalous. 'My half-sister thought Mother was dreadful and she said "You ought to be ashamed of yourself. You should be past all that at your age",' says Elsie.

And now her daughter, the product of faintly scandalous midlife goings on, is married to Alf and will give birth in a makeshift maternity hospital in Ruskin College, Oxford, to twins. Alf is given leave to visit. 'I was lying there with me legs in the stirrups and he came in with a big bunch of flowers and I told him, "Take your flowers away, I'm not dead yet."' But there is a death 'The baby boy died as he was born.' Daughter Jan survives, a 'lovely little baby'. Elsie and Alf will move into 39 Auckland Road, 'the posh end of Bethnal Green'. Elsie will go on to lose three more, all boys, until the doctor will say, 'Don't be stupid, Elsie, you're ruining your own health trying to get a boy that's not meant for you.' But it never goes away, that feeling of loss, the grief for the boys that never were and should have been, and many years later Elsie will say that when she thinks about her dead children 'it's the only time I can sit and cry'. But all that is in the future. Now it is wartime, and Elsie and Alf have carved from a dismal situation a small still shelter from the storm.

All over the East End men and women are finding in the devastation a new and urgent reason to love. For some this might amount to no more than an anonymous knee trembler in a blacked-out passageway, for others something more innocent and longer lasting. Among these is the courtship between Marian Stratford, machinist, and Jim, costermonger. The Olds are a long-time coster family, not quite as rooted in the Roman as the Da Costas but not far off. They've been in the market since 1860. Old man Old runs a fruit and veg stall in the market. Old mother Old runs another. The young Old brothers each have their own within spitting distance of Kelly's pie and mash. When the war is over, Marian and Jim's sons, Peter, Tom and William Old, will supply the shop with potatoes. Now, in late 1942, potatoes are becoming hard to get, but love, it seems, is off the ration, and so it is, at the age of nineteen, after a short and innocent courtship, that Marian Stratford and Jim Old are married and almost immediately forced to say goodbye as Jim heads back to the front. In December 1943 Marian gives birth to Peter in Bishop's Stortford, and prays that Jim will make it home to see his son.

Not far away in Severalls in Colchester, Beatrice Bundock, still unmarried and pregnant for a third time, most likely by an American soldier, will give birth to a daughter, Shirley. But she will not be allowed to keep her. It's hard to say from the vantage point of the twenty-first century what Beatrice's problems were, but losing her children could only have added to them.

16

We didn't understand what was going on, really.

Ted Lewis

By 1943 there are almost as many women working in the forces as in the home. Many of those still at home are doing voluntary work or taking in bomb-outs or evacuees. One way or another wartime lives leave them with little time for the routine household chores which only a few years ago might well have taken up their waking hours. Among these is Ray Gipson's mother, who arrives back from Northampton with her new son, and is immediately conscripted into war work making uniforms. From then on, Ray hardly sees her. Nearly eight decades later, reflecting on his life around the Roman, never more than ten or fifteen minutes' walk from Kelly's, Ray recalls sitting around a coke fire with his father Charlie and a bunch of old men discussing the progress of the war, while his mother puts in the late shift machining uniforms at Compton's. Ray doesn't recall what his mother thought about the work, but will wonder whether those long hours she spent at the factory when he was so little might account for why, in later life, he never seemed to have much luck with women.

At least the Gipsons still have a home. Among those not so lucky is Ann Simmons, the little girl who was hop-picking in Kent with her nan when war broke out and who arrived back to London only to discover that the family home no longer existed. Like Ray,

Ann, too, will spend almost the whole of the rest of her life around the Roman. In 1942, though, with the East End half-blown to bits, the family is forced to move in with Ann's maternal grandparents, the Stapleys, in Southall, a distance of 16 miles from Bethnal Green, and another world. When Ann's father, James, a sergeant major serving in Egypt, returns on leave, he quickly decides the place is 'too posh' but there's no choice except to stay, at least for the time being. The East End is still being pummelled. In any case, Ann's mother is off doing war work and needs to be able to leave her daughter in the care of her parents. Ann remembers Nan Stapley with more fondness than Grandad Stapley, who was born a Romany and a bargee, and drinks to forget the family who cut him off for marrying a gorger.

By 1942 rationing has really begun to bite. In London there are long lines outside the butcher's, the grocer's, the baker's and the greengrocer's. To answer the need for cheap, hot food off the ration, British Restaurants have sprung up around London, over 200 in all, and at half-mile intervals across the East End. Originally opened in autumn 1940 to provide hot meals to bomb-outs from the Blitz, new branches rapidly open round the country. Here anyone can turn up and be served a simple hot meal from a counter manned by WVS volunteers. Soup is 2d, a plate of mince and mashed potato or a rissole and cabbage is 8d, a sweet 3d, and a two-course meal with a cup of tea is 10d. No one is allowed more than one serving of meat, fish, eggs or cheese. By the mid 1940s the British Restaurants are dishing up 600,000 meals a day. That said, a survey indicates that only 20 per cent of the population ever eats in one. In the East End the deciding factor is always cost. At Kelly's, two meat pies, mash and liquor and a cup of tea can be had for 6d, making it much cheaper. The rationing of coal, gas and electricity makes life difficult for the home cook, and it's this, coupled with the endless queuing and unreliable supplies of food in the markets and shops, which drives men and women exhausted by long working days, difficult commutes and night-times spent fire-watching or on ARP, WVS or AFS duties to the pie and mash shops of the East End.

At the Bethnal Green branches of Kelly's, Matilda Kelly and her daughter Tilly try to keep up with the demand while Theresa Kingdon and her mother, also Theresa, manage the two shops on the Roman. The glass is repaired after the bomb blast which blew out the windows at 526* – it hardly matters about the lights because of the blackout – and the shop is soon trading once again. Demand is high. The deal Bill Kingdon negotiated with the Ministry of Food helps. Customers can enjoy meat pies without using their ration coupons. The problem is supply. Flour isn't rationed but fat is very difficult to come by until margarine begins to be made from whale oil. Beef is hard to source, and expensive, but there are other meats: sheep, horse, pig's head, whale. Eels at least are plentiful and the supply unrestricted, though, after the Nazi invasion of Holland, Dutch imports dry up. Still, the shops get by. The pastry on the pies might be a little thinner the meat might be sparse and of somewhat unreliable provenance; there might be rather more jelly than eel; the scoops of mash may be more modest. But all through 1942 the Londoner's meal of pie, mash and eels remains on the menu.

---

* The shops on the Roman Road were renumbered after the war. Numbers 236 and 310 became 526 and 600.

17

My dad wasn't right, he was crumpled because of the war, they used to lock him in the coal cupboard.

Alfie Burns

The hit-and-run raids on the East End continue through 1943. The shelters fill and empty, fill and empty. This far into the war the shelters are both sordid and unwelcoming, which is partly a function of how many are using them and partly an active measure to ensure that no one is tempted to decamp underground until the war is over. The government does not want its bunkers to create a bunker mentality. In Bow the feeling is that deep shelters like those in the Tube stations are the only places safe from a direct hit. People remember 15 October 1940 when a bomb landing on a trench shelter in Kennington Park killed 104; they've heard of basements caving in and burying occupants. Many know someone who knows someone who has been lost when a high explosive landed directly on their Andie.

There aren't many Tube shelters in the East End because there aren't many Tube stations. The largest is at Bethnal Green. This station was built in 1936 as an extension of the Central Line from Liverpool Street and track has yet to be laid, so it is more like a vast cavern than a station. Five thousand bunks are set up on the platforms and the track bed, and shelter tickets are handed out with assigned bunk numbers. In addition to the bunks there's room for another 2,000 sleeping sitting up or standing. Entry is from 5 p.m. through to 7 a.m. The shelter has to accommodate a wide, overcrowded area where there are relatively few backyards and thus a shortage of Andies. It is noisy, humid and stinking but is the only deep shelter serving Bethnal Green and Bow and the people living around the Roman. There are rats and lice and all manner of tribulations. There is also a measure of safety from the tumult above ground.

But only a measure of safety.

The horror begins shortly after 8 p.m. on 3 March 1943, a day when the mood is particularly tense. On 1 March the RAF began bombing Berlin and everyone is bracing themselves for reprisal attacks. By 8 p.m. a couple of hundred people have already taken up their bunks. At the King's Row cinema a few minutes' walk from Bethnal Green Tube station, a popular picture house with people living in the turnings off the Roman, Irving Berlin's musical comedy starring Ronald Reagan *This is the Army* is playing. The nearby Rex is full, as is Smart's cinema and the Museum Picture Palace on the Green. Just after 8 p.m., at the whine of air-raid sirens outside, notices are flashed up on screens to warn audiences and reassure them that the film will continue for those who wish to stay. Most do not, and, rising from their seats, begin to make their way out of the cinemas and towards the Tube shelter. Within five minutes the entrance to the shelter is packed with men, women and children.

A single blue bulb illuminates the flight of nineteen steps that descends to the ticket hall. The entrance is narrow. Usually a policeman controls the flow of human traffic, but tonight there is no one. The ARP wardens who would normally assist the police-man aren't there either. No one seems to know why. The local council has applied for funds from central government to widen the entrance and install a central guard rail, but it has been turned down, so though there is a bannister on each side of the stairs there is no rail. The front edges of the steps have not been painted white. It has been raining and the concrete is wet and slippery. A couple of steps down, beyond the feeble reach of the single blue bulb, it is impossible to see even as far as the person ahead.

Seven minutes after the sirens go off around 300 people are wedged into a stairwell 15 foot by 11 foot. No one can see much further than the back of the person ahead of them. On one of the lower steps, a middle-aged woman carrying a baby trips and, with no central guard rail to reach out for, loses her footing and tumbles. The elderly man behind her stumbles too. That instant, in Victoria Park a rocket battery manned by the 128th Battery of the 6th Royal Artillery Regiment, 37th Brigade fires an exercise salvo and sends up a red flare. Mistaking the sound for enemy rockets and unable to see the unfolding turmoil at the base of the steps, the crowd at the top surges forwards. People begin falling over one another, on top of one another. Screams and shouting alert the people further up the stairs to what is going on at the bottom, but they are powerless to stop the press of the crowd at street level. As more and more people surge forwards onto the stairs, those below are squeezed and jostled. Unable to see into the stairwell and with the sounds of screaming eclipsed by the roar of guns, the crowd continues to edge forwards, unaware of the crush of bodies beginning to pile up. What is needed now is people to hold back the crowd at street level. Instead, the press of people thickens on the stairs. People are packed so tight that their breath is squeezed out of them. Unable to escape the vicelike pressure of the wall of people, they begin turning purple then blue. One or two, young boys mostly, manage to squeeze through gaps and make their way over the sea of heads to alert those at street level, but by the time anyone understands what is happening it is too late.

The guns at Vicky Park are silent. Muffled screams and groans issue from the tangle in the stairwell. Reaching the scene minutes later, the police, the AVS and ARP hardly know where to begin. The rescue workers, among whom are Ray Gipson's father Charlie, who may well know people in the crush, are having to work in near darkness, pulling out the living and the dead, some men, but mostly women and children, some with life-threatening injuries who are still, miraculously, alive, along with others whose bodies are so bruised they are unrecognisable or heartbreakingly unblemished save for the blue-purple death blush that comes from the exertion of extreme, unsurvivable breath-extinguishing pressure.

There is a particular irony to dying while taking shelter, and all the more so since the bombing has been insignificant. Between the sirens sounding and the all-clear a single bomb has fallen, in Ricardo Street, Poplar, a couple of miles away. At Bethnal Green Tube the corpses of the dead are taken away on open trucks to the mortuary at Mile End Hospital, and when that fills, to the Salmon and Ball pub just across the road. The injured are taken anywhere that can accommodate them. Civilians have arrived by now, anxious for news of loved ones. Everyone who can is helping see to the injured and offering comfort to the survivors. It's a long job. When midnight arrives, four hours after the incident began, rescue workers are still pulling people alive from the pile of the dead. Relatives are being asked to identify the bodies. One father is only able to recognise his seven-year-old daughter from the child's shoe, from which he has recently pulled a nail.*

By the time dawn turns the sky rosy, 173 people – 27 men, 84 women and 62 children – will have lost their lives. Among them are Ron Moss's sister and niece. In the makeshift schools scattered across Bow and Bethnal Green there are empty spaces in morning assembly. The clean-up team tasked with going down into the Tube by daylight finds a mess of books, hairclips, keys, matches, handkerchiefs and children's shoes, and everything is coated in human hair.

---

* I am grateful to Alf Morris's contribution to the BBC's People's War archive for this story. See article A7466079 www.bbc.co.uk/history/ww2peopleswar/stories (accessed 16 August 2016).

A message goes out to the survivors and to loved ones of the victims that news of the incident could badly affect morale and lead to people avoiding the Tube shelters, which could lead to further deaths. The official line will be that there has been a terrible accident. Survivors and the families of the victims are told not to speak about it. A memorial will go up in 2012, but by then many of the survivors will be gone.

18

It wasn't all glamour, believe me . . .
Hazel White, Mapping the Change

By 1944 Londoners have grown used to day raids, night-time bombing, blazing buildings, people trapped under rubble, the *ack-ack* of anti-aircraft fire, rubble and dust and bits of bodies everywhere. On the streets and in the pubs gallows humour predominates. But no one accustoms themselves to the telegrams. There's no getting used to those. One arrives at Marian Old's house. Marian is machining uniforms at Compton's, her baby son Peter being looked after by her mother-in-law Liz. Perhaps it's Liz who first reads the telegram, since reading is not Marian's forte. Either way, its message is unequivocal. Private James Old – her Jim – has been killed on 28 May 1944 while serving in the Pioneer Corps. The corps' motto, *Labor Omnia Vincit*, 'work triumphs over everything', turns out not to be true. James worked like a demon but his work did not triumph over death. Many decades later Marian still cannot bring herself to talk about it, so the circumstances remain a mystery. The record shows it happened in England. Was James caught in a bombing raid on an army installation? Perhaps he was brought down by one of the many bombs dropped on London while he was on leave, or killed on exercises. In a way it doesn't matter. James Old is dead, and Marian is left widowed and bringing up her boy alone.

A few weeks later, at the beginning of June, another telegram arrives, this time at Ripporth Road on Fish Island. The Artful Dodger's brother has been killed in Operation Overlord in Normandy. It's hard to imagine how Melinda copes with this news. Five children have died in infancy, she's lost a daughter and a granddaughter at Bethnal Green, her husband is dead at sea and now she has to say goodbye to a grown-up son. Decades later, Ron remembers her as a bitter woman, angry and liable to lash out. Is it any wonder?

There's hardly time to mourn this latest outrage, for only a week later, on Tuesday 13 June the D-Day reprisals begin. Ron Moss hears a giant lawn mower monstering across the sky, followed by an eerie silence, and then, a few seconds later, a great blast. It's the first V1 rocket, the Nazi war machine's not-so-secret secret weapon.* Fired from Cap Gris Nez near Calais, it lands in Grove Road, Bow, destroying the railway bridge, an office building and houses in Antill and Saxon Roads, killing six, including a young mother and her six-month-old boy. Among the more surreal of the bomb's effects is to send the supply of sanitary towels from a chemist shop falling like giant snowflakes through the early summer sky. Minutes later in Antill Road an old man is found wandering dazed, his arms outstretched as if trying to catch the sanitary towels as they make their way to the pavement.† As the dust cloud begins to clear, a crowd gathers to inspect the damage and look for the pilot, not yet knowing there is no pilot.

Some days later Ron Moss is in the garden at Ripporth Road when he hears what has become by now the distinctive *burr*, but this time, when the terrorising silence falls, it appears to fall right above him. There's a crimp in the air. No time to do anything but

---

*The intelligence services are aware of the existence of the V1 but they have considered it wise not to let the British public in on the secret. What they do not know is when the Germans plan to deploy it.
†I am grateful to Joan Barwell for this story from the BBC People's War archive. See article number A3066446, 29/9/2004, www.bbc.co.uk/history/ww2peopleswar/ stories (accessed 16 August 2016).

dive deep into the water of the canal. Down, down he goes, the water a-tremble then roiling and bubbling around him. He can hear the roar of the explosion a little distance away and he's still under the water when the shockwave hits – *Ba-boom* – and tumbles his body about like a pebble in the rapids. Lucky for Ron that he's a strong swimmer, a regular water-boy with a water-boy's lungs, because the canal seems to hold his body in a vice. He cannot come up for air and he cannot swim. And now all he can hear is the tinny ringing of pressure in his ears. It seems an age before the water finally lets go its grip and allows him to rise, gasping, to the surface.

As the VIs continue to fall through the summer, a campaign begins to re-evacuate returned children. Ron, never having left, isn't one, nor, most likely, would he wish to be, for the more empty and ruined Fish Island becomes the more completely it is his kingdom. An island paradise for an artful boy. But thousands of children are packed off once more to the countryside. Among these are Bet and Edna Chorley, who having returned to Bow from Somerset after the death of their father from TB, manage to persuade their mother to send them away to a children's camp in the Surrey hills. Ann Simmons, the little girl who was hop-picking when the war started and has been staying with her maternal grandparents while her mother does war work, will be sent to Barnsley, Yorkshire. Brian Baker, son of Len, the former tram driver and barrow maker, recalls the train leaving Hatfield and passing the fields of planes at Hendon, and reaching a house in Medway Road, just off the Roman, a home he has never yet seen, and his mother taking one look at what remains and bursting into tears. That night the two of them sleep across two chairs in a room full of brick dust with a partially collapsed ceiling. But there's no way they can stay. Not in a ruin, not with doodlebugs churning overhead.

It's been so long since Phil Shratsky saw his home in Brady Buildings in Bethnal Green, and he was so young when he left that he's all but forgotten it. He's a Welsh boy now, a Jewish Welsh boy living in the Rhondda Valley, spending his mornings at a Welsh school and his afternoons clambering across the hills looking for birds' nests and rabbits' burrows. His dad, Solomon, a private in the Royal Electrical and Mechanical Engineers, has been away fighting for most of the war. His mother has been doing war work in Bethnal Green. She's been to visit when she can, which isn't often, and Phil has adjusted, in the way children do, to not having his parents around. So it's a surprise when, one day in March 1944, Solomon arrives to take him to Hitchin in Hertfordshire, where his mother has just given birth to the newest member of the family, Rita, at an evacuation hospital. Father and son travel by train, a long haul from Rhondda, and by the time they arrive Phillip, who is six now, has worked himself up into a state of wonder. His mum! A new sister!

It's not to be. A nurse at the hospital explains they can't have children around the newborns. Who knows why? An infection hazard? Maybe just the times. So, having come all the way from Wales, Phillip is left sitting outside looking at the sky and 'all the American planes going over'. Later, he remembers, 'Dad coming out and [he] said you got a baby sister and I said Dad how do you get babies and he said what happens is, if they're 7 lbs 3 oz you pay £7 3s'. This sets off a number of other questions in Phillip's mind, such as, why pay for a big baby when you can get a smaller one cheaper? But he is six so he doesn't question the principle that babies must be paid for by weight, like cabbages or bacon knuckles, not least because the information has come from his dad, who is in the Royal Electrical and Mechanical Engineers and knows a thing or two.

Six months later, in mid October, Phillip is upstairs in the house in Wales when one of his aunts calls him down. He's seven by now. A telegram has arrived, and he is the reader in the family. His aunt hands it to him and asks that he read it out loud. And so he does, though the words don't really sink in. Nineteenth of October, Private Solomon Shratsky. Antwerp. Killed in Action (later this will be amended to accidentally killed). Phillip stops reading and looks up, the telegram between his fingers. Suddenly everyone around him is crying. And then Phillip too is crying, and while part of him knows why – because he is young and his father has been away at war for so long – another part isn't quite sure.

In 1942 another evacuee to Wales, Harry Da Costa, returns to London as a sixteen-year-old newly trained baker keen to find work. Moving in with Hyam, his grandfather, and the maiden aunts in Barkingside, he begins looking for work. Market trader, his family's occupation, won't do because the Roman has more or less closed up and Harry's too young to get a licence anyway. When a cousin by marriage, the manager of a firm making coats for C & A, says there's an opportunity at the machining tables, Harry jumps at it. So he puts himself to machining coats, but it's no life. Fiddle and dust and poorly paid. The aunts fuss over him in the evenings, but he has to sleep in the same bed as his grandfather Hyam, who snorts and snores like a defective train. By 1944 Harry can stand it no more. In February, remembering the trip he made as a seven-year-old to Plymouth in the company of the family's Irish maid Elsie, Harry volunteers for the navy. He'll make his way to the HMS *Buke* training camp in Worcester for basic training, where, ironically, he'll be prevented from shipping out to sea by an attack of German measles.

While Harry is in Worcester, Ted Lucioni is heading back from his evacuation posting in Devon to Bow. He's thirteen now and his father, Teddy, thinks it is high time his boy got a proper job. No matter that, not long before Ted is due to arrive, a VI lands in the back garden and blows out the interior walls of the house, leaving one big bedroom where there had been three and clouds of dust everywhere. Ted is put on a train and given his first pair of long trousers, cast offs from a cousin, and once back in London apprentices at a bookbinder's, curving the spines of hard covers where the pages meet the stitching. The work is boring and Ted spends his days dreaming of reaching eighteen and being able to join his father in Billingsgate. So dreamy is he, so numb, that one after-noon, when he manages to crush two fingers in the machine, he keeps on going as though nothing has happened. A naval doctor stiches the ends of his fingers back on and bandages them up, and Ted goes back to work. In the evenings he eases his frustrations in the boxing ring. South-East Division junior champion. Born with a punch.

On 8 September 1944 there's further mayhem as the first of Hitler's V2s overshoots its target in the docks and lands in Chiswick, killing three and injuring seventeen. From then on they keep coming, fired from longer range than the V1 but with more accu-racy and power. Now instead of bombs taking out one house or two, flying rockets are routinely destroying entire terraces, roads of houses and shopping parades. The most lethal, in November, hits Woolworths in New Cross in south-east London, leaving 168 dead. In separate attacks, Bow and Old Ford are both hit. The Bow rocket lands in the back garden of Ted Lewis's aunt near Bow Road Station. Ted is on his way home from work that day on the underground and hears the explosion. He carries on to the next station and runs back to his aunt's house in a sweat of anticipatory anguish, to find the upstairs of the property completely gone and, thank god, his aunt and baby cousin shaken but alive. The aunt had taken the boy into the living room and put him in the armchair when the bomb blew her under the stairs and turned the arm-chair upside down over the baby. That saved them both.

The rockets leave craters that are irresistible as playgrounds for the children who are still in Bow. There's a giant one not far from Olga Street school. Kids congregate there with their bikes, spin-ning round and round the crater's walls on what was once marsh-land, then a terrace of homes and is now a smoking bowl of rubble doubling up as a children's playground, a thrilling wall of death.

19

I didn't want to go back to London . . .

Phil Price

As the sun goes down on Sunday, 1 April 1945, the lights come on in London. On Monday, 8 May the war in Europe is over. On Sunday, 2 September it's finished across the world.

From the Kellys' shops in Bethnal Green and Bow the views are of drab, pinched, exhausted ruins of rubble from which buddleia and old man's beard burst in cheery sprigs. The area looks like a bad set of dentures: discoloured, smelly and uneven, full of gaping holes. Over a million London homes have been destroyed and most of these are in the East End. In the Roman, Bow Baths, the dairy behind Arber's and the Needle Gun pub are all as good as gone. On Fish Island, Clarnico's is wrecked and the timberyards devoid of timber. Five minutes to the north, the lido where Ann Simmons swam and the pagoda where Ted Lewis picked up girls are collections of wreckage now. The ironwork railings and ornate gates which once surrounded Vicky Park are gone, and where there were once neat grass lawns there are now gun emplacements and prefab lodgings for POWs. The formerly immaculate flower-beds are sprouting cabbages.

At the end of 1945 a steady stream of demobbed soldiers and sailors are arriving back in Bow, among them Gary Arber's brother Stanley and Ron Moss's brother Charlie. One of the first to arrive is Harry Da Costa. Since February 1944 he's been serving as a cook in the Navy, making an old childhood dream come true. He's in Malta when the war ends and is judged eligible for early release only so long as he agrees to go back to tailoring for at least six months. There's a need for civilian clothes. The journey back home by boat to Toulon and from there by train to Marseille and all the way across France to Calais then to Dover and London takes two and a half days. By early 1946 Harry is back in Bow cutting cloth, but he soon decides he's not cut out to be a tailor. Costermongering is in his blood. Once his obligatory six months is over, he packs in the tailoring game and sets up a stall in the Roman with his brother Joel. Among their first items for sale are deflated barrage balloons, which the brothers repurpose as vehicle covers for vans, barrows, cars, carts, what have you. Tremendous success, they are, those barrage balloon-cum-vehicle covers.

A few stalls down from Harry and Joel, Bill Old, newly back from a Japanese POW camp, resumes selling fruit and veg, but it's quiet now and for the most part supplies are harder to come by than they were during the war. Even with the children returning from evacuation and the men from the fighting, London's population has fallen by 2,250,000; it won't reach its 1939 level again until well into the next century. The bulk of the loss is felt in the area where there is most damage, which is to say, the East End. More than 20,000 civilian Londoners have died.* There's hardly a family in the East End that has not lost a loved one.

Inside G. Kelly's Noted Eel and Pie Shop the conversation is framed by questions. What will London be now? What will the Roman be? Who will buy cauliflowers in the market, and who will sell them? Who will wheel the barrows and eat pie and mash for dinner followed by Randolfi's ice cream? Who will roll into The Aberdeen for the singing or sit in The Albert after a long day at the market or the factories with a pint of Mild and a Player's,

---

* To put this in perspective, the second highest number of civilian deaths recorded is Liverpool, with approximately 4,000.

putting the world to rights? What will become of the factories at Old Ford and Fish Island? Who will cut timber at Malinson's, pack matches at Bryant & May, machine uniforms at Compton's, wheelbarrow fish at Billingsgate or heave coal in the docks? Who will fish the eels and roll out the pastry and grow the parsley for the liquor and keep the oven up to temperature?

What will the East End look like? Who will East Enders be?

20

All the prefabs, now they were the elite, you know . . .
Brenda Wood, Mapping the Change

The immediate priority is housing and home. It's hard to see how this broken, rickety corner of London will ever be able to serve the people who live in it, even though there are many fewer people than before the war. Some of London's evacuees have made other lives with other families away from the capital, and have no desire to return to the reek and rubble of their old homes. Others prefer to start afresh in newer, less ruined countries. A steady flow heads out from the docks towards new lives in the old colonies. Among these are the Da Costas, who, in 1946, pack up their 400 years of family history in the East End and head out for the untroubled pastures of New Zealand. Only Harry Da Costa stays behind. It's now that he meets Marie from the flower shop just up the road. What does he like in particular about Marie? Many decades later, aged ninety, and Marie long gone, he ponders the question for a while. He hasn't been asked that one before. Has to stop and think. 'She was a girl.'

In Bethnal Green the newly widowed Ruth Shratsky is looking to start again closer to home. The flat in Brady Buildings has been war damaged and is in any case marked for slum clearance, and Ruth is keen to move elsewhere. She's eager to reinvent her family in other ways too. When Solomon was alive the Shratskys were always saying they'd help him out in business if Ruth converted to

Judaism and made Jews of her children. But she wouldn't and so they didn't. His sons are still subject to Jew jibes at school, though, and, now that Solomon Shratsky has given his life in service of his country, to jokes about being fatherless too. From now on, Ruth decides, the family will be known by her maiden name, Price, and if her husband's family won't help them out, then she'll have to hope the council will.

It isn't long before the newly reinvented Price family is rehoused in a prefab in Lessada Street near the Palm Tree pub off the Roman. Ruth has to work all hours cleaning other people's houses, washing other people's laundry and making up bird cages in a factory till her fingers are raw and bleeding from the wire, to be able to afford the rent. But oh, it's a beauty! Small, yes, but with a fitted kitchen, an internal bathroom and, of all things, a little refrigerator. Deluxe!

There are prefabs going up in Monier Road out on Fish Island too, though the Plenty family, who are long established there, won't be eligible for one. The Plentys are among the more respectable families in the neighbourhood, with men in work and a house of their own. Linda Plenty, who is not quite born yet, will go on to work at Randolfi's café on the Roman and at the local bingo hall. The house where very many of the family live is one of the few to have remained intact on Monier Road. There it sits, a lone galleon in a sea of rubble. Though owned by the Plentys, there is absolutely nothing plentiful about it. With the houses on either side bombed or torn down, the old party walls now have to function as exterior walls, and what with moist London air leaking in through every line of cracked mortar the place quickly becomes a green and sprouting cave. The damp is so bad the whole family falls ill.

Still, they are lucky to have somewhere. In the spot where the Simmons family home in Lydia Street once stood there is now a pile of brick rubble sitting in a V2 crater. ('Mr Hitler made sure it wasn't there no more,' says Ann.) Instead, the family finds a modest Victorian with two bedrooms and a boxroom to rent in Antill Road just off the Roman. It's not far away from their former home and it's dusty, the bricks coated in a film of cordite from the bombs and soot from the fires, but the rent is cheap and it does at least contain the possibility, perhaps even, with a great deal of elbow grease and care, the promise, of a home.

Gradually the East End begins to pick itself up and dust itself down. Then, because East Enders are used to misfortune and struggle, and remarkably resilient in the face of both, this dirty, raggedy corner of London shakes off the dust and dirt of six years of war and gets on with the business of living. There are bright spots – the return of lighting as blackout restrictions are lifted, the end of daily fear and the jostle for places in the Tube station shelter, the return of nights undisturbed by air-raid warnings, the relief for some from overcrowding, the reseeding of the city with children and, with them, the resumption of a merry street life. And though the air is full of dust and factory fumes, there's a feeling of being able to breathe once more. Before long, elderly women past the age of factory work are back out on their stoops peeling vegetables and gossiping, while their daughters, either counting their blessings to have their husbands home or else steeling themselves for widowhood, head off through thickening smog to humdrum jobs at Cundle & Eve's, Compton's and Bryant & May's. Once more the early morning streets are full of men jostling to work or pouring into the pubs from the docks and timberyards and factories at work-day's end. In half-ruined turnings all along the Roman Road steps are scrubbed, pavements swept, rag rugs beaten, coppers heated and ham hocks and sheep's heads and trotters put on to boil. Out in the yards washing's hung out, Andies are filled in and planted with flowers and vegetables, and on the Roman shop windows are reglazed, doors painted, street signs rehung, market barrows spruced up, pitches marked out and supplies brought in. Girls play skipping games and the streets are once more chalked up for hopscotch. On the marshes, boys back from evacuation pit their footwork skills against teams from Eton at the Eton Manor Football Club, snare rabbits and race pigeons, knock together stilts and go-karts from the floorboards of bombed-out buildings, or make camps in the old POW huts in Vicky Park and let off stink bombs made from the rolls of old surveillance film they find there. War babies and kids too young to remember how it was before the war play war games on bombsites or sift through the debris of ruined lives hoping to uncover some treasure or other. And from the ashes a proud and shabby phoenix rises.

In the harsh winter of 1947 the Regent's Canal and the Hertford Union Canal ice up and kids dare each other to slide across. Brian Baker, whose father Len owns the barrow business in the Roman, comes across a gem in Mile End. The place was once a terraced house but now resembles an elaborate if broken ladder. Up on what was once the second floor sits a wardrobe, teetering on broken floorboards like a high-rise Aladdin's cave, a 'wossname', Brian recalls decades later, a word that stands in for all manner of things and feelings in Brian's world. But the sheen in Brian's eyes at the memory is both moving and eloquent. He sees himself, as a boy, skipping across a moraine of broken bricks and mortar. Finding a foothold in the rubble of a wall, he creeps along splintered joists until he draws nearer to the treasure chest. Fifty feet aloft now, balanced on a tiny bridge of broken boards, he edges close enough to the cupboard to reach an eager hand around the handle. Holding his breath to keep himself steady, he twists and pulls until the door cracks open, then pulls a little more. All of a sudden a cloud of dust billows out and the door swings wide and he waits, poised precariously on the boards, blinking and coughing the dust away, until the air clears and before him sits the deep interior of his Aladdin's cave. Only this particular treasure chest turns out to be completely empty. All that effort's been for nothing, but still, six decades later,

Brian remembers it. And when, from the vantage point of old age, he talks about following in his father's footsteps on the market barrows and how he never went for no fortnight holidays and never left England, it may be that the empty wardrobe, which as a boy he risked his life to reach, comes to mind.

21

We seemed as if we had so much to look forward to . . .

Ted Lewis, Mapping the Change

Just after the war . . . were the best times for years. Everyone was
better off then. It was just a better time. We were looking forward.
The National Health Service had come in, we were guaranteed we
were going to get good pensions and all sorts – I mean half these
things never happened. But they seemed like they were going to
then. Everything was good. We had some good politicians as well
– they was real politicians. People just got on with their lives and
seemed contented. People seemed a lot more contented.*

And so Bow emerges, blinking, from its six-year nightmare, rubbly,
darker and down at heel but by no means out, and while there's no
doubting the streets and turnings of the East End have changed in
very visible and material ways, what's less clear is how the war has
changed East Enders. What will become of the old world, the
Friday night dog races, Saturday morning markets, the eel, pie and
mash dinners, the Sunday shellfish teas? The elderly women sitting
on their stoops, the kids playing hopscotch in the street, the boozers full to the brim on a Saturday night? What will remain of the
camaraderie of the turnings, of the borrowed sugar, the midnight
flits, the annual beanos to Margate and Southend? For those left in

* Ted Lewis.

the East End, what of the old life can, or even should, be preserved? What will become of neighbourhoods and neighbourliness among all that rubble? And for those rehoused on new postwar estates on the eastern fringes of London, what deep and as yet intangible price might there be to pay for the small and reasonable pleasures of a fitted kitchen and an apple tree in the backyard?

The immediate postwar years are a good time for reinvention, for a severing of old ties. Ron Moss is eighteen at war's end. His father, brother, sister and niece are all gone now. The house on the Fish Island sits among ruins awaiting slum clearance. It feels like an ending, a time for new beginnings. On the surface of things Ron is exactly the kind of young man who might get sucked into villainy, of which there is no shortage. It's hard for a young man with no money or education to make a fresh start. But the teafing life is not for Ron. He wants a regular life; work, wife, home, some kids and enough money for a pint or two down the pub. A job comes up in the building trade. Plenty of that around in the postwar East End too. All those wrecks, bombed-out shells and slum clearance. Any amount of work in repair, rebuild and demolition. With his first proper wages Ron gets a tattoo of a heart with a dagger with the word *Mother* written beneath. It's supposed to be a tribute, but the moment Melinda sees it she goes bananas and hits Ron over the head with the frying pan. Not long afterwards Ron's brother Charlie turns up, newly demobbed, for a family visit. Bit of a chancer is Charlie. Bit of a wheeler-dealer, bit of a Jack the Lad. Normally Ron gives him a wide berth, only this time is different, because he's got £500 for his younger brother, to help see him on his way. 'I don't know why because we never hit it off at all,' Ron says. But he's hardly one to say no. Ron has never seen so much money. 'I thought I was a million-aire.' Five hundred pounds is worth more than £17,000 today, enough to start somewhere fresh, perhaps, even to set up a small business.

The following week Charlie reappears with his tail between his legs and gambling debts on his mind. The money will have to be used to honour them. What's more, Charlie wants to move back in to the family house in Ripporth Road because he's now broke and up to his old tricks. At the time Ron is working as a slinger at Gliksten's, fetching logs to slide on to the cutting machines. Most lunch hours he goes fishing in the canals for eels, bream, roach and pike. At the weekends he snares rabbits. Evenings he fries the fish and stews the rabbits for Charlie to scarf down before going out on the town. Ron's nineteen now and tired of being exploited, especially by his elder brother. 'I told him to piss off and sling his hook,' Ron says, and when Charlie refuses to do either of those things, Ron packs a bag and waves goodbye to the only world he has ever known.

In 1948 Parliament passes the National Service Act. From 1 January 1949 all males aged seventeen to twenty-one are obliged to put in eighteen months of national service followed by four years in the reserves. Ted Lewis is twenty when he's called up, and desperate not to have to go. He's officially Ted Lewis now, his father having changed the family name towards the end of the war, his thinking being that it didn't do to be going about with a name reminiscent of the enemy. Lewis is a good name, the family's official boxing name, going way back to Teddy's father, old Bill Lewis. Young Ted has his Billingsgate licence and his boxing and his new girlfriend, soon to be first wife, whose name he can no longer remember.* He's doing well. Only last year he paid for his mother and brother and the girlfriend to go on holiday to Ilfracombe in Devon. The only holiday they've been on if you don't count hopping, which you can't really, seeing as that's three weeks of hard work. The way Ted sees it, his young life has had enough interruptions, what with the war and that. No way he wants to be spending his days shining boots and doing drill. But there's no getting away from it. If he refuses National Service he'll be disgraced. How

---

* He marries Sophia Dornan in June 1951 in Ilford.

could his father who fought in the war ever forgive him? Besides which, he might also wind up in prison.

Predictably, he hates all the parading and being bossed about, first at Catterick then at Bovington. 'I'd always been my own governor, and to salute someone and call them sir when they're giving you three shillings and I'm earning a lot more at home didn't sit well.' Besides, the whole thing seems pointless. 'We weren't supposed to have any more wars.' What else has all that privation been about? Every weekend he gets a pass to go home. 'It was a waste of time because I did more or less what I liked.' He hates it so much that it makes him ill. He's relieved to be given early discharge on health grounds, and after his years in the Z reserves are up and he's required to return his uniform and all his kit, he takes it round to Old Ford Halt, where once the Artful Dodger snared rabbits, and before dropping it off as required removes the trousers and the boots from the kit bag then loosens the ties so that anyone receiving the bag will assume it has been broken into en route. For a year or two his old National Service boots and trousers serve him very well at Billingsgate – and that, he figures, is the least the government can do.

For Gary Arber, National Service is a dream. The family's print business has had a good war printing government stationery, but Gary has never really taken to the work and he's happy to be called up. It's a chance finally to be the man flying the plane instead of the kid watching it from his backyard. In 1949 he signs on with the RAF for four years, long enough to qualify as a pilot. He'll love it in the RAF, flying single engines then twins, then graduating to four engines. 'It's the life of Riley.' Soaring above the clouds gives you space to think. And what Gary thinks is that he never wants to go back to the print.

22

I've never left England. I like to travel in the Roman Road . . .

Marian Old

In 1942, when Private Jim Old was conscripted into the Royal Artillery, he told his new wife, Marian, that if anything should happen to him, he'd be glad if she'd give his brother, Bill, a look. 'Nothing will happen to you because you're too handsome,' Marian had said back then. But the war took no account of handsomeness, and on 28 May 1944 Jim was killed. His brother Bill, a lieutenant in the Mechanical Engineers, was languishing in a Japanese POW camp, but after his release and return to London, Bill and Marian took Jim's advice and began walking out. In 1946 they were married at St John's Church, Bethnal Green, where Marian had wed Jim four years before. For Marian, the marriage is a tidying of loose ends, a way to pay tribute to Jim and provide a father for Peter. And Bill is a lovely husband. A lovely, kind, delightful other half.

The newly-weds move into lodgings in Tapp Street, Bethnal Green, spitting distance from Samuel Kelly's eel, pie and mash shop, and Bill returns to selling fruit on a stall in the Roman Road with his mum Old Liz. 'Everyone knew her as Old Liz. She was separated from her husband and she had two lovers. She pulled a barrow all the way to Spitalfields. Worked hard all her life. She had two children with somebody else but I never got friendly with them,' remembers Marian, who is soon pregnant with the second of her three sons. Pressing men's apparel at Schneider's in Whitechapel Road surrounded by all that heat and steam and in constant danger of burns is no work for a pregnant woman, plus it's ruinous to her beautiful red hair, but money's tight and she cannot give up work altogether. She's wondering how to solve the problem when Bill comes home one evening with news that the council is looking for a toilet lady. Keep the facilities clean, hand out toilet paper, make sure everyone behaves. Marian throws her hat into the ring and, much to her satisfaction, is appointed.

'I was lucky in a way considering I wasn't normal in the head,' says Marian now, adding, 'Well, it wasn't my bleedin' fault I couldn't read or write.' Her first assignment is the conveniences in Whitechapel by the Royal London Hospital, then the ones in Cambridge Road, now Cambridge Heath Road, next to the church where she was twice married, and finally, after the family moves to St Stephen's Road, to the toilets in the Roman, where, for the next twenty years, she will remain. The daily routine is this: up at seven, set the fire, make breakfast for Jim and the kids, do the housework then don the white apron and head to the conveniences in time to meet the man from the council who will open them up. Once inside, she'll start mopping the floors and scrubbing the toilet bowls, replacing the soap and handing out the sheets of crunchy Izal paper to those who need it. She likes the work, the chat, the business of being her own governor. Plus there's the array of mirrors. 'I've always been a bit vain.' It's sociable and gossipy down there in the bowels of the earth. The wireless is always on. Marian likes to dance and sing while she mops and cleans. Benny Goodman, Frank Sinatra, later Cilla Black, Shirley Bassey. All the greats. Regulars bring cups of tea and chat about their husbands, kids, the latest scandal, things they've read in *Reveille* and *Tidbits*. Sometimes she'll work with the wife of the bloke next door, Charlie (she can no longer remember the woman's name, only that she was a smoker and a drinker). In any case, Bill is only a few yards above ground, selling his fruit. Over the years she'll see women become grandmothers and girls grow into adults and bring their own children to the toilets. Every day the same but ever so slightly different. Something satisfying about that.

At 4.30 Marian locks up, goes back to the flat, cooks the tea, and forgets about the conveniences. Evenings are spent crocheting, darning, dressmaking, painting and decorating. No holidays to speak of, but there's always Saturday night at the dance in York Hall to look forward to, Marian dressed in her finest, twirling about in Bill's arms, her long hair following on like a Roman candle.

Twice a week for two decades, Marian heads to Kelly's on the Roman at opening time and treats herself to an early lunch of hot eels and mash. They know her in there as Aunty Ginger, and often she'll be the first customer. From time to time she'll have a pie, though the meat supply to Kelly's remains rationed, but there have always been plenty of eels and it's the dense, almost muddy taste of the slippery, wobbly fish that brings Aunty Ginger back. 'I gollop 'em down.'

It's not hard to see the practical attractions of an eel, pie and mash dinner. Cheap, filling, comforting, and since Bill Kingdon won his battle with the Ministry of Food, customers don't need to use their coupons so they'll often come in when they've used up their meat ration. But there's something else too, the feeling that in amongst all the postwar ruin of East London, the Londoner's meal survives. For this reason the Kelly family has prospered. In Bethnal Green, Samuel and Matilda senior still run the shop at 468 Bethnal Green Road and live in the flat above. Their son, Samuel, is at 284 Bethnal Green Road, where one of his regular customers is Violet Kray, mother of Ronnie and Reggie. His brother Joe Kelly and married sister Matilda Searle run Kelly and Searle's at Green Street, now Roman Road. In Bow, Theresa and Tom Kingdon have taken charge of the shop at 310 Roman Road with their son, Tom, just back from the war. Their daughter Theresa

Kelly runs number 526 with her brother Bill Kingdon and his wife Bea who are also living in the flat above.

In 1947 Bea will give birth to Sue at the German Hospital in Dalston. The infant will spend her most formative years in a Silver Cross pram parked in the shop, surrounded by the comforting smells of baking pies and boiling eels and the *ooh*s and *aah*s of cooing customers. Each morning before the lunchtime rush, Bea will walk her over to Vicky Park to look at the ducks or have a go on the swings or in the sandpit near Lauriston Road. Now the park is restored somewhat, in the summer they'll venture to the lido, though Bea won't let her daughter play in the sandpit or swim there because there's polio about and Bea doesn't want Sue catching anything nasty. There's an old-fashioned garden in the park, leastwise that's how Sue remembers it, with herbaceous borders stuffed with cottage garden flowers, and here Bea will pause and while Sue rushes to the sundial in the middle, her mother will daydream about having her own cottage garden one day, somewhere far from Bow. Before long it will be time to return for the lunchtime rush. Sue will go back in her pram, and Bea will wheel her to the shop and either park up by the kitchen or else take her up to the front bedroom of the flat upstairs. From there the little girl can peer out along the market at all the heads and all the stalls, and opposite to the sweet shop run by Mr and Mrs Chester, to the toilets where Marian will be scrubbing and singing, to Mrs Davis sitting outside the grocer's on her chair, and she'll fall asleep to the racket of traders and auctioneers.

Theresa Kelly, now in her late forties, doubtless loves this new addition to the family, though how she feels about her own child-less state it's not possible to know. Most likely sad, Sue thinks, since Theresa loved children and would, on family occasions, gravitate towards them. She and George are living out in leafy Walthamstow now, in separate bedrooms, though the long hours in the shop keep Theresa tied to the Roman. George is rarely there. When he's not in his eel yard on Old Ford Road he's driving round Essex and Kent supplying eels to pubs and cafés for the area's new population of cockneys displaced by bombs and slum clearance from the East End. Eels thrive in mud and where there's muck, so the saying goes, there's brass. That's true for George Kelly. When he's not on the eels, he can be found working on one or other of his expensive American cars. A photograph from 1948 has him in a Lincoln Continental, the motor Frank Lloyd Wright called 'the most beautiful car of all time', sporting one of the wide-lapelled, double-breasted suits that were so fashionable at the time, and looking more like a minor gangster than a man obsessed with a fish.

23

I was born with a punch.

Ted Lewis

It's 1947 and eighteen-year-old Ted Lewis is a registered Billingsgate porter, like his grandfather, father and uncle before him. This means he's up at three thirty in the morning and on the Becontree train into Liverpool Street with his dad, to arrive at the market at four thirty in time for breakfast and a chat in the pub. Work starts at five or five thirty, depending on who hires him that day. From then till one o'clock he's heaving hundredweight fish boxes on his head, the ice sliding around, fishy scales jamming under his finger-nails. 'You had to have the strength of Goliath and the memory of someone . . . I forget who,' Ted says decades later. 'You earned your money then.' But he's young and his family is in the fish, and for someone like Ted who's always ploughed his own furrow, the job's independence and camaraderie sit well. The market is 'known for its good fish and bad language'. Often, after close of play, he'll sit with Jimmy Wicks, the union chair, and they'll talk 'about religion, sex, the lot'. Sometimes hours will pass before he realises it's time to go home.

Weekday evenings and weekends find Ted in the boxing ring. In less than two years he rises from London and South-East junior flyweight champion through the Amateur Novices leagues to the pro game. Suddenly he's fighting four three-minute rounds at Mile End Arena for £5 each, nearly a week's wages at Billingsgate. In his late teens through his early twenties Ted seems unstoppable. His first twenty-five fights he's undefeated. Only four even go the distance. The 1949–50 edition of *The Ring* magazine cites him as the world record holder for knockouts in the featherweight category. He loves the fight. 'When I got into the ring I thought, this is my area. I'm in charge,' he says. For a kid brought up to believe 'all the working class is good for is manual labour', it's a shot in the arm.

While working on the fish and boxing, Ted takes time to court his Becontree neighbour, Bet Chorley, the gal who was evacuated with her sister Edna and lost her father to TB. Ted and Bet meet at Campbell Youth Club in 1947. Bet is fifteen to Ted's eighteen, shy but 'with an edge'. Ted only has to take one look at her to know she's the girl he's going to marry. The feeling isn't reciprocated. Bet thinks Ted has piggy eyes. On the other hand, he's a slick dresser, all tailored suits with hand-stitched lapels, a little flash with his money, and seems to have access through his boxing connections to nylon stockings, plus he's sweetly protective, so, really, what's a girl to lose? The couple go to the pictures and Bet finds herself warming to Ted's wry company, his kindness, and the way he looks after her. Before long she's coming to watch him fight at Mile End. Afterwards he'll take her for ham, egg and chips in one of the local cafés and then on to the pictures. Within a year or two they're engaged. Then, disaster! Success goes to many a young man's head and it goes to Ted's. He begins walking out with the sister of some young toughs he knows from the boxing club, the Dornans. Name Sophia. Even though Ted loves Bet, and he doesn't love Sophia, the lure of the Dornan brothers and their rough sparkle proves too much.

So that's that. Or perhaps it isn't . . .

It's 1950 and Ted is twenty-one when the National Service recruiters finally catch up with him and send him first to Catterick and then to Bovington. By now he's something of a celebrity and the officers are lining up to spar with him. But he hates it. 'To salute and have to call people sir when I'm earning more than them back home.' In the evenings he always goes out in his bespoke suit, never in uniform. Sometimes he goes AWOL and no one seems to notice. It's the boxing booths that keep him sane.

No one betters Ted in the booths. In the late forties and early fifties he's at the height of his powers, boxing the 'six-threes' (six three-minute rounds) and making fifteen quid a fight (about £500), signing autographs, fans writing to him from Australia and South Africa and Ted sending back signed pictures. He's suddenly getting a lot of respect from the faces in the Roman. The Bolters and the Carrs know him and he knows them. Before the war Joey Carr boxed Luigi Lucioni a few times. After the war Jerry Carr's usually to be found causing trouble at the racetrack. But the Carrs and the Bolters don't bother Ted. 'They're wise enough to take their business elsewhere,' he says. Joey Carr is running a stall selling apples outside Mile End station one time, the same evening Ted is boxing in the Mile End Arena. It's an open-air venue, next door to the station, gone now of course. This is when fruit is still hard to find so there's a queue for the apples, but Ted is the kind of man who can skip queues now, so he goes right up to Joey and he says, 'Here, sell me a few', and Joey looks about and in a low voice so only Ted can hear, replies, 'They're bleedin' hard as iron, mate, I wouldn't *give* 'em away to you.' So Ted and Joey have an understanding.

Elby Corser is another one, a bookie, who comes to see Ted box, and every now and then he slips Ted a fiver because he's making money off him. A sign of respect. 'That was the sort of people they were, they never forgot you, and they treated you as one of them,' says Ted.

Sometime in the midst of all this, Ted marries Sophia Dornan. It's a mistake from the off. 'When I went to the wedding I never got in the car, I walked round to the church and even then I thought shall I just walk away, but it was different times and you had to go through with it.'

'What was your first wife called?' Bet will ask years later, struggling to summon the name.

'Marie?'

'No, that was your first girlfriend, Mickey Duff's wife. Now what was the wife's name? God, Ted, you should remember that.'

Ted shrugs. 'Well, I haven't got a clue.'

Needless to say, the marriage between Sophia and Ted doesn't last. By the time he's released from National Service on health grounds (dizzy spells, fainting), Ted's marriage to Sophia is dead and buried. Back in Becontree he files for divorce then writes a letter to Bet and posts it through her door. Not long after that he spots her walking by the house and calls her back, and she comes. Only now Ted has to wait three years after the decree absolute before he can marry again. But he and Bet don't have to wait another minute before moving in together.

'We was naughty, wasn't we, Ted?' says Bet.

'Yeah, but it was good though.'

An opportunity arises to rent a flat above a fish and chip shop in Forest Hill where Ted and Bet aren't known, and so can pretend they're married. They are happy there. Bet takes a job at Bryant & May, the factory where sixty years ago as a little girl, Ted's grandmother, Martha Robertson, now retired and with only a few years left in this world, toiled over matchboxes. In their time off, 'we'd listen to the Goon Show and we'd go out for a walk on a Sunday and it was as quiet as the country out there'. They're both readers: Ted likes Dickens while Bet prefers contemporary fiction. But a great deal of Ted's spare time is taken up with boxing.

My manager Tommy Woods used to come down from Scotland and I used to go on the booths for him. I'd go from work. You weren't supposed to box unlicensed then so I boxed under Teddy

Barlett. That was the name James Cagney used in the film. There would be a spieler who'd stand outside the tent and call out. You'd stand beside him and show your body off and challenge people. And if they could last three rounds they'd get £1 and £5 if they could knock me out. Me and Mickey Duff would be up on the front doing a bit of shadow boxing. You'd get people come up and if no one came up you'd always have two or three boxers already lined up in the crowd who'd put on a show.

They'd get into clinches and Ted would throw a punch but 'you didn't hit him on the chin, you hit him on the shoulder and his head would go back and it would make a helluva noise and it would look like a terrific punch. We'd go head first through the ropes and end up in the crowd and people would love that.' But it didn't often come to that.

Me being the smallest one, everyone wanted to fight me. After the fight Tommy Woods would ask everyone to show their appreciation and we'd go round with the hat. Sometimes you could earn quite a bit. Epsom on Derby Day was always good. There was a big marquee with a ring in the middle and a platform outside where you'd show yourself off and people would pay to come in. You'd get people who'd lost their money on their races and they wanted to earn their fare home and they'd come up and challenge you one after another. I could get four or five fights in one afternoon. I had one come up once, he's just come out of prison for GBH and he might have been all right in the street but he couldn't fight in the ring. It was fun. You learned a lot. A lot of good fighters used to travel in the booths with us. They were a big thing in fairgrounds, people would come regular. I don't know why they stopped. To me it was a good way of life. People begin to recognise you in the street and talk to you and you think, 'At last, I'm somebody, I've got somewhere.'

The Bow of the late forties and early fifties is all about getting ahead. It's a game, and the East End is full of canny players. In the pubs, up the dogs in Hackney Wick or at the West Ham speedway, down Upton Park, in the queue outside Kelly's and most definitely down the Roman. Snobs and toffee noses might call it 'spivving' but the preferred term down the Roman is 'ducking and diving', and as anyone who knows this part of the world understands, it's a continuation of an old East End tradition, a direct result of the decision by the old medieval guilds to exclude artisans living east of Aldgate. Remember the Bow bakers barrowing their bread to Cheapside every morning to undercut the City bakers? That's enterprise East End style, and it takes resourcefulness and no small degree of nous. Take Charlie Gipson, who before the war laboured in a carpet dyeing factory but afterwards parlays his ARP experience and contacts into a job working for Poplar Council as the borough's rat-catcher. It's a step up for Charlie, not because of the pay, which is pitiful, or the conditions, which involve rooting around in the dark and fetid corners of the docks, but because the job makes him much more his own boss and, crucially, gives him access to those alleys and quiet backwaters where wagers are laid and deals are done, and a man can make a mint running off-track betting. It's not legal, but the frequent ten-shilling fines are just a cost of business. There's a spot of trading to be done in the docks too, just bits and pieces really, not much more than taking excess stock off people's hands. If some of that stock happens to have fallen off the back of a lorry, then that's not Charlie's problem, is it?

Off-track betting has always been common around the East End but never more so than now. And hardly surprising. East Enders have every reason to believe in their luck. They've survived the Blitz, the doodlebugs and the war. They're still standing even if most of their architecture isn't.

One of Charlie's competitors in the docks and at the racetracks is Jono Smith.* They might well have known one another. Looking back now, Jono can't be sure. Born in 1925, in Gray's Place off the Roman, he's the fifth son of coach driver Henry and wife Sis. As the family expands they move to 22 Norman Grove, a few doors down from the house where Sylvia Pankhurst set up her crèche and toy factory in the years before the Great War. Jono's is the kind of feral childhood common among boys born into conditions of poverty and overcrowding in the East End. Officially he attends Roman Road School, next to the Needle Gun and opposite what is then still Arnold's pie and mash. Lou Randolfi, whose parents run Randolfi's café on the corner of the Roman and St Stephen's roads (the Randolfis are still running it today), is in the same class. It's fair to say that Jono is not an attentive pupil. He'd rather play football or cricket up at Vicky Park in the morning, though he likes to spend lunchtime in Arnold's. Young Jono will always have a penny helping of mash and liquor, and as Old Arnold spoons it out he'll say 'That'll last you until you get home tonight.'

Home is tiny and bursting, and Jono and his siblings have to play on the street in all weathers until teatime and then often again until it's time to sleep, which they do, top and toed four to a bed, with the baby nestled in a drawer. Jono is fifteen when the Smith family house falls down. It happens during the Blitz when a bomb lands in the street, killing the neighbours on both sides. The Smiths are saved by their Anderson shelter, but the house is a ruin. There's no choice but to move back to the two tiny upstairs rooms with a kitchen at Jono's grandmother Lilly's house in Gray's Place, where Jono was born. The overcrowding eases as one by one the Smith boys are called up, first Henry then Alfred and finally Jono. He's in Colchester awaiting a posting abroad when he's pulled aside by a medic asking to see the growth on his head. Been there for years, Jono says, family never had no money to do nothing about it. An operation is arranged and by the time Jono

* The name and a few identifying details have been changed.

has recuperated the war has more or less ended. Counting his luck, he returns to the Roman, and buys a horse and cart to fetch wholesale fruit from Borough Market, Covent Garden and Spitalfields for selling on wherever he can get a pitch. On market days you'll find him down the Roman flogging apples. He's friends with Bill Kingdon and Lou Randolfi though he keeps his distance from George Kelly. 'Funny looking fella,' he says now. Doesn't quite trust him. The summer will find Jono selling peaches up at the fair on Wanstead Flats with his brothers, but mostly he prefers to work on his own.

What Jono likes more than almost anything is a bet. Several evenings a week and on Sundays you'll find him and his friend Bob at the dog tracks at Hackney Wick, Clapton Pond, Walthamstow and West Ham. They don't pay an entry fee – if you sneak round the back you don't have to. On a Monday, Wednesday, Thursday and Sunday he'll be at a Spurs game or at the horses laying a few bets for himself and a few more for friends. Weekends he can be found at the flapper tracks on the marshes. Strictly speaking they're illegal, but the organisers pay off the police and no one bothers them. Come the weekend the whole of Walthamstow and Hackney marshes is one giant outdoor bookies. If it's not the dogs it'll be the pigeons. Sunday lunchtimes, the pigeon racers will be in the Nelson or the Top of the Morning with their clocks, waiting for their birds to come sailing over the marshes or across the dark water of the docks, over rubbled buildings, past the smoke stacks at Tate & Lyle's and Clarnico's, over the timberyards and back to the little huts strewn at the backs of ruined Island gardens.

Before long Jono has branched out into the cards, first at the racetracks then around the Clairmont in Berkeley Square. He's playing Find the Lady. Sometimes known as Three Card Monte, and with a provenance dating back as far as the fifteenth century, the game is essentially a short con involving sleight-of-hand and misdirection. Jono and his loose team of shills have no trouble finding marks to con. Drunks and degenerate gamblers can be persuaded to bet on virtually anything. At the Clairmont one time, Jono has his picture taken with Lord Lucan. 'He used to walk through Shepherd Market and we used to give him a couple of bob 'cos he's lost all his money,' says Jono half a century later. 'His ancestors were in the Battle of Waterloo, but he was a big gambler.' He feels for Lucan. The man may be a toff but he's got no class.

Shepherd Market after the war is a red light zone. Streetwalkers on the pavements and working girls in the flats above the shops. Jono knows them to talk to; Sherry and Ann and Cathy and June, runaways from Scotland and the north mostly, though there are French girls and even Russians. Jono treats them just like anyone else, will sit down for a cup of tea with them before they start work. Feels protective of them, even. One time he's in a café and spots a couple, man and woman, plain-clothes peelers looking to make arrests. Just then Cathy comes along and seeing Jono, puts her head around the door of the café and Jono says, 'Don't do any business because you're being watched.'

Cathy, looking worried, says, 'I've got a lot of things in my pocket.'

'What things?'

'Rubber things.'

Jono checks to make sure the plain-clothes couple aren't looking, then hisses 'Here, give 'em to me.'

She's a nice-looking girl is Cathy, and Jono feels for her, out on the street all night. Ann – one of the madams he knows – has got a space in a flat, so when Cathy comes for her condoms a couple of days later, Jono mentions Ann's room. It's safer there than patrolling the street. Cathy says, can you vouch for me? Jono can. Within a few days Cathy's off the street and conducting her business in the flat. 'She finished up with a lot of money and went back home to Leicester.'

Cathy is one of the rare ones without a pimp. Most of the girls are controlled. The Maltese dominate the West End racket. The pioneer, Eugenio Messina (real name Debono), arrived with his

French wife Colette in 1934 and established a sex business in Clerkenwell in the years before the war. His brothers followed in the forties, importing often destitute women from Belgium, France and Spain. By the end of the decade the Messina brothers are actively recruiting British women for some thirty brothels in the West End, and paying off the police to leave them alone.[*]

Some of the men are okay, Jono says, others are vicious. June is run by one of the bad ones and comes to Jono one day with a black eye saying she wants to get away. Her pimp is knocking her about and taking all her money. She can't tell the police because they'll only arrest her, and the moment she's released she'll be back in the same boat. 'I hate this business, I want to settle down.' She'll give Jono twenty quid if he'll come and move her things out of the flat she shares with a couple of other working girls in Lewisham Way, New Cross Gate. They'll have to be quick. Her pimp's away but he'll be back any time. Jono has a van by then, and he's keen to help, not just for the money but because he likes June and feels for her. It's really not that simple, though. If June blabs, Jono will be up against some heavy muscle. Still, he decides the risk is worth it.

For reasons of self-preservation Jono keeps his hands off girls like June and Cathy. He's rarely without offers – that compact but muscular physique, the lush black hair, those beautiful deep-set brown eyes – but Jono doesn't fancy getting bashed up. He's in Shepherd Market to make money, not to spend it. In any case, by this time he's got Iris.[†] In 1953, when Jono is twenty-eight, they'll marry. Their union won't produce any kids, but it will last. There will be ups and downs. In the early seventies they'll have a bust up, but a week or two after Iris moves out there will be a knock on the door and when Jono goes to open it, Iris will be standing on the

---

[*] After Duncan Grant's exposé in *The People* on 3 September 1950, the police finally began to take action against the Messina brothers. But while some were imprisoned and others fled, the Soho sex industry continued to be dominated by Maltese criminal gangs until the 1970s.

[†] Not her real name.

doorstep. She'll say, 'I'm only coming back because I miss the dog', but they both know that's only half the story. Jono will say that the secret to a long marriage is 'not to want the hassle of a divorce', but there will be a smile on his face as he says this.

Maltese pimps aside, the ducking and diving life usually involves rubbing up against the law. It's a cost of business. One time, Jono is arrested for gambling at Rippon racetrack. 'The copper handcuffed me to his bike and he's walking me down this country lane and he says, "See that cottage? That's your police station."' The station is little more than a house with lockable room. The copper's wife puts down a rubber mattress on the floor, 'and in the morning she give me poached egg on toast'. Jono's arrested at Newmarket too – Clement Freud, the humourist and grandson of Sigmund, is there – but it's all just box-ticking, no one really takes a short con terribly seriously.

Some of Jono's other activities *are* more likely to get him into hot water, however. One time he's in a van with 'these fellas' and the van is full of stolen goods:

> . . . we was along Marylebone Road and they have a puncture and we have no spare wheel so I'm sat there and one of the fellas goes into a shop to make a phone call and the law comes and they says they'll give the van a pull. And I can see the fella I'm working with come out of this shop and see the law, and off he goes. So the law says, how do you know the fella? And I says, all I know is he's called Harry and I met him down the dogs, so they remand me in custody at Wormwood Scrubs. It's at the time Ivor Novello was arrested for misuse of petrol and he was in there. But I keep me trap shut and after a time they drop the charge.

It's a portfolio career of petty crime. For long periods between times Jono will go legit, flogging fruit and veg and anything else he can get his hands on cheap, down the Roman. The market life might have none of the thrills of the peripatetic life, but there's none of the risk either. The law rarely bothers anyone. Plus he gets to have his morning breakfast in Randolfi's and lunch at Kelly's, and a chance to catch up on all the gossip. Because a man like Jono knows all the faces around Bow and Bethnal Green. And all the faces know Jono.

24

He wore so much gold you only had to rub him to get your pension.

George Beech

It's 1953 and life in Bow and Bethnal Green is about to get a lot sweeter. On 5 February that year, candy of all sorts comes off the ration and children from across the East End empty out their savings and pour into the sweet shops. Toffee apples prove most popular, followed by nougat and licorice. At Clarnico's on Fish Island, which has been partially rebuilt since the war, they celebrate the occasion by handing out free cough candy and pear drops.

Bit by bit food and clothing and petrol become more freely available. Slums are cleared and replaced by brand new high- and low-rise tower blocks and council estates, and for the first time a great many families find themselves living in flats with internal bathrooms and fitted kitchens. Among these are Ron Moss and his new wife who are allocated a small flat on the ground floor with a patio in a large low-rise brick block just off the Roman. Unlike most couples, encountering each other for the first time at the dance halls, sports clubs or factories or down the pub, Ron and his wife meet on a bench in the park where Ron's been sleeping rough. 'She told me to get off the seat because she wanted to sit there. I says, "It's my bed!" . . . She said, "This is for people, not you, lay-about." She thought I was a tramp.'

Evidently, Ron puts her straight. In any case, he's working at the time, at Mallinson's, driving cranes and earning a decent wage. There are so many jobs going in the factories and timberyards that a man or woman can walk out of a job in the morning and start a new one in the afternoon. That's exactly what Ron does. He's at Glicksten's one time driving the cranes operating the gantries loading logs into the saw:

> . . . the blade itself was 45 foot long, about a foot wide with great big teeth and the saw doctor used to drive it, he was in a little box at the side of the blade . . . it used to build up a great speed, and it made you nervous, you was over the top of it when you was driving the crane . . . and I didn't like what I saw, so I said to the foreman, I said, 'I don't like this job up there' . . . and he said, 'You got to do it,' so I said, 'I'm not!' 'Well,' he said, 'if you don't do it there's no other job.' And I left there and I walked down Wansbeck Road and I went to Turner and Hunter's lumber yard and asked for a job and got a job straight away.'

Ann Simmons is another one. She was the girl picking hops in Pluckley when the war came. During the war she and her family were bombed out and move to Libra Road a few steps from Kelly's. After the war, when Ann is fifteen, her mum decides her daughter will get on well as a machinist making ladies' underwear in a sweat shop in Whitechapel. Neither Ann nor her mother take into account that she's 'very bad with colours, you know, colour blind'. Pink fronts are matched to orange backs and trimmed in blue lace. It's a disaster. After three or four weeks it's clear to both sides that Ann is never going to be the queen of ladies' smalls. 'I thought, I know what I'll do, I'll go up to Bryant and May's. And lo and behold, you had 3000 people then at that factory.' Her first day they give her an apron and a green snood to keep her hair away from the machinery, and just like that, she's a box girl, sitting at a machine on the second floor, working on the 'outers', checking that the matches are straight when the outer box goes on. Hours 7.15 a.m. to 5, Friday a half day; £3 a week pay, of which £2 goes for the housekeeping at home, leaving £1 for Ann. After a while on the outers she's switched to 'front girl', making sure the boxes of matches are aligned on the conveyor and there are none sticking out which could strike and cause a fire.

They're decent employers, Ann thinks, not so much with the pay, maybe, which, despite the efforts of her forebears back in 1888, remains poor, but there's a bank on site, a subsidised canteen, social club and sports ground plus a swimming club at the baths in East Ham, and the management puts on dances at Poplar Dance Hall. Every so often a dentist comes round to check everybody's teeth (no one has forgotten phossy jaw), an optician checks eyes (in parts of the factory, splinters are a big thing), plus there's a nursing station you can go to if you get burned with the matches, which happens. In fact, it happens often, particularly in the summer when the light shines in through the windows. This is why the glass is whitewashed over. It's why the factory has its own fire engine. Sometimes in the summer the matches won't dry, and then it's enough of a fire risk that everyone has to go home.

For the most part, though, match work is plain sailing. Ann's never bored because they swap her between inners and outers and packing and even the compo machine, where the splints are topped with match heads. And she makes a few good friends – Ivy, Sheila and Mary. They go on holidays to Margate together. 'We wasn't treated no different to the men, and the only time it got wossnamey was when they started learning the women to feed the machines and the men didn't like that, because it's a man's job, which it was for all them years. But then, you know, it's the sixties and they decided to put women on it. We had some good crowds working the machines.'

After hours, Ann and her friends will head down to the Ilford Palais for a Babycham, or to the Repton Social Club to flirt with the boxers, or sometimes to the Sally Army for games. And in the summer they'll pile into the lido at Vicky Park 'and watch all the men's muscles, creaming themselves up, you know.' There'll be flirting, though according to Ann she doesn't 'get a lot of attention because I wore glasses all my life and I had buck teeth'. Nonetheless, she's a keen swimmer – a champion swimmer, and a member of the Neptune Swimming Club at York Hall Baths – with a swimmer's body.

Saturday mornings Ann and her mum will head down to get their weekly fix of the Roman. 'We'd get bits and pieces and have something to eat in the pie and mash, sometimes a drink in the pub, then go home.' From time to time they'll bring pies and mash home for tea. Saturday afternoons Ann might go down to York Hall for a swim or, in summer, to the lido, while her parents disappear to the pub. By the mid fifties she's got herself a curly perm and on weekends she gets dressed up in her finery and high heels and heads off to the Palm Tree by Vicky Park or the Duke of York in Antill Road for the customary Babycham before heading out to the Ilford Palais, the Lyceum ballroom or the Empire, Leicester Square. She meets a couple of local likely lads and steps out for a while with each of them – it's all very innocent – but no one really clicks with her until Shirley at number 34 Antill Road invites her on a blind date and introduces her to Jerry. Originally from Jacksonville, Florida, Jerry is in the US Navy on shore patrol, and is presently stationed at the American Embassy. He's tall and glamorous and exotic, and if it's not quite love at first sight, it's not far off. 'I loved the Americans and I liked going out with them because they treated you so good. They was generous and well mannered. Our blokes were pigs sometimes, but Americans knew how to treat a woman.'

The year is 1957 and Ann, who has never thought of herself as pretty, discovers that there is someone out there for everyone, even if that someone is a foreigner and about to make your life a good deal more complicated. The following year they're married at a church in Morgan Street. There are people in Bow who think

Ann should have married a Londoner, but Ann doesn't care. She and Jerry are happy. In the early days of their marriage they spend a bit of time out in Florida then return to Norfolk, where Jerry is stationed with the US forces, training sailors in radar technology. By 1960 Ann is pregnant but in June that year, just before she gives birth, her father dies unexpectedly, and being an only child, and a daughter to boot, Ann returns to London to look after her newly widowed mum. She and her baby, Dale, now spend their time shuttling between Jerry in Norfolk and Antill Road in Bow. Whenever Jerry is given leave he drives down. Before too long Ann is pregnant again and Joanie is born. And very soon after that Jerry is posted permanently back to Florida. Ann, who has a hard time with her pregnancies, is advised not to fly for a while. They decide it's best if Jerry goes on ahead and Ann and Joanie will join him in due course.

Only a matter of weeks after Jerry's return to Florida, his car is involved in a collision. Jerry does not survive. Ann is given the news in a long-distance phone call. Jerry is buried in Florida but Ann, who still cannot travel, remains in Antill Road, widowed at twenty-seven and with a heart to mend and two small children to bring up alone. 'I loved him to pieces. My mum loved him to pieces, and when he died you'd have thought her son had died all over again. Your world ends for a while, and [then] you gradually bring yourself around because you have the kids to think of.'

Ann and her mum return to shopping in the Roman together. After a few quiet years the mile-long market is back to its pre-war heave. There's root veg from Mick the Sticks, Ronnie Down's stall specialising in curtains and jackets, and beside him, on the corner, Jim Old selling veg. On the opposite side Jim's son Peter flogs fruit and Tom Old runs the potato stall a few minutes' walk down the road. There are golden cutlets of smoked haddock from Tom the Fish, live eels outside Kelly's plus every kind of clothing, lingerie, haberdashery, crockery, silverware, rugs, towels and cutlery. There are shops: Cohen's the men's outfitters, Cater's the grocer's, Percy

Ingle the baker, Abbott's carpets, Dennington's the florist, Applegate's for faggots, saveloys, head cheese, sheep's heads and brains, Brown's for spectacles, Kelly's for eels, pie and mash, Randolfi's for ice cream and sandwiches, and Woolworths for everything else. Presiding over the spending of pennies in order that the shillings may be handed over, you might say, is Marian Old, Aunty Ginger, keeper of the public conveniences, hot eel fanatic and self-confessed 'bunny rabbit'*.

Among the few notable absences are the Da Costas, all of whom but Harry are now settled in New Zealand. Harry himself is at sea, with Marie and two daughters back in London, though the moment his ship docks in Sydney he'll jump ship and head to New Zealand to see his family, intending to stay for a few months but stopping in the finish for seven years. He writes to Marie asking her to bring their two daughters. The Da Costas will furnish her with a bustling little furrier shop to run in Christchurch, he says. They can all be happy. The only one who remains unconvinced is Marie, who has no desire to leave East London, even if that means being apart from her husband. In the market, the Da Costas' spots are soon filled by newcomers, among them the Christadoulous escaping the war in Cyprus. The family moves into a house on Antill Road, a few doors down from Ann Simmons, and before long they have taken up positions at Maria's Fashions, Tony's the hairdresser and The Saucy Kipper fish and chip shop, all in the Roman.

Otherwise, it's business as usual. The Baker family is still supplying stallholders with their trolleys and barrows. The business has expanded enormously since Len carved the first barrow in his cellar back in 1915. Now there are 250 trolleys and barrows supplying five or six of the East End's markets and three generations of Baker men working in the yard just off the Roman. The most recent addition is Brian Baker, who, at fourteen, leaves school to

---

* From 'rabbit and pork,' cockney rhyming slang for 'talk'.

start in the family firm. He's always known this is what he wants to do.

I was always up the old yard and we got caught one day by the council who said you're not allowed to work, you're too young, and I said it's me family business, you can't stop me. The phone would always be going – Chrisp St, Rathbone, Chatsworth, all the markets. A lot of people never had vans or nothing and a lot of the stallholders lived round local and you'd put the stall out for them so they could work.

Brian turns out to be a chip off the old block, a grafter. Tall, well built and strong, too.

I used to pull 'em up from Walthamstow. I used to get a trolley to Stratford, the 669 I think it was, used to get to Walthamstow and drag the barrow home. It used to take about two and a half hours and when you got home your legs hurt, but because you was only fifteen you cracked on. The furtherest I ever took one was one Tuesday afternoon, a mate of mine, we had a customer at Aldgate, the old man took one up there, a trolley, a big 'un an' the bloke couldn't use it so he says, right take the small one up there, change it and pull the big 'un up to Stoke Newington. So I set off and I got there about 6 o'clock. There was a fruit stall there, I always remember the bloke's name was Batey, and he says lovely, thank you, and all of a sudden the cramp set in me legs because I'd stopped walking. Oh it hurt! I got the 106 bus home. Me wages then was £3 a week.

Kelly's has no need of the Bakers' offerings, though they benefit mightily from the market. On Saturdays pie-making starts at 8 a.m., and there are queues at opening time at all the Kelly shops – by midday they're round the block. At 256 Roman Road Theresa Kelly has to take on extra staff. Even so it's not uncommon on a

Saturday to have to wait an hour to be served. On Saturdays too Bill Kingdon's army friend, George Burdett, mans the purpose-built eel stall outside the shop and shouts out, 'Everyone's got a bright eye and a silver belly.' His wife works in the shop and sometimes helps out on the stall. Friday and Saturday nights they're often still there at 11pm. When things get mad busy there's a Saturday girl too, though there are usually arguments about it in the winter. Young people aren't so tough these days. Standing in the freezing rain for hours dishing out jellied eels makes them whiny. Being from a different generation, George Burdett never complains. Compared to human combat, killing eels is a walk in the park. You put your hand into the barrel and catch up the fish, and grasping it firmly hold down the head and *wump*, bring a sharp knife down and lop it right off. The old ladies complain that they don't want their fish nutted. Regulations specify they have to be dead, but they're as near to live as makes no difference. Seconds after the head's off you're scooping their guts, wrapping them, still squirming, in newspaper and handing them over to the customer while in the bucket below the chopping board surprised-looking eel heads carry on gulping.

Business is booming in the two Kelly's shops in Bethnal Green Road, though the market there is much smaller. George Kelly has sold his shop in Broadway Market and bought 414 Bethnal Green Road from the Vickers family, bringing the couple who managed the Broadway Market branch, the Cooks, with him to live in the flat above and manage the shop. It's a modest place, with no bathroom, painted a shade of shit, but the Cooks are glad of a decent home so near their work. George lets Johnny Cook get on with things. 'We had an old green ship's oven and you had to stoke it and you couldn't wear any jewellery because it go so hot it would burn you, and you'd have to get the hot clinkers out or the oven wouldn't stay to temperature,' the Cooks' daughter Terri remembers. 'Twenty minutes before you closed, if you was going to sell out of pies, he'd make you get all the stuff out and start again.' Terri

– Theresa Georgina, named after George and Theresa Kelly –
starts work in the pie shop at age five, clearing tables. Before that,
she recalls, 'I used to be in a big Silver Cross pram and there was a
bowl and there were little tiny eels to play with.'

At one time, the Cooks, Terri, Terri's nan Beatrice Jones and
her great-aunt Caroline Martin are all working in the shop. Each
week George Kelly sets aside a portion of Johnny's wages until, by
the 70s, there's enough saved for Johnny Cook to buy out his boss.

In 1954, three things happen. The 'match girl' Martha Robertson,
Ted Lewis's grandmother, dies. George Kelly sells G. Kelly Noted
Eel and Pie Shop in the Roman to Bill Kingdon. Lastly, with the
proceeds of the sale George buys one of only two Plymouth
Belvederes in the country (the other is owned by Bob Monkhouse),
billed in America as a car 'for the young at heart', and most days is
to be found tooling up and down the road between his house in
Waltham Cross and the shop and eel yard in Bow. George is fifty.

25

Proper Kray Country

Ray Gipson

It's the late forties, and on the instructions of their mother, two boys are heading up Valance Road in Bethnal Green to Samuel Kelly's for pies and mash. Samuel knows the boys and watches out for them because they have a habit of making a nuisance of themselves. Pranks, mostly, like loosening the caps of the vinegar shakers, but an irritant all the same. If he catches them at it, Samuel will give them a thick ear and 'chuck 'em out without serving them'. They will 'run home and tell their mum and she'd give them another clip'. When Violet Kray asks her twins to run an errand she expects Ronnie and Reggie to do what they're told. Truth is, Ronnie and Reggie only ever do what they want. But they're very good at hiding that from Violet. At home they're sweet and obliging, Violet's own twinnies, but on the streets of Bow, Shoreditch and Bethnal Green they're scrappers and, even as boys, slightly unhinged.

Pugilism runs in the family. Paternal grandfather 'Mad' Jimmy Kray is the kind of street fighter men cross the road to avoid, while Ronnie and Reggie's dad, Charlie senior, is more of a pub brawler. On their mother's side, grandfather Jimmy Canonball Lee is a former welterweight world champion. By the time they're ten, the twins' seventeen-year-old brother Charlie is taking them to box at the Robert Browning Youth Club, hoping to instil some discipline in the tearaways. At twelve they're at the Repton Boxing Club fighting each other, and by their mid teens they're performing in the same boxing booths as Ted Lewis, Reggie in lightweight, Ronnie in welterweight. Reggie shows promise. In 1949, the year Ted Lewis is listed in *The Ring* as world champion for knockouts in his weight, Reggie is declared London and South-East Division youth club champion, a title Ted himself once held.

Most likely Ted and the twins know one another from Billingsgate. The twins work as porters there for six months, their only legitimate jobs, before turning to a life of crime. They won't be the only criminals to hone their muscles, stretch their sinews and broaden their backs hauling fish. George Cornell, the Richardson crime family associate Ronnie Kray will later gun down at the Blind Beggar pub, is also a fish porter, as is jewel thief Lenny Hamilton.

Jono Smith runs into the twins at the Mile End Arena. He's friends with Charlie, the twins' older brother. 'He seemed a nicer person,' Jono says, though, to be fair, the bar is set pretty low.* If the twins have a rep around the manor, it's not for niceness. Jono will tell you. He knows a couple of fellas, runs into them in the clubs in Mayfair sometimes, Limehouse Willie and Nobby Clarke, who are stupid enough to get tangled up in the Firm, as the Kray gang is known, and can't extricate themselves. 'They put things in your way, you couldn't get out of it,' Jono says. Nobby Clarke winds up getting shot in the leg by Ronnie supposedly for stirring up the trouble that leads to the killing of George Cornell. Limehouse Willy 'didn't want to do murder, but they put wreaths outside his door and everything. Eventually he was found dead in a hotel in Blackpool.' Draw your own conclusions.

Anyone with any sense steers clear of the twins. 'They done a lot of bad things. I didn't have a lot of respect for them,' Jono says.

* Charlie Kray was convicted of helping to dispose of the body of Jack 'the Hat' McVitie, murdered by his brother Reggie and, in 1997, of cocaine trafficking.

One time he walks into Pellici's, the café on Bethnal Green Road not far from Kelly's and a favourite Kray haunt, only to find Ronnie and Reggie 'and all his team' sitting at the front and Reggie's father-in-law, Frank Shea, on a table by himself at the back. This is not long after Frank's daughter and Reggie's wife, Frances Shea, has committed suicide.* The atmosphere is tense, barely holding together. Who Jono chooses to sit with may determine his fate. The decision has to be quick; to go over to one table before the other may well lead to retaliation by the rejected party, and to stand by the door hesitating makes him look weak. At the back of the room Frank is waving. 'Jono, mate, you come sit here with me. Them lot's the ones what murdered my daughter.' So Jono sits with Frank because he knows that the Krays won't do anything to Frank or his friends because, in their dark little hearts they know that what Frank says is true.

Not that murder generally means much to the twins. On 10 March 1966 Ronnie shoots George Cornell in the Blind Beggar despite the fact they have been childhood friends. 'The one who they shot, Georgie Cornell, I talked to him the day he got shot,' says Jono.

> He told me he was meeting a girl in Brady Street [the same street Phil Price grew up in]. He was with another fella, a Jewish sort of a fella, I didn't trust him at all. Georgie went to the south London mob and he slagged off Ronnie a few times, called him a queer and all, and there was a right needle and he was back in town and someone tipped [the Krays] off.

And that is the end of Georgie Cornell. Jono also recalls:

---

* Frances had made previous suicide attempts, so this would not be surprising, though there is also a theory that Ronnie Kray killed her because he was jealous of her.

Jack the Hat was a great friend of mine, they murdered him and all. He lived over by Stratford, he wouldn't stand for their rubbish. One day we'd come back from the dogs and went into the Green Gate and he said 'Drop me over Stratford', and I dropped him and he threw two tenners at me. Real nice fella, he was . . .

The twins disagree. On 29 October 1967 Reggie stabs Jack McVitie to death at a flat in Stoke Newington.

It's a wonder Jono Smith doesn't end up the same way. He's sitting in his old van up by the Salmon and Ball in Bethnal Green one day, waiting for a delivery, and 'a fancy car pulls up and a fella gets out and it's Reggie Kray, and he's laughing at me as if to say, watch what you're doing'. And ever after, Jono does. He understands he's been given both a warning and a reprieve.

When the twins were boxing, they had their flyers printed at Arber & Co. on the Roman. Gary Arber, the little boy watching the plane at the start of the Second World War, was the man at the linotype. In the early fifties Gary had joined the RAF, and by 1954 he was flying four-engine bombers, but that same year his Aunt Emmy wrote to say Gary's father, Francis, was very ill with nephritis, and she would need someone to help in the shop. Brother Leonard had moved to Rustington on the south coast with his new wife Winnie, another brother, Stewart, had gone into antiques, and the youngest, Gerald, was still a kid. Reluctantly Gary discharged himself and returned to the Roman. 'It ruined my life. But that was my duty. I couldn't let the family down, especially my brother.' So there he was, back in the print shop, letter-pressing boxing flyers for two psychotically violent criminals. Though Gary never had any trouble from them. 'They were decent blokes,' he says. 'If anyone mugged an old lady in Bow they'd end up in the Cut. The twins had standards. They wouldn't attack the weak and they paid their bills.'

The twins weren't so decent to a few of Gary's customers.

There was this man, he'd come in the shop and buy a Royal* and he used to draw a gambling game on it called Crown and Anchor, and when it got tatty he'd come and buy another one; but he upset the Krays and he 'fell into the canal'. The police weren't interested.

You knew they were a bit nutty but you didn't say anything that could provoke. You watched it. One time there was this thick fog and I had a customer in Hackney and the road went through Vicky Park. While I was out there the fog suddenly cleared and I saw a crash in front of me and I had to go round on the other side to avoid the crash but there was this big black car stopped and I made a gesture to ask it to move and a bloke gets out and it's Reggie. And he come up to me and goes, 'Oh, it's you.' I says, 'Sorry Reg, didn't know it was you, mate.' And he replied, 'Just having a look [at the accident], mate,' but if I hadn't been a 'mate' he'd have gone for me.

From time to time the twins round off a visit to the Roman with a cup of tea and a sandwich at Lou Randolfi's café, a few doors from Kelly's and Arber's. Lou Randolfi is one of the few small businessmen the twins leave alone – they never pester for protection and make sure no one else does either. Randolfi's always attracts plenty of teenage boys, 'the little mob in trilby hats, not gangsters like, but young men, they all used to congregate in there after they came out of the Ritz pictures in St Stephen's Road,' remembers Brian Baker. There was a pinball machine, and Randolfi kept late hours. Ronnie Kray was partial to young men, and the twins would recruit them as spies – 'my little info service,' Reggie calls them. Which might explain why the twins keep Lou Randolfi on side.

By the mid fifties Phil Price (Shratsky as was), the kid from Brady Buildings who came back from evacuation in Wales to live with his mother in a prefab, is hitting puberty and rapidly becoming exactly the type of young blade the Krays routinely recruit to be their eyes

* A piece of card 25 x 20½ inches.

and ears; troubled, fatherless and in and out of reform school, street hustling and running with the wrong crowd. But Phil is smart enough to know that staying safe means staying small and not getting noticed, although this is more difficult than it sounds in the closed, claustrophobic world of 1950s Bow and Bethnal Green. He's in the tailoring trade, is Phil, working with an associate on the Jewish side of the family in Whitechapel as a cutter.

[But] the wages were poor so anything you could earn on the side was a bonus. The pubs was the place. You'd go in there with a lorry load of cigarettes, sell it easy. So I went in for a patch of that then I got into the criminal fraternity a bit when I was twenty because my wife's brother lived with us for a time and he was a bit of a villain and it didn't take me long to get into a bit of villainy. I used to be a fence. They used to steal and I used to sell it. I remember going into the Regency Club [the drinking club in Stoke Newington then owned by the Barry brothers] and drinking with the lads who were doing the stealing, called jump-ups because they used to jump up on the back of lorries and nick whatever. We were sitting there boasting about what had gone on and then through the door walked the Kray twins and their entourage, and as they walked in everyone went quiet. If you let them know what you were doing they'd want to bash you unless they got a cut of it so you didn't want to tell them anything. They walked around the side of the bar in a little mob, order drinks off the Barry brothers, I never see them pay for it. They'd walk out and travel on their little journey. There was a pub up in Stepney, the Black Lion, and they walked in there one day and one of their lads was a bit of a singer and they asked the compere if he could sing and the compere said, in a while, but he didn't call their lad up, so eventually they went and smashed the compere's head on the beer pumps.

As adults the twins rarely went to Kelly's, but neither did they ever ask any of the Kelly family for protection money. Their mum had been a regular customer and they had grown up into the men they were on a diet of pie and mash. They had a rule not to shit on their doorstep and, besides, they had something in common with the Kelly's. Like George Kelly, the Krays were lovers and owners of American cars.

26

In all your refinery . . .
Rose Rawlings, Mapping the Change

Saturday Night is dance night. At York Hall, the Ilford Palais, the Hackney Empire, the Regency and a dozen other dance halls around about the East End, young men and women are dressed up to the nines and moving to the old dance tunes and the new rock 'n' roll. The monkey parade, they call it, the girls lined up along one wall waiting to be asked to dance, boys ranged along the other working up the courage to ask them. 'The only way you could meet girls was to join a club, become religious or go to a dance hall. You get the religious ones but they was a bit toffee-nosed and not such fun. The dance hall was the best place,' says Gary Arber. 'If you're a good dancer as a man you can whisk a woman around the dance floor and make her look good and you've got a girl-friend.' The first step is learning to dance, so having picked up the basics at Harry Doughty's dance school by Dagenham Heathway station above Burton's tailors, Gary heads out of a Saturday even-ing to the dance hall at East Ham. In 1956 (or is it fifty seven?) he's up there when twenty-year-old Ruby catches his eye. Moments later he's asking her to dance, and though she says yes he has to almost pull her on to the dance floor she's that shy. Sixty years later if you ask Ruby what she liked about Gary then, she'll reply, half-joking, 'nothing really'. And it's true, that first dance fails to set Ruby's heart on fire, but when the couple run into each other some while later a spark ignites and after two years of courting, they are married in Old Dagenham village church. It's a union that will last a lifetime.

Around the same time, a few miles west, in Hackney, Phil Price is pitching up at Barry's Dance Studio on Mare Street, 'supposedly to learn dances but really to pull girls'. Phil never does become much of a dancer. Over on Fish Island, Brenda Wood is more dedicated. Heading to Pilgrim House on Dace Road twice a week after school, she sits on the wall waiting for the doors to open and scratching the name of her latest crush into the soft red brick. It's at Pilgrim House dance club that she meets a boy, who wants to take her up the Prom, but it's common knowledge that if a boy wants to take you up the Prom there's going to be a bit of hanky-panky, 'so you either went if you was that kind of girl or you didn't'. It so happens, Brenda isn't that kind of girl, but she does love to dance and pretty soon she's out five nights in seven at the 59 Club in Hackney Wick, or up the Ilford Palais swishing around to Lonnie Donegan and Bobby Vee.

It's at the Palais in 1956 that sixteen-year-old local singer Kathy Kirby first encounters dance band leader Bert Ambrose. By this time rock 'n' roll has arrived and Bert is in his cups, but sensing an opportunity in Kathy he takes her under his wing and – despite the forty-two-year age gap – into his bed, and soon Kathy is topping the bill at the Rising Sun in Green Street (now Roman Road) with Ray Martine; a few years afterwards, between mental collapses brought on by as then undiagnosed schizophrenia, Kathy is topping the charts with 'Secret Love' and 'Dance On'.

Clubs are springing up on every corner in the late fifties, most notoriously the Kray Twins' Double R and the Regal but also the Regency, the Moonglow and others, places where men and women can meet in a more intimate environment than the dance halls, to enjoy jazz and live bands and risqué shows. At the Earl of Aberdeen, more usually known as the Aberdeen, on the corner of Grove Road and the Roman, Nancy-boys wedge themselves on to the tiny stage, crack blue jokes and sing songs with know-ing lyrics and no one bats an eyelid. 'If you didn't know them you'd think they were ordinary fellows,' remembers Pauline Ausling. A decade or so later it'll be the heyday of drag act Gay Travers at the Deuragon Arms, Homerton (recently demolished to make way for twenty-nine one-bedroom flats) and of Mrs Shufflewick, Lily Savage, Michael Barrymore and Danny La Rue, inheritors of the old-style music hall and not averse to a bit of slap and tickle, a few double entendres and a pint of Mild down the East End.

This is also the era of the Dansette record player. And where there are records and record players, there are parties, often huge ticketed affairs (Gary Arber prints the tickets – a hundred, two hundred sometimes) in private houses. Jamaicans run the best ones. Like the parties themselves, the hosts are new arrivals in the East End, joining the flow of immigrants and refugees pushed or pulled or otherwise persuaded to make the journey to London for centuries past. The East End has had a sizable population of black sailors for many years – Canning Town, where many settled, is often known as Chequerboard Town, and East Enders are well used to black GIs from the war – but it's only now that numbers are growing following appeals by London Transport and the NHS for Caribbean workers. Trinidadians, Bajans and, most of all, Jamaicans are really making their mark on the Roman Road scene. You pick up a ticket to Count Clark's house in Tredegar Road or to Lord Roy's, the Downbeat King of the Blues in Lyle Road, stock up on pie and mash at Kelly's and beer from the pub, and walk down there and they've got the airy doors between the living room and the dining room opened out and huge loudspeakers set up on either side of the room and a hundred people dancing, the space so packed that guests are lining the stairs and spilling out on to the street. Afterwards you might head down to Randolfi's on the Roman for a cup of tea or an ice cream float. Fridays and Saturdays, Kelly's pie and mash shops, Randolfi's and the Saucy

Kipper chippie on the Roman are rammed with youngsters and not so youngsters at either end of some big night out.

In other parts of Bow young people are discovering rock 'n' roll. From the mid fifties onwards Phil Price finds himself more and more drawn to the new American music. One evening in May 1956 or thereabouts, he is walking from the prefab home he shares with his mother towards Bethnal Green clutching his radio and a song comes on that's so catchy, so lush with sex and regret that it stops him in his tracks. He's frozen, not making a sound, holding his breath so as not to miss the name of the singer of 'Heartbreak Hotel'. It's a fella he's never heard of: Elvis Presley. As Phil carries on through the dank, sooty East End streets, he repeats the name. Within a year he's bought a gramophone with savings from his tailor's wages, and on weekends he's to be found in Paul's record shop in Whitechapel looking for fresh tunes. By 1959 he's listening almost exclusively to American rock 'n' roll.

Phil's too young to be one of the Cosh Boys, the original Teddy Boys, and he's not at the Trocadero in Elephant and Castle when a group of tearaway Teds run riot during a showing of the teen-sploitation film *Blackboard Jungle* (theme tune: 'Rock Around the Clock'). But he's got the Tony Curtis hair and the drainpipe trousers, and he's no stranger to trouble.

Tel Willets is cut from the same cloth. Tel is a proper Bow boy, born and raised inside the bright, welcoming beam thrown out by Kelly's, and an enthusiastic eater of pies from boyhood to pensioner. Lived all his life in and around the turnings either side of the shop, on speaks with all the staff, who know him as a cheeky chappie, a Jack the lad and all round small-time hellraiser. Unlike Phil, Tel goes in for the hardcore Ted look, with drape suits custom made at Harry Mars Tailoring Stars up the Bethnal Green Road. (Four fittings per coat – Tel's got two, a grey and a black stripe). In his drapes, as Tel himself will tell you, he looks the business: tall and handsome, a regular cock of the heap. A ladies' man if ever there was one. Leastwise, that's what Rita thinks.

They meet at the Gaumont picture house in Stratford, where Tel and his mates are making a nuisance of themselves throwing popcorn and cracking jokes during a screening of Norman Wisdom's comedy *The Square Peg*. Tel doesn't recall which of his two drape suits he's wearing that day, but he remembers Rita* and Jean. Rita was wearing a circle skirt with an enormous net underskirt which she's saved up for with her earnings from boxing up matches at Bryant & May's, and a tight top which makes her waist look tiny. Rita remembers Tel's green eyes. Tel remembers the tight top.

Not long after the evening at the Gaumont, Rita and Jean are in the chippy at the top of their turning when the owner says 'You seen them two geezers come in here in drapes, walking around like they own the place?', and Rita and Jean exchange looks and smile and say, no, no idea, but crack up on the pavement outside because not only do they know them geezers in drapes, they're actually stepping out with them. They're fun, and they make Rita and Jean laugh. Only the other day they've gone round to Tel's flat in Libra Road just off the Roman. It's dark and they've got the Dansette on and they're kissing and cuddling and whatnot when Tel, reaching for another beer, says 'Put a record on, will you, Rita.' So Rita gets up and goes to the Dansette and in the dim light picks up a record, only there's something funny about it, so she brings it over to the lamp and bloody hell, if there isn't a spider on it! Feeling her stomach lurch but not wanting to drop the record, which is fragile, she holds the thing up, pinched between two fingers, and gives it a good shake, and that's when she sees another couple of spiders. She's shaking the record like mad now, but the spiders are staying put, which is when she realises that the entire surface of the record is covered in spiders. Over on the sofa Tel and his mate are in fits. And this is the

* A different Rita from Rita Price, Phil Price's mum and widow of Solomon, who is by now living in a prefab off the Roman and working as a bird-cage maker.

moment Rita realises two things: first, she's been had; and second, Tel is a man who will never bore her.

Tel's in a skiffle band called the Roman Road Ramblers, inspired by Lonnie Donegan. They're a bit raw – the drum kit is a tea chest and the sticks broom handles – but they could use someone on accompanying percussion and they're very relaxed about adding Rita to the line-up. She'll keep rhythm on an old film tin filled with rice. None of the band members seems to mind that she's not all that good, maybe because they're not all that good either. The whole band thing is really a marvellous excuse for buying a bit of clobber. Clothes have been off the ration since October 1949 but the Utility Clothing Scheme doesn't fully wind up till 1952. By then women have had enough of sensible twills and plain gabardines in fabric-saving shapes. The Ritas of this world want something cheery and extravagant, a brightly coloured circle skirt, net petticoats, beading, sequins, angora, silk and jewel-coloured prints. And nowhere are such garments to be had at better prices than down the Roman. Oh, the cabbage laid out on those stalls! Winklepickers, Capri pants, circle skirts, girdles, bullet bras, nylons, bobby socks, stilettos, trapeze and bubble dresses, shirts with Peter Pan collars, round-neck cardigans, baby doll nighties with matching negligees, shifts, mini-dresses, kinky boots – you name it, every fashion craze of the fifties and sixties will be stocked by someone in the Roman at half the price of the same up West.

It's hardly surprising that women and men of the East End are so particular about their outfits. This is the hub of London's garment-making district, the beating heart of working-class Londoners' pride. Here you're not just a working man or woman, not just a Londoner, you're an East Ender, and that means doing your best to look the part.

The East End's association with the rag trade goes back to the late seventeenth century and the arrival of around 25,000 French Protestant Huguenots in the city after the 1685 Edict of Fontainebleau effectively endorsed their persecution in France.

Many were weavers who settled in Spitalfields, then just beyond the city walls. There they built houses with tall windows to let in the light, and set up tenters for stretching and shaping cloth. Skilled textile workers, they developed a method for fixing scarlet dye, then (sweet revenge indeed) sold the red cloth back to the Catholics for fashioning into ecclesiastical robes. Over the centuries gradual assimilation took place, many Huguenots anglicising their names and moving outwards from Spitalfields to Bethnal Green, dispersing into the general population and becoming cloth cutters, tailors and, after the commercial introduction of sewing machines, machinists.* In the late nineteenth century Jewish immigrants began to populate the East End's garment factories and tailoring workshops. Phil Price's grandparents, the Shratskys, are among them, while Bert Ambrose's father is listed as a 'dealer in rags' on his immigration papers. After the Second World War this workforce too begins to assimilate and move out to the suburbs. Greek Cypriots take over for a time, but by the seventies they in turn are being replaced by Bangladeshis. In every successive wave of immigration, cloth cutters are overwhelmingly men and machinists and finishers overwhelmingly women.

So East Enders are surrounded by fabric pressers and garment factories, and they know what makes a well-cut outfit. And when all around is rubble and grime, a good suit or a pretty dress is a declaration of sorts. It has always been a tenet of respectable working-class life that you look on the money. And that means paying homage to the latest fashion. By the early sixties the Teddy Boy drape suit and the circle skirt are beginning to look dated. The Mod look is signalling a change in style and if you want to be anyone in the East End you need to go with it. All across the area young women are swapping their circle skirts for Capri pants and

---

* It's believed the children's rhyme 'Pop Goes the Weasel', which became a craze in the 1850s, originated in the East End as a song about the rag trade. 'Pop' is a cockney term for pawn, a weasel both slang for the machine that wound yarn and, as part of 'weasel and stoat', cockney rhyming slang for coat.

leather jackets. Among them is Pauline Ausling who, with her first week's wages buys 'The Night Has a Thousand Eyes' by Bobby Vee, and by the end of 1962 has saved for a three-quarter-length jacket in brown suede with a leather collar 'in a lovely leafy green' to go with two dresses with mandarin collars, blouses and matador trousers in the new style.

The sixties finds Ray Gipson, rat-catcher's son and budding politician, newly married (the couple's first son, named Perry after Perry Como, comes along in 1968) and living in a council flat off the Roman. Growing up Ray was never much bothered about fashion. Couldn't afford to be. But all that changes once he's out working as a driver for an antiques transport company on Fish Island. Money's tight, but a man in a sharp suit can always hold his head up high. What he wants is a couple of the new Mod-style suits, bespoke, with single-breasted, wide-lapelled jackets, and a couple of pairs of narrow-cut, tapered trousers made up at Conriche's on the corner of Grove Road and Mile End Road, or at Albert's on Whitechapel Road. That's where the Kray twins get their tailoring. They cost a packet, but there's none better. Real East End glamour.

On a Saturday the Roman is one long fashion parade, from eight in the morning, when the first women arrive with their hair in rollers looking for something to wear on their Saturday night on the town, to eleven at night, when the crowds spill from the pubs and start making their way to some after-hours club or private dance party. Tight dresses with matching boleros, pencil skirts and nylons, beaver coats in the winter, kinky boots, everything newly laundered with Sunlight soap or borax or at the launderette, hair washed with soft soap, eyebrows plucked, makeup thick and immaculate. By lunchtime the queue at Kelly's will be full of young men in drainpipes and Brylcreemed pompadours and girls in their ready-to-wear Capri pants and kitten heels laughing and flirting and giving it some lip. Kelly's has never been busier. At the marble tables elderly women tuck into hot eels beside courting couples.

Theresa Kelly will be standing at the counter scooping out mash from a vat while beside them Chris serves pies and jellied eels from the takeaway window. Two Saturday girls will be bussing the finished plates to the kitchen for the washer-up, and out in the backyard Bill Kingdon will be bringing in coke to stoke the oven before sliding another tray of pies onto the top shelf. Out front, beside the line for pie and mash, another queue has formed for Kelly's stall, where George Burdett is working. By six it will all be over, at least with customers. Families will have bought their pie and mash to take home for tea, and there will only be the sweeping up and cleaning down to be done. Sunday will be the family's day off and on Monday morning, around 7 a.m., it will all begin again, with deliveries of flour and margarine and beef and potatoes; by 10 a.m. the porters from Spitalfields, Billingsgate and Smithfield will be in for their lunches, at midday it's the turn of the school kids wanting mash and liquor and half an hour later the shop will be buzzing with housewives and factory workers.

From her spot in the ladies' conveniences, Marian Old – Aunty Ginger – sees little of what goes on but seems to know everything. She's grown accustomed to handing out everything from fashion to family to romance advice with the sheets of crispy, disinfectant-smelling Izal toilet paper. On market days women young and old troop in to the toilets, keen to try on their new togs and wanting Aunty Ginger's advice and expertise. Does the length suit? Can I get away with that neckline? What about this blue with that green? How do I look from the back? All day long you'll find them primping and pouting in the mirrors, unsmudging mascara, slapping on pancake, reapplying lipstick, backcombing hair. Some days the toilets feel more like a social club cum holiday camp than a subterranean khasi. Aunty Ginger doesn't mind. In fact she enjoys the company. She's always been one for clothes. In the old days, just before the war, her mother would buy the material in the Roman or at Petticoat Lane and she'd take it over to Ivy, the old dressmaker in Whitechapel, to get it made up into a dress. Then the war came and she was pressed into machining uniforms. After the war, with all that accumulated experience, Marian began to make her own clothes. Then Peter arrived along with rationing, and there was never enough time or money or fabric. And while clothes came off the ration in 1949 and clothes factories diverted their production from uniforms back to civilian wear, most remained far too expensive for the likes of Aunty Ginger. It wasn't really until the late fifties the ready-to-wear revolution began, with many of the overstocks or seconds coming out of the clothing factories around the East End landing up in the Roman. Big brands too. Marks & Spencer, C&A, one or two of the major designers. All at less than half the shop price.

One of the perks of arriving early to open up the toilets is you get to shift through the market stock before the hoi polloi arrives, and as the fifties slip into the sixties Marian, now in mid-life but by no means behind the times, makes the most of everything the 'women's market' has to offer, flirting with Capri pants, jersey trousers and ready-to-wears in modish polyester and nylon and newly fashionable orange and pea-green.

All manner of new ideas are flooding into the East End by now. In the Roman, old shops close and new, more modern ones open. A branch of Woolworths arrives. Rumbelows follows. Cater's, the long-in-the-tooth grocers, gets a revamp, goes self-service, expands its product range and begins calling itself a 'supermarket'. Bet Lewis works there part-time now. The Lewis family has moved from Becontree back to Bow and is living in a tidy Victorian house rented from the council. Ted is still at Billingsgate hauling fish. He's had to give up his boxing career after a cut above his left eye kept opening up. It's a devastating blow because he loves boxing, lives for it really, but what can you do?

There's another new-fangled idea: a launderette. Ray Gipson's wife works there, and oh, what a godsend it is! Rita goes often – there's no washing machine in the new tower block flat. Some- times she takes her mother-in-law, who has endured a lifetime of

Mondays standing in the scullery at the back of the house scrubbing and boiling and blueing and starching. 'It could be freezing but she just used to get on with it.' Well, no more. All over the East End, in fact, coppers, mangles, washboards, starch buckets and all the rigmarole of a Monday wash day are slung out or converted into children's playthings.

All this leaves a bit more time for leisure. Saturday night is down the pub or in the clubs. Georgie Fame plays at the Rising Sun on Hackney Road and Lennie Peters is on the bill at the Green Gate in Bethnal Green Road. If a young man is short of a girl to take to a party, he can go down to the Blind Beggar (where Ronnie Kray killed George Cornell) and pull one there. They might go up to the Two Puddings in Stratford, the East End's self-described 'first' disco, entrance fee 2s 6d.

Young women are mostly working. Around here most of them have to. It's at this time that Linda Plenty, whose family still live in the stranded house on Fish Island, leaves school aged fourteen. Linda will spend most of her adult life around Bow and will eventually work just a few doors up from Kelly's at the Randolfi family café. For now, though, she's off to work in a car showroom up the West End, then, more conveniently, in the office of a small furniture factory making tables and chairs for John Lewis in Violet Road, Bow. Her first pay cheque at the factory is £5 10s (of which she gets to keep £5 2s 6d after tax), and with it she buys a skirt, a bag and stockings on the Roman.

As a young widow with two small children and a husband buried on another continent, Ann Simmons has no choice but to spend every spare penny she earns at Bryant & May's on the kids. She misses Jerry, but doesn't want to spend the rest of her life alone, and that means finding a decent fella to walk out with. Not so easy for a woman with children. Friends suggest she invest in some new clobber, park the kids with her mother for an evening every now and then, and get back out into the world. Finally, after years of having her ear bent, she agrees. By putting away a shilling or two every week from her wages, she is eventually able to save enough for a plum astrakhan coat, beige shoes and a hat. In the winter of 1966, all dolled up in her new gear and looking 'the bees knees', she meets John in the Prince of Wales pub. He's quiet and sweet and interested. For Ann, bruised and wary, it's not love at first sight, and in the course of their courtship there's a good deal of breaking up and getting back together again. Finally, John loses patience and delivers an ultimatum. Marry or split. So they marry. 'And my mum loved him because he married me with two children,' says Ann. It's a good marriage. John is a good man.

Meanwhile, after nearly eighteen years rotating in and out of Severalls asylum (partly for being an unmarried mother, partly for unspecified mental afflictions which may or may not be related to the loss of her children), Beatrice Bundock is finally getting married too. Her bridegroom is George Lee, seventeen years her senior, once married to a bigamist, but now thankfully removed from Margate and that situation. Having had to give up her first three children, Ann, Shirley and Robert, Beatrice is fragile, but she's on the road to recovery. Soon after the wedding she gives birth to another daughter, Susie, who dies aged four, but then Georgia and Christine come along and life finally appears to be looking up. After many, many years of loneliness and isolation, Beatrice is finally married and settled and working in Woolworths in Hackney, arriving at the shop each morning immaculately turned out in fishnet stockings and pencil skirts with her red Max Factor lipstick and jet black hair put up just so, artfully designed to turn heads. There will be no more spells in Severalls. Money is tight but there's sometimes enough left at the end of the week to go down the Roman, buy Georgia and Christine a little jumper or a dress and stop off for pie and mash in Kelly's. Other times, when there's no surplus, Beatrice will take what she wants or needs. Her daughter Christine remembers her mother returning from a shift in Woolworths and shaking out her belt until small items of makeup, one or two lipsticks, a mascara pot, some face powder, fell to the floor. It was never anything much, and all these years later Christine doesn't really know why her mum did it. Maybe it's because life had brought her so little joy she felt the need to take some. Maybe in a life full of knockdowns stealing lipstick was the only way she knew how to get up again.

27

People used to say 'Aren't you fed up with pie and mash?', but I never was.

Margaret Bradley

Margaret Bradley watches the weekly parade down the Roman from Kelly's front window. In 1962 Meg ('my pie name') is four-teen and has just begun work as a Saturday girl at 526 Roman Road. One perk of the job is that she gets to walk by the youngest of the Old brothers, Tommy, who is now running a stall in the market selling potatoes. Hard-muscled, rangy, with the genial cockiness necessary to survive as a coster, 'He made my heart throb,' says Meg. The Bradleys have long ties to the Kelly family. Aunty Chris is on the pie counter at the 526 Roman Road branch, now owned by George Kelly's brother-in-law, Bob Kingdon. And until recently, Uncle George was working for George Kelly at the Bethnal Green branch.

Having no children of their own, Aunty Chris and Uncle George like to spoil their niece, and that year Chris offers Meg a trip to Italy to celebrate the end of her schooldays and the start of her working life. The trip is conditional on Meg earning her own spending money, and it's a dream. Every Saturday morning around eight, starting in the early months of 1962, Meg alights from the bus at Parnell Road and makes her way up the Roman past stallholders still setting out their wares, and checking out the blouses and skirts and dresses as she goes and asking anything she particularly likes the look of to be put by for later. She knows she's supposed to be saving for the trip, but she figures that she'll need clothes for the Italian climate. Plus there's Tommy Old to impress. By 8.30 every Saturday morning. she is washing down tables and mopping floors. Two weeks into the job Bill Kingdon says, 'I'm going to try you on the pie bench.' It's an instant success. Meg is a natural pie-maker, judging just the right amount of filling and handling the pastry with delicacy and care. 'Sometimes it's me and Iris, sometimes me and Susan, with Aunty Chris cutting up all the pastry by hand.' Together, the pie team will make 200 pies then slide the trays into the big coke range to cook before setting about making the next batch. They can easily sell 600 pies in a single day. There's no time to get bored. At lunchtime the queue stretches all the way to Randolfi's on the corner and round into St Stephen's Road. No break until mid afternoon, when Meg will take another look round the market to see if she can spot any bargains. And, if she's lucky, exchange a smile or two with Tommy Old. She finishes her shift at 6.30 p.m. Pay is half a crown plus two pies and mash and a jubbly.*

   In June Meg finally leaves school and goes off to Italy with Aunty Chris. The trip is a life-changer. The warm sea and the outdoor life. Many, many years later she will succeed in her dream of returning more permanently. But that's all in the future. For now, work, marriage and children beckon along with a permanent position at Kelly's on the Roman Road. And so begins Meg the pie-lady's career of nearly half a century on the eel, pies and mash.

---

* An orange squash drink packaged in a waxed paper triangle with a straw and, presumably, the origin of the phrase 'lovely jubbly.'

28

It must have been moonglow
That led me straight to you

'Moonglow', Will Hudson, Eddie DeLange
and Irving Mills, 1934

In the summer of 1962, the same year Meg Bradley sets off for Italy
with Aunty Chris, an ageing passenger ship, the *Ascania*, departs
Kingston, Jamaica bound for Vigo and Lisbon, stopping off at
Southampton. By then the vessel has already given nearly forty
years of service. Built in Florida in 1926, it was sunk by the
Germans off the coast of France during the Second World War,
then raised and refitted to accommodate 183 first-class and 932
tourist-class passengers. The refit has left it with a permanent list.
If you set a marble on the starboard deck it will roll slowly portside.
No one seems to know why, and the ship still appears perfectly
seaworthy. In 1962 it is owned by the Italian firm Grimaldi and
used to shuttle passengers between Spain, Portugal and the UK,
and the Caribbean, a journey of some 3,728 miles (6,000 km).
Setting sail from Kingston in the summer of sixty-two in first class
are American tourists, colonial service Brits and a few, mostly
white or light-skinned Jamaicans. In steerage are several hundred
others, almost all Jamaicans, heading towards what they hope will
be a better life in what is about to cease to be the mother country.
On 6 August 1962 Jamaica is due to become independent, and
while this is a happy prospect for most, there are few who think it

will be a smooth one. For everyone on the *Ascania* that summer the journey will take two weeks.

In Old Ford, O. G. Pettigrew will be awaiting the immigrants' arrival. A war veteran originally from Jamaica, he settled in Bow and by the sixties runs a successful construction and nightclub business. On the side he assists Jamaicans wanting to reach London, maybe to work in his businesses, maybe to live in his rental properties, maybe out of a feeling of patriotic duty. Gary Arber prints the tickets and flyers for his club, the Moonglow in Old Ford Road, and also the immigration forms for O. G. to send on to his clients in Jamaica, so he knows O. G. personally and likes him. Deals are done round a table at the club with a bottle of rum and a game of dominoes, but no matter how much rum is drunk, O. G. Pettigrew always sticks to the agreed terms. 'Black people have standards,' says Gary.

In September of that year, to mark Jamaican independence, the new prime minister, Sir Alexander Bustamante, makes an official visit to London and O. G. has Gary print up a special gold Moonglow membership card for him, in case he fancies escaping from the dignitaries to enjoy a few shots of good Jamaican rum and some calypso tunes.*

'London is the place for me . . .' So goes Lord Kitchener's popular calypso song of 1951. But it's hard, at first glance, to see how. For a Jamaican brought up to believe London's streets are paved with gold, the state of the city must come as a shock. These people had an empire, but here they live crammed into row upon row of damp and frigid little terraces† and seem grateful just to be able to

---

* Bustamante's first official visit to the UK as prime minister of newly independent Jamaica was on 7 September 1962. I have not been able to establish whether or not he used his gold membership card.

† The 1958 Clean Air Act gradually put a stop to London's smog, but not before the 'Big Smoke' of December 1952 had killed thousands (government sources at the time estimated the death toll up to 8 December 1952 at 4,000, though more recent research has revised this up to 12,000) and made more than 100,000 ill.

feed their kids and have enough left over to drown their sorrows. This isn't how Jamaicans pictured London. Look at the bomb craters, the ruined buildings, the terrible slip of decay, and on the streets snot-nosed, half-clad kids running wild and raggedy old people peeling their endless potatoes. This isn't how London was sold to them. This wasn't how it was supposed to be.

To come so far only to wind up under this dead, ashy sky; to feel your backside being prodded by some halfwit in the street asking 'Where's your tail?' To see some, not all by any means but a notice-able minority, puffed with pride, the signs in the windows reading 'No Irish, blacks or dogs', even here, in the East End, where Irish and blacks have been living at least since Roman times. It would make you laugh if it weren't so misguided. Who do they think cut the cane for their sugar and planted their tea and helped win their war? Well here's a fact: dogs in Jamaica live better than some people in these squalid, dark, damp little houses with their leaky windows and brown backyards. Who are they to imagine themselves better than their Caribbean cousins? They all live under the same queen, after all.

The first black immigrants to Britain were almost certainly from Africa. No one can say for sure when they arrived in Britain, but it's fair to surmise that at least a few of the Roman warriors march-ing across the Lea at what is now Old Ford were of North African origin. So far as the official written record is concerned, there are notes of sub-Saharan Africans living in London from the twelfth century onwards. They began to arrive in numbers during the seventeenth and eighteenth centuries, mostly as slaves to planters and colonial officials. Many of these unfortunates were sold on the quayside or in coffee shops in Bristol and Liverpool. A few were taken up by aristocratic families and put to use as butlers or mascots. Over the years some escaped while others were dismissed or given their freedom, and of these many ended up in the East End where they could eke out a living undisturbed around the docks, putting out to sea, busking and begging. By and large East Enders were supportive and protective of these new arrivals. Sir John Fielding, brother of the playwright Henry, noted that it was almost impossible to recapture a runaway slave in the area because they would have 'the Mob on their side'.

Two became famous: Billy Waters, who probably bought his freedom by enlisting in the British Navy and, complete with violin and feathered hat, busked on the streets of the West End; and 'Black Joe' Johnson, an ex-sailor who had been wounded out of the British Navy but, since he wasn't born British, was not entitled to a pension. To make ends meet he would walk the streets with a model of HMS *Nelson* on his head, touting for change. There were many others. In fact, so successful were black buskers and street musicians, at least relatively speaking, that by the mid 1850s it wasn't unknown for white street buskers to 'black up' in the hopes of attracting better tips.

All through the seventeenth and eighteen centuries the maritime trade brought sailors from Africa and the Caribbean to the East End, and unscrupulous ship owners, unwilling to provide passage back, would often dump the sick, the injured or anyone who had become surplus to requirements. Invalided out or unable to get passage back, sailors often had no choice but to stay in London. The Committee for the Relief of the Black Poor supplied food, clothing and medical aid to former slaves loyal to the British during the American War of Independence. Many of these men were resettled in Nova Scotia, but several hundred made their way to London. There were attempts to set up makeshift job centres for the men at the White Raven pub in Mile End and at other locations, with the aim eventually of establishing a community of free blacks in London. After this came to nothing, in October 1786 the committee funded an ill-fated expedition of 280 black men, 40 black women and 70 poor white women from London to Sierra Leone in an attempt to found a colony there. That too was a disaster, though very few of the settlers survived to return to London. As British trade expanded, other immigrant mariners found themselves in the capital, such as the large population of Chinese who settled in Limehouse and Shadwell. In 1827 the Destitute Sailors' Asylum opened in Dock Street, Whitechapel, to assist sick and stranded mariners. Thirty years later the Strangers' Home, otherwise known as the Home for Asiatics, Africans, South Sea Islanders and Others, in West India Dock Road, Poplar, catered specifically to sailors of colour. By the mid nineteenth century there were around 10,000 black people living in the capital, mostly in the East End. Around 80 per cent were men. They were usually poor, working on ships or around the port, in tailoring or as street musicians. Among them were a large population of African mariners concentrated in the Canning Town area.

The end of the First World War brought in demobbed African and Caribbean soldiers and sailors. Many struggled to get work and lodgings. As a response to the growing numbers of men of colour on the streets, in 1926 a Methodist minister of Indian origin, Kamal Chunchie, founded the Coloured Men's Institute at 13–25 Tidal Basin, Canning Town, in a former lodging house for Chinese sailors. The institute provided black sailors with lodging and food, but also advice and company. Most eventually found passage back, but some stayed and by the 1930s East London, specifically Canning Town, just east of Bow, was home to the largest population of black men in Britain, many of whom were second generation Londoners, married to local women and with bi-racial children. So commonplace there that the district came to be known throughout the East End as Chequerboard Town.

What we now think of as mass immigration from the Caribbean began considerably later than the arrival of the *Windrush* in 1948. It wasn't until February 1956 when London Transport began actively recruiting from Barbados and Trinidad, and then Jamaica, that large numbers of Caribbean men and women began to arrive in Southhampton and the Port of London. The first black couple to settle on Fish Island were called the Powells. Being of a literary bent, Mr Powell was known by the neighbours as Mr Poem – by all accounts a very polite man who worked in the flour mill in Bromley-by-Bow. Since Mrs Powell worked too, neighbours would look after their son. At the weekend Mrs Powell would show the local women how to cook Jamaican dishes: jerk chicken, mutton curry (in the absence of goat), rice and peas, and Jamaican patties.

West Indians, particularly Jamaicans, have been eating their own version of meat pies since the British introduced Cornish pasties to the islands in the eighteenth century. The Caribbean patty is spicier than the London variety served in Kelly's, incorporating other colonial influences such as cumin and curry powder (brought to the islands by indentured servants from India), cayenne pepper from Africa, scotch bonnet peppers and turmeric. Along with egg yolk and goat fat, these ingredients give the pastry crust of a Jamaican patty its sunny hue. The patty filling is traditionally beef, like the London pie, though many other meats and fish are used, and it is seasoned with vinegar, which is left out of the London pie but always served with it. Mash, too, has its Caribbean analogue in boiled yam, which is traditionally cooked with a piece of dried salt fish. All in all, the London and Jamaican versions aren't so far apart, so it isn't so surprising, perhaps, that from the sixties onwards you'd find Caribbean immigrants lining up outside Kelly's eager to get a taste if not of home then at least of something like it.

Ann Simmons remembers that the newcomers 'got treated very badly, which I thought was wrong, 'cos we're all entitled to live. And it wasn't taking nothing away from us, they was just helping out. There was always heavy heads as they used to call them – you know – heavy boots around, letting [black immigrants] know they were here. And they were wrong. All the time.'

The newcomers have their own way of dealing with prejudice. In the early days, they do their best to ignore it. They're outnumbered after all, and not well supported by the police and the courts. In short order, though, they open their own cafés and clubs, where they can play their own music and drink rum punch and eat rice and peas. Having their own places gives them new confidence. White folk are welcome to attend so long as they never get the idea that any of these places or the Caribbeans who go there belong to white people or to white culture or to the white world.

They go to work on the buses and the trains and in the hospitals and schools. Men like O. G. Pettigrew do their best to employ their fellow countrymen. A few of the incomers marry white women or white men. Others live as far as possible within their own communities. For all the prejudice that meets them on their arrival, and for all their dreams of returning home one day, many settle, mostly into privately rented rooms in multi-occupancy dwellings, planting the yards with cassava and yams. At the end of the working week, they go down the Roman and do their shopping, where it's cheaper, and when they're done they join the line outside Kelly's with everyone else for what's almost a taste of home.

29

Life isn't all fricasseed frogs and eel pie . . .
C. S. Lewis, *The Last Battle*

While the *Ascania* is at sea, another, much larger group of migrants is travelling in the opposite, westerly direction. Unlike many of the human beings heading east, the approximately 1 million mature adults of the species *Anguilla anguilla*, or European eel, are already familiar with their destination, the Sargasso Sea, to the north of the Antilles, because it is from here they first came into being as eggs a decade or so ago.

Each fishy migrant has already made the trip to Europe as a tiny transparent larva or *leptocephali*, a journey of two to three years and some 3,100 miles (around 5,000 km), making the most of the North Atlantic Drift. Arriving around April off the coast of Ireland, Britain and France, the larvae begin to metamorphose into glass eels, or elvers, recognisable as eels now, if still tiny and transparent. There they gather in vast shoals, waiting for the water to warm before heading up the Severn and the Thames estuaries, among others, and into rivers, growing darker as they travel, until they become 'yellow' eels, actually more brown than yellow. And this is where they remain for a decade or so (though the oldest known eel grew huge and fat in a well in Denmark for 155 years) before some alchemical process spurs them on to swim back down towards the sea. So potent is the call that where the journey is impeded they will clamber on to land and, so long as it is marshy and wet, travel across country until they reach the estuaries and back out into the Atlantic on their final, epic return to the Sargasso. During the journey every fish transforms from muddy green (when they are sometimes called Shannon eels) to silver in order to be better camouflaged in the Atlantic waters, their eyes enlarge and become pigmented to optimise their vision in dim light, and their stomachs dissolve so they cannot stop to eat. The eels travel at night close to the surface, swimming about 9 miles (15 km) before dawn (by contrast, the *Ascania* will travel roughly 108 miles (175 km) in the same time period), when they dive to a depth of around 3,280 feet (1,000 m) to rest in the sand on the seabed. As they travel the males develop sex organs and the females grow full of eggs. The journey will take them a total of around 175 days. By spring, after a journey of nearly five months, the eels that left Britain's rivers and estuaries the autumn before will have arrived in the Sargasso Sea. They will not have eaten, and will reach the waters of their birth exhausted, hungry and ready to breed and die. Their eggs will hatch into *leptocephali* and make their way back to Europe, and so the cycle will go on.

Aristotle gives us one of the earliest accounts of eels. Since their breeding habits remained mysterious – no one saw any eggs, elvers looked so different from mature eels, and it seemed as if mature eels spontaneously appeared in lakes with no outlet to a river or stream – and since they had no scales, Aristotle concluded they were 'born of earthworms' growing through the 'guts of wet soil'. It took naturalists till the eighteenth century to work out that eels were fish, albeit fish which could leave rivers, but still they remained exotic and mysterious. In 1876 Sigmund Freud dissected hundreds of them looking for male sex organs but conceded defeat (males only develop sex organs on their return journey to the Sargasso Sea). The eels' brilliance and adaptability make them the third most abundant fish in Europe's rivers and estuaries; indeed, they are so common that a description of the Thames from 1904 describes the riverbanks as black with eels feeding in the mud.

Evidence suggests that eels are a very ancient food. Iron Age people almost certainly didn't eat fish generally, but they very likely did eat eels. Certainly Anglo-Saxons consumed them in the fifth century, fishing for them in the shallow waters of Britain's estuaries in the early autumn by lantern light using pronged spears. The only other sources of fats – livestock, game and dairy – being prohibited during periods of religious fasting, eels were particularly useful, being 48 per cent protein (more than meat, eggs and nuts) and a rich source of fish oils. One medieval recipe boils them in soup, a pound of eels to one pint of soup, adding mace, whole pepper (this last being expensive, the poor would substitute horseradish, which is still often served with smoked eel), and flavoured with parsley, nettles or goutweed (ground elder). Another more substantial version adds roots and crab apples. It was noted that eels would keep longer if cooked in vinegar, and they naturally formed a jelly when left to cool. By the fifteenth century silver eels (the ones on their way back to the Sargasso Sea), which taste less muddy once they have left fresh water, were fetching three times the price of salmon. In the fifteenth century, when Bow was London's bakehouse, Bow's bakers may well have made eel bread featuring eels baked into the crust, or eel cakes, where the dough was formed around a filling of eels and dried figs. The medieval historian Bede mentions people living in Chichester who did not fish but did catch eels in traps made of woven willow, and there are plentiful medieval illustrations of eel bucks – traps lined up to block a river. In the Fens of East Anglia and elsewhere, eels were a form of currency used to settle debts, a 'stick' being twenty-five eels.

Raw eel blood is poisonous to humans and other mammals, and burns if it comes into contact with the eyes. To 'feague' a horse was to insert a live eel into its anus to make it prance and seem more lively, and feaguing or gingering (when raw ginger was used in the place of an eel) was common practice at horse fairs well into the Victorian era.* The process of cooking and digestion destroys the toxic protein, however, and reactions in humans are vanishingly rare. It is why eel is always served cooked. Having toxic blood is evidently a survival mechanism, making the eel unpalatable to marine predators, but very little is known about the toxin. At the turn of the twentieth century Charles Richet used eel blood in experiments on dogs to investigate for the first time the process of anaphylaxis or severe allergic reaction, for which he won the Nobel Prize in medicine in 1913.

By the mid eighteenth century, long before itinerant piemen wrapped them in pastry and sold them as fish pies on the streets, hot stewed eels and cold jellied eels were already one of the staple foodstuffs of the London poor. Wealthier Londoners turned their noses up. The creatures were snake-like and slimy, and because of their habit of feeding on decaying matter caught in the mud, had to be bought live and eaten quickly after they were killed. Eel flesh is subtly flavoured and easily overwhelmed. Its bones make it awkward to eat, and when it is fished from fresh water the flesh can be muddy-tasting.

In the late nineteenth century, as beef became both cheaper and the population more affluent, beef replaced fish in the pies, but the attachment to the eel was still such that eels continued to be served, either hot and stewed or cold and jellied. Around the East End they have long had a reputation as an aphrodisiac. Way before marketeers and advertising executives used the phrase 'sex sells', Tubby Isaacs, whose eel and shellfish stall in Aldgate became famous, used to shout out 'Every one's a baby'.

Because of their association as a food of the poor, we've taken eels for granted, overfished them and decimated their populations. So little is known about them and their extraordinary journeys.

---

* 'Feague' is likely the origin of the word *fake*.

No one knows why they migrate or what triggers their epic journeys, and indeed it was only recently discovered that they do so at all. These long, slimy fish, which have over the centuries brought nourishment, comfort, pleasure and a sense of belonging to so many East Enders – and made George Kelly a wealthy man – remain one of nature's mysteries.

30

You had to be a Geezer for anyone to look up to you with any respect but before that you had to be a Jack the Lad.

Chris Christadoulou

The East End has always been a wild outpost, a shifting, teeming, dynamic law unto itself where the forces of anarchy and conservatism grind together to bring a restless, ceaseless energy to the surface. There is no stillness here, no quiet and leafy backwaters, no fixed boundaries, no real definition even, for the streets and turnings, the parks and markets, the pubs and clubs, the flats and wartime fill-in constitute an idea as much as a place, a high-spirited whorl of people and trade, in and out and in and out, of tides and unpredictable marsh and industrial miasma cut through with waterways, sewage pipes and railway lines, never finished, never completed, never done. Always on the move. Wherever you look, sparks of energy, rumbles and japes, flashpoints and scuffles, the routine Friday- and Saturday-night punch-ups. One time the Elliots beefing over a stolen coke, a knuckle duster hidden in the piano at Pilgrim House, another time skirmishes between Teds leaving Randolfi's café and the Greasers waiting for them outside, on Saturday nights a spot of bother between the Roman Road Gang and their rivals, the Boaters, up at Vicky Park.

In the fifties and sixties there's always something kicking off down the Vicky. One time, Tel Willets remembers, he's in the park and there's a band playing at the bandstand and women in silver and gold sandals dancing about, all fancy like, and he's there with his mates, about thirty of them counting the girlfriends, and they've sent an advance party down to the lake to hire four boats. They're small boats, maximum four people, but when the boatman isn't looking seven or eight of the gang pile into each and out they row to the middle of the lake, and there they are in the centre of the lake getting shouted at by the man, who can't do a blind thing about it, when some bright spark gets the idea of trying to fit everyone into one boat. So now there are thirty young men and women doing their best to cram into a rowboat designed to fit four, and the little vessel is beginning to sink from the weight, but there's no going back because the three other boats have drifted away so they're all stuck in a single, rapidly sinking vessel, madly paddling towards the landing stage, trying to make it before everyone gets dumped in the water. Suddenly a Black Maria appears at the lakeside and a dozen coppers pile out, and the lake is completely surrounded and there's no way to get back on to dry land without getting nicked.

But it's all just high jinks, like the time Tel and Rita are at a dinner at the Bryant & May's social club 'looking lovely – we could have been going to a royal do the way we looked'. Tel's brother Tommy's there with his wife Val, 'who only come from Stratford but she used to be a bit la-de-da', and there's been a few drinks and on the spur of the moment Tommy lobs a chicken leg and within seconds 'the chicken legs was all coming over' and Rita's got great globs of chicken skin and grease down her dinner frock but no one really cares because everyone's having a ball. At least until the maître d' turns up. After which, well, Tel and Rita and Tommy and Val are asked to leave immediately and barred from ever coming back.

The East End has always had more than its share of scuffles, the fights that spark outside the pubs after closing time when everyone's had a skinful and there's a bit of aggro in the air. The place is full of hard men and tough lives. It's what you expect. People are going to want to let off a bit of steam, but these days, the sixties, it involves young people, and the papers act as though it's the end of civilisation. Like the time Phil Price gets caught with his crew trying to break into a shop. He's with Theresa now, a dark-haired half Italian beauty who lives down the road in Palm Street. Theresa's brother is in the villainry, but the shop incident is nothing more than a bunch of kids larking about, really. Phil, the oldest at seventeen, makes it on to the front page of the *East London Advertiser* – 'Teddy Boys Terrorise the East End'. A closed shop on a quiet street at night. Against the law – wrong – but terrorism, really? Once it's in the papers though it's a big deal, so the Old Bill gets hold of Phil and some time later the probation officer comes round to the prefab and reports back that he's never seen a home so immaculately clean and well furnished, the new Dansette on the sideboard, food in the cupboards, all perfectly spic and span. If Phil Price is the end of civilisation, there's no hope for any of us.

There *are* teen gangs of course, and trouble kicks off in Vicky Park sometimes, in the summer, when the fair is there. The Roman Road Gang versus youth from Hoxton or Haggerston, the crew from the Isle of Dogs, Mods versus Rockers, Teds versus all-comers. Tel knows when it's coming. Some sort of thickness in the air. He's up there a lot now, working on the fair, spinning the Wurlitzers, giving out tokens for the dodgems. They don't pay him. You have to make your money any way you can. 'You don't mug people but you do give 'em short change.' He's got the technique down, has Tel. Say the customer is expecting three shillings back from five. You wait till his ride has started then you go over to his car and you tap out two coins on his palm but when you tap the third it's an empty tap. No coin. The mark's not looking, he's messing about with his mates or showing off to his girlfriend. He can feel there are coins in the palm of his hand and he doesn't think to count them. He just slides them into his pocket without even looking and carries on enjoying the ride, leaving Tel a shilling ahead and another mark about to get on another dodgem he can game the same way. Mostly it's uneventful. So long as Tel's not greedy, no one gets hurt, just a little bit poorer.

Tel's not one to court trouble, though when you are a young Ted or Mod or Rocker in sixties Bow and Bethnal Green, there are times when trouble steps out with you, like it or not. One of those times a mob from Elephant and Castle comes up to Vicky Park and a big fight starts up, turf war between Bethnal Green, Bow and the mob over the Other Side, otherwise known as Indian Country, the East End's catch-all for everywhere south of the river, and a friend of Tel's says

> We got bother with the Bethnal Green boys and I said, 'When we going to sort them out?' and he said 'At the weekend, I'll bring a team down', and we was over the park and they all come across and we was talking and a copper rode by and said, 'Move on', so this bloke took his leather coat off and threw it under the copper's bike and tipped him over, and as the copper's gone flying the geezer's flung the bike into the canal. And that kicked it off.

Another time there's been a fight over in Vicky Park, the Roman Road Gang versus the crew from Hoxton, and Tel is in a café in Coborn Road and he's wearing a cut-down motorbike chain over his hand as an improvised knuckle duster. Defence only. So he's at the table drinking his cup of tea, and when he looks out there are two rows of policemen outside the door and they're wanting to search anyone who looks like they might be a bit of a likely lad, so they haul Tel out and they see the chain and they say, 'That'll do, Lofty.' Handcuffs, and he's bundled into a Black Maria and taken to Bow Station and bound over to appear the next day at the magistrates' court. When he gets to court there's PC Davis saying 'I didn't think you'd turn up today, mate. Because you ain't half got a bad thing going with that chain,' and straight away Tel's quaking and regretting the chain 'because they put the fear of god into you'. But when his case comes up the magistrate lets him off with a fifteen-pound fine and some while later he receives a letter from PC Davis saying, 'I'm glad you handled that in an adult manner, keep away from cafés in future and good luck to you.'

Keep away from cafés! Not likely! Tel's far too partial to pie and mash to give it up. Besides, you never know who you might bump into. This is when Barbara Windsor and Tommy Cooper and Terence Stamp and the Kray twins and even the Beverly Sisters are showing up at Kelly's. Tel's round there too one time when a friend challenges him to a pie-eating competition. Eight pies later, Tel's all done in, but next day he's back at it. Two and double mash with liquor. He'd eat pie and mash every day if he could. Never tires of the stuff. Why would you? It's the taste of London: that's why it's worth defending.

We was on the bus once and one of the fellas had a pie and the conductor said 'You can't have that here', and we went upstairs and they called the police and the boys went crazy, jeering and shouting and smashing all the windows because you can take away all kinds of things from an East Ender, and the authorities, the powers that be, regularly do, but you can't take an East Ender from his pie.

31

In them flats you got four plugs in the kitchen but that wears off
after a while.

Terry Willets

In 1964, the Queen drops into Bryant & May's. Rita Willets
remembers the occasion, because every female worker in the
factory receives a powder compact. (Rita doesn't remember
whether the gift is from Her Majesty or the management, but she
remembers the compact.) And because she's in early pregnancy
and suffering awful morning sickness. She and Tel are married
now and living in one of the old terraces in Libra Road (which,
for some reason, is always pronounced Lybra). Rita's walk to
the bus stop in the morning takes her to Blondin Street where the
buses turn. For the last month or so she has been sick most days
over the same garden wall and so, as the date for the Queen's visit
draws near, she begins to worry. What if she's overtaken by a wave
of nausea while curtseying, or worse, pukes up on the monarch?
The only way to guarantee this does not happen is not to see the
Queen, and Rita really wants to see the Queen. In the end, though,
after much deliberation, she judges the risk too great and decides
to take the day off, thereby missing the opportunity to meet Her
Majesty but avoiding the possibility of being sick on her. It's something she still thinks about now – the path not taken. Not that the
Queen will ever be aware of her lucky escape. Unless, of course,
she reads this book.

A few months after the royal visit Rita gives birth to a daughter, but she still needs to work. The hours at Bryant & May's being inflexible, she finds a 6–10 p.m. shift at Lipton's tea factory on the corner of Brick Lane. She waits for Tel to return from his painting and decorating job before handing over the baby and heading off to work herself. This means the couple barely see one another, but this is what it takes to pay the bills.

Meanwhile the council moves the Willets family. The house they are renting in Libra Road is about to be demolished to make way for a new estate, and Poplar Council has allocated them a flat on the fourteenth floor of a tower block just off the Roman. 'You got a good view all round and there was an indoor toilet but there was often no electric,' Rita says. When the electricity fails the lifts don't work, and for a woman with a young baby and shopping to carry this is a major inconvenience. Often she'll spend all day in her father's flat on the fourth floor, just in case. Things only get worse when Rita finds herself pregnant once again. The night she goes into labour there is a very bad storm and the electricity cuts out. The nuns at Nonnatus House in Poplar have promised to send a midwife but neither Rita nor Tel can get through to them on the phone. The couple don't have a car, there are no black cabs in Bow, and this is well before the era of the minicab. In any case, the lift is out and Rita knows she won't be able to make it down fourteen flights of stairs. They are effectively prisoners in their own home. In the old days someone like Martha Robertson would have been summoned from the next road, but in this new world of flats and slum clearing and high-rises there's nothing for it but to wait, keep trying to get through to Nonnatus House, and hope for the best. The storm continues to rage, and by 2 a.m. the contractions are coming on fast and there's still no reaching the nuns. The electricity has come on, then gone off a few times, but the lifts are still not working. In the intervals with power, Tel takes it upon himself to vacuum the carpets – what else is there to do? There's no rest to be had while Rita's in this torment. Around

2.30 Tel decides that the situation can't go on. The only thing for it is to call 999.

Minutes later, an ambulance pulls up at the tower block, and in its headlamps is illuminated the windswept, rain-drenched figure of a nun on a bicycle. While the paramedics are getting their equipment together, the nun wastes no time. Rushing up the fourteen flights and bursting through the door to the Willetts' flat in a spray of water droplets, she assesses the situation – even if they could move Rita now, it would be too risky, and she's in a great deal of pain – and instructs Tel to head down to the ambulance immediately and fetch up a tank of gas and air. As Tel battles up and down the stairs he can't help thinking that it's all too much, this living-in-the-sky lark, when your wife is trying to give birth.

Life in the tower block doesn't get any easier once the baby is born. Now the couple have a school-age daughter and a baby son and are still having to live with the lifts suddenly not working or, worse still, getting stuck inside them. And then there's the shopping. It's all very well, the bathroom and the fitted kitchen and the indoor toilet, but, oh, the sheer drudgery of dragging bags up to the fourteenth floor. Someone hasn't thought this tower block business through. For housing that was supposed to offer great amenities and the freedom of modern living, it's strange how often the place feels more like a prison. For all its faults – bug-infested walls, tiny, overcrowded rooms and draughty windows, there are times when even the memory of the flat in Libra Road is enough to make Rita weep.

Of all the East End's political hot potatoes, none has remained hotter for longer than housing (it's the biggest political issue in the area even now). With the exception of the posh enclave of Tredegar Square, the houses in Bow and Bethnal Green in the fifties and sixties are drafty, overcrowded and damp, having been thrown up in a hurry by Victorian speculators eager to cash in on the huge influx of migrants from the countryside or abroad looking for work on the railways or in the docks in the mid-nineteenth century. There are tenements, mostly charity run, which were a little better built but no less crowded. In Bethnal Green there are turnings of better-built weavers' houses with their generous windows, and in Bow you can find terraces of more spacious homes, but by the sixties most of these are multi-occupancy households. Take Linda Plenty's three-bedroom house on Fish Island. In the fifties the house is home to twelve people. The largest of the upstairs bedrooms houses Linda's aunt and uncle and their four children in two beds. Across the passageway, in the second bedroom, sleep Linda's nan and granddad. You have to walk through their bedroom to reach the 'off' room, a tiny box with just enough room to squeeze in a bed, which Linda shares with her mum. At night a put-you-up in the front room serves as a bed for Linda's great-nan, and an aunt sleeps in the kitchen.

Very few of the residents of Bow and Bethnal Green except, perhaps, those in Tredegar Square, own their homes. They're renting from private landlords, the women passing their tenancies down to favoured daughters. Newly-weds live with the bride's parents until they can save up enough money to rent a room or two from the same landlords who collect rent from their mothers and fathers. It's common for children to be sent to the door on rent collection day to tell the rent collector that their mother has told them to say she's out. It's a rare family who hasn't had to do a midnight flit.

There are a few decent landlords, but many more are happy to take the weekly rent and give very little back in return. For most people, conditions are pretty bad. At night cockroaches appear from behind the wallpaper. In warm weather beetles breed in the damp plaster. Often as not, there are rodents camping out under the floorboards or in the cellar. Even for those who can afford the fuel, the open fires are barely adequate to warm the rooms. The sash windows rattle in the slightest wind, and during winter icicles gather on the inside of windows. For three or four months everyone will have to put up with chilblains.

After the First World War an era of government intervention and council house building results in 100,000 East Enders, among them Ted and Bet Lewis and their families, being relocated from terraces and tenements condemned as slums to Becontree and other newly built estates on the fringes of London. Brenda Wood remembers: 'We all looked forward to slum clearance . . . We thought we were going to so much better.' In many ways that was true. The houses in Becontree and elsewhere offered better accommodation than those the residents had left behind. All the houses on the Becontree estate had indoor toilets and private gardens and a copper boiler in the kitchen for heating water. In the summer the council sent gardeners to trim the privet hedges, or 'evers' (evergreens) as they were known, but the sash windows let in the cold, there was no roof insulation, and it was costly to keep the fires burning in the bedrooms. And the rent was, relatively speaking, high. But more importantly, perhaps (East Enders being already accustomed to drafty sashes and freezing rooms), there was very little in Becontree besides houses. For people used to living a short walk from markets, dance halls, picture houses, factories, pubs and social clubs, parks and a lido, the place seemed quieter than the grave. Worse still, what had once been a short walk or bus ride to work was now a commute. The social connections, support of extended families and neighbourliness that was necessary for survival in the turnings mattered less in Becontree, and because tenants also had to sign an agreement to the effect that, once their children were grown, they would have to find homes elsewhere, the estate never felt like somewhere you could put down roots.

If the First World War was the spur for government to begin to involve itself in housing, particularly in poor areas, the Second World War injected a terrible urgency into the situation. By 1945 24 per cent of all dwellings in the boroughs of Stepney and Poplar (which includes Bow and Old Ford) were deemed to be irrevocably damaged or destroyed. In Stepney nearly 40 per cent of the housing stock had fallen down, either as a direct result of being bombed or because the stock was so shoddily built it could not withstand the earth tremors resulting from bombing. Many who moved out to safer places returned to find their homes obliterated. But by then their ties to the East End had weakened and they'd grown used to lives in other places.

In the immediate aftermath of the Second World War, London County Council, judging the area to be overcrowded, set the goal of reducing the population to 42 per cent of its pre-war figure. In fact, between 1931 and 1961 the populations of the boroughs of Stepney, Bethnal Green and Poplar dropped by more than half. A few bomb-damaged factories, such as Clarnico's, were rebuilt, but many were left empty while the industry and enterprise they once housed set up anew elsewhere. Despite this, the urban planners of the postwar period seemed remarkably confident. In 1947 the Stepney and Poplar Reconstruction Area Board compulsorily purchased a thousand Victorian tenements and terraced houses, demolishing the rows of terraces and displacing the tenants to Roehampton in south-west London in order to make way for eleven new 'neighbourhood units', more or less self-contained estates, each with its own schools, GP surgeries, shops and open spaces. Construction on neighbourhood unit 9, the Lansbury Estate, named after the Borough of Poplar's radical MP and friend of Sylvia Pankhurst, George Lansbury, began in December 1949. In November 1950 King George VI and Queen Elizabeth paid a visit, and a few months later, on Valentine's Day 1951, the first occupants, Mr and Mrs Albert Snoddy, their two children and the family tortoise took up occupancy of a three-bedroom flat in Gladstone House, rent £1 9s a week. The same year 79 per cent of East End dwellings still had no bathroom, 37 per cent no internal toilet and 35 per cent no piped water.* The Snoddys' new flat had all these things.

---

* Geoff Dench, Kate Gavron and Michael Young, *The New East End: Kinship, Race and Conflict* (Profile Books, 2006).

Twelve weeks after the Snoddys moved in, on 3 May 1951 the Lansbury was opened to visitors as part of the Festival of Britain. The brochure read: 'Here at Poplar you may catch a glimpse of that future London which is to arise from blitzed ruins and from the slums and chaotic planning of the past.' The Snoddys had officially become an experimental family plucked from obscurity and thrust into a brave new world.

By the mid fifties the hub of redevelopment in the area had moved to Bow and Old Ford. Ripporth Road on Fish Island, from where Ron Moss ruled his Fishy Kingdom, was one of the first roads to be demolished. Almost overnight the chilly front parlours, sculleries, outdoor privies and long backyards sloping to the canal disappeared in clouds of brick dust. Gone with them were the people and their stories. Among the relocated was Ron Moss, who was found a flat just off the Roman. By 1958 it was the turn of Monier Road. By this time the Plentys' house was more or less the only one remaining, a stand-alone in a sea of rubble. The Plenty family was moved into a flat in Jodrell Road – 'Just me, my gran and my granddad on the first floor.' At first they liked the place; it was well laid out, light and warm. But all that cosiness came at a price. A few months later 'gran got an electric bill and went mental. She said, "I can't stay here," so we moved to the first floor of a house in Devons Road because it had an open fire with a back boiler and the water was cheap and bloody hot.' Brenda Wood and her family were moved out to a tower block in Hackney Wick. 'Rain just run down the walls . . . they leaked like strainers.'

The story repeated itself across the East End. In a contemporary report on the Lansbury Estate, J. M. Richards described the development as 'worthy, dull and somewhat skimpy', where 'new appears as but a pale imitation of the old'[*]. As part of the Lansbury development, Chrisp Street Market, where Brian Baker and his

---

[*] J. M. Richards, 'The Failure of the New Towns', *Architectural Review* (July 1953).

family had rented out barrows for half a century, was converted into London's first pedestrianised shopping centre. The developers offered to design new stalls for the traders, but they were happier with their old ones. A few years later a new market square was built in the Roman – a branch of Kelly's opened up there – but neither Chrisp Street nor the new square were much liked. If the planners had asked Harry Da Costa, whose family had been coster-mongering and market trading in London for 300 years, he could have told them a square wouldn't work. In a linear market people can walk up and down and compare prices; in a square it's harder to go back to a stall once you've left it. 'People lose interest,' Harry says. People did.

Ten years after the Snoddy family took occupancy of the first flat on the Lansbury, 58 per cent of East End homes had no bath-room, a reduction of 21 per cent, only 29 per cent no indoor toilet, and just 7.6 per cent no piped water. But redevelopment had come at a high price. Children no longer played out on the street while their mothers or grandmothers sat on the stoop peeling vegetables, gossiping and keeping an eye on them. Extended fami-lies could no longer guarantee living within a few moments' walk of one another. Daughters could no longer secure accommodation near their mothers. Families could not expect a garden or even an outside yard. A few years after their move, Mrs Albert Snoddy was interviewed by the press: she felt moved to note for the record that, even though it had no internal bathroom or toilet, she preferred her old house and would move back in a blink if only it hadn't been pulled down.

Back to the sixties, and the Kingdons have followed the Kellys out of the East End and are living in one of the leafier parts of Essex. Business at both branches of Kelly's in the Roman Road is buzzing. At number 526, Bea Kingdon and her daughter Sue have taken over the management of the shop from Bill, whose health is failing. Meanwhile, the area of land bounded to the west and east by, respectively, the Regent's Canal and the River Lea, to the north by the Old Ford Road and to the south by the Mile End Road (a square that for so long has made up the neighbourhood of Bow) is about to be transformed once again. A major new throughway, known locally as 'the motorway' but officially as the Bow flyover, part of the A12, is about to cut Old Ford and Bow in half and maroon Hackney Wick. Over the course of a couple of years most of the turnings to the east of the railway line through Old Ford at Fish Island are acquired by compulsory purchase and the residents moved out of the Island to Millwall on the Isle of Dogs. Demolition begins and within months the railway yard that was once alive with rabbits, the tree in Ripporth Road where the Artful Dodger trapped linnets, the watercress beds, the cut-throughs to Vicky Park and the Roman Road market, the Jewish chicken abattoir, the home of four generations of the Plenty family and the Prom where Brenda Wood wouldn't go with her date because she wasn't that kind of girl – are all gone and in their place traffic rushes south to the Blackwall Tunnel and north to Hackney, Tottenham and on to Cambridge. Meg Bradley, manager at Kelly's, says,

> When more flats were built there was still some community around, but I remember when I used to walk up to the Parnell Road from the pie shop there were still terraces and people would be sitting out and chatting to one another. They were used to sitting outside watching the sun go down. But once they'd knocked the little houses down that feel had gone.

One story more than any other captures the sense of loss that came with the building of the flyover. This is how Gary Arber tells it. During construction Gary was working in the family print shop, which then also sold toys. A customer of Gary's, one Mrs McGrath,[*] lived in Stour Road on Fish Island with her sister and brother-in-law, Mr and Mrs Stone. All three were elderly, and Mrs

[*] No relation to the author.

McGrath was housebound and passed much of her day and all her nights lying on a chaise longue in the kitchen. The women worked for a millinery company making funeral hats with veils and bobbles, Mrs McGrath working on her chaise longue and Mrs Stone sewing at the kitchen table. Each week Mrs Stone would collect her sister's weekly pension, and Mrs McGrath would put a small amount by to spend on a present for her grandson and granddaughter. When Christmas came round Gary Arber would appear with his van loaded with toys so housebound people like Mrs McGrath could do their Christmas shopping.

The house next door to Mrs McGrath and the Stones had been bombed to rubble in the war and the party wall was soaking and green with damp. Mrs Stone would have to keep a fire going in the back kitchen to make the place bearable, but even then the damp bothered them terribly. Dr Taverson, who was new to the area, was so concerned about the living conditions that he managed to arrange to have the trio rehoused in a basement-level flat in a large new block near the flyover. They moved into this new accommodation, and there they were one day, Mrs Stone and Mrs McGrath, sewing the bobbles on funeral veils, Mr Stone reading the paper or pleasing himself, when the contractors building the flyover hit a water main. In moments the water had flooded the raised flyover and the ground below, and within minutes the trio's flat was 6 feet deep in water. 'I could imagine them calling for help with their weak little voices,' Gary says now, but back then there was no one to hear them or come to their aid. None were strong or could move fast. Mrs McGrath couldn't move at all. Their bodies were found once the water had cleared, Mrs Stone at her table, Mr Stone at his chair and Mrs McGrath on the chaise longue. Damp now. Very damp indeed.

If the building of the flyover feels like the end of an era, that's because it is. On 27 October 1967 Reggie Kray stabs hitman Jack the Hat McVitie to death (though it's two years before any arrest). A rumour goes around the district that the Krays have dumped

McVitie's body in the wet concrete of the flyover's foundations, and none of the more plausible alternatives ever has the same purchase on the public imagination, because the flyover is more than a throughway, it's a sign that the Krays' grip on Bethnal Green, Mile End, Bow and Old Ford is over, and that, in some raw, vital and as yet indefinable way, nothing in this part of the East End will ever be the same again.

32

There were happy times because we were out of our heads . . .

Christine Yeend

Christine Lee, daughter of Beatrice Lee, is as wild in the seventies as her mother was in the forties. In 1970, fourteen-year old Christine is doing her best to get sacked from Barratt's shoe shop in Hackney. 'Our flat was full of clocks but I was late every single day and it was only two minutes down the road. My dad used to say, she'll be late for her funeral, that one.' The pay is £9 a week, of which Beatrice takes £3, which leaves Christine with plenty of money for going out. The moment she's home Christine pulls on her glad rags, does her makeup and steps out into the big wide world – she often stays out all hours. More often than not Georgia comes too, the sisters togged out in hot pants and leather over-the-knee platform boots, with false eyelashes, white lipstick, panstick and black eyes.

My dad used to say 'You ain't going out like that', so we used to take clothes with us and change round the corner. I remember going round to my friend Jill's house and her dad saying, 'The panda's at the door' . . . We lived on the ground floor and my mum would leave the window open a little so we could climb in but my dad put a saucepan lid in the window so if we opened it up it would go bang. Then there'd be a big argument.

Things aren't good at home. In his sixties now, dad George Lee seems to his daughters to belong to a long-distant past. He and Beatrice don't get on. Both drink a bit; George likes a flutter, Beatrice likes to flirt. Christine will often retreat to her Aunty Jane and Uncle Fred's flat on the floor above. Fred works in the print in Fleet Street, and they don't seem short of money. 'Uncle Fred and Aunty Jane used to have this glass cabinet full of beautiful trinkets, and he used to have a little teddy bear you'd wind up and it had a little bottle of Guinness.' Christine suspects her uncle has been sweet on her mother for years. Sometimes, when they're riding around on George's motorbike and sidecar and Fred sits pillion, he leans over and touches Beatrice's hair behind George's back. Years later, after Fred dies, Christine writes a letter to her uncle to be put in his coffin, telling him how much she will miss him. Asked to choose a keepsake to remind her of her uncle, Christine selects the wind-up teddy with the Guinness bottle and in a drunken rage one day her father breaks it. Christine's father broke most things: plates, household knick-knacks, his wife's spirit.

At the weekends Christine, Carmela and Margarite will often take the bus to Hackney Baths at Clapton Pond. Christine can't swim, but that doesn't matter. The point of the Baths is to meet boys. 'I remember coming out of the water and this boy followed me home and gave me sixpence to phone him. He had beautiful black curly hair. I remember giving him a kiss in a phone box, my mum would have gone mad if she'd found out.' But Beatrice never finds out. For one thing, she's rarely home these days.

After years of institutional living at Severalls, and then with George and his drinking, Beatrice has finally struck out for herself and is working in the kitchen at the Wimpy in Mare Street. 'There used to be this old woman, Annie, who worked in the kitchen with her, with a real long nose, and it would always be dripping,' Christine recalls. The Lee family avoided eating there. Saturday lunch is pie and mash, with lambs' hearts for Sunday dinner, 'and Dad would make a rice pudding and egg custard in those lovely old-fashioned tins'. Then he'd be off to the pub and that would be that for the day. 'Mum and Dad had no life together,' says Christine.

Maybe that explains why Christine never aspires to be like her mother. Elder sister Georgia is the one she looks up to. 'She was my idol. I wanted to be like her, seeing her working and all her nice clothes.' Georgia has a thing for clothes and a figure that makes her look spectacular in everything.

She had these white leather and suede hot pants. She had beautiful white leather boots that came over the knee with a little platform in khaki suede. And she had this beautiful brown suede waistcoat and if she was out I'd borrow it and I'd always try to be back before she came in, but one day I got in later and she'd put all my clothes in the dustbin. My mum got them out.

The sisters fight and hiss at one another. 'She could be a cow to me, she had long nails and she'd scratch and sometimes she'd bite, but I just wanted to be the same as her.' The animosity never lasts, there's too much shared pain. Mostly, they spend their time planning their escape.

As Christine remembers it, 'Me and Georgia went off the rails.'

[Georgia] went out with this bloke, Mickey McCartney, one night and she took half a Mandrax and I wanted to do the same because I looked up to her. We went through a bad spell of not knowing how we got home or not coming home. There was this flat in Bannister House in Homerton and this girl used to have all the hard junkies up there and she had two children and I can remember seeing them stick a needle in, and that was shocking. We didn't do that, but anything we could swallow we did. We was down the West End, Soho, nightclubs like Samantha's, the Experience, the Spooky Lady at Hackney Wick, Cherry's, the Gucci Club, a lot of the time we'd just be on drugs, bottles of Old English Cider, barley wine and not remembering where you was or how you got home.

Mostly me and Georgia together, or maybe with my friend Jackie and her friend Leslie.

When Georgia got pregnant the first time at eighteen she didn't even know who the father was, but when you're on drugs and drinking it happens. One of her boyfriends was Bert. He was about eight years older than Georgia and he had a shoe factory and a fancy car. Georgia was a manageress in a wallpaper shop, she was intelligent, she'd sit indoors and read, but she was also a topless dancer and a stripper and that's how she met Bert. So she's going out and about in this fancy car and I'm about fifteen or sixteen and I begged to go in this car. Bert brought a friend along, his name was Monty, and he seemed like a great-great-grandfather to me. They took us down this club down the West End and I remember Bert bought Georgia a Dunhill lighter and a coat and we ended up going to his penthouse in Bayswater. I remember having a little dance with this fella, he was a film producer, but I was sixteen and all I wanted was to go in the fancy car. Bert and Georgia went into one room and this old fella leaned over and tried to kiss me and I screamed and cried me eyes out and they had to bring me home.

This Bert used to treat Georgia so we could afford to go to the Purple Pussycat in Swiss Cottage, a beautiful club. Then Georgia met this bloke Peter, he had an orange mini with black windows. One night she was going out with Ray Sheldrake who used to do an advert for Ultrabrite toothpaste on the TV, and they wanted to take us down Chelsea Wine Cellars and we was only in there ten minutes when Georgia wanted to go to the toilet and I was standing with Peter and Ray and someone come behind me and pulled me to the floor by my hair and it was these two fellas' wives. Georgia was in the toilet, I had thick eyelashes on and panstick and my hair was all bouffed up, and when Georgia come out the toilet my face was all black where I'd been crying and these two blokes had scarpered because their wives had come along and me and Georgia was walking along Chelsea and this man come up and said, 'Are you OK? You can come to my hotel room and clean yourself up.' We could have been murdered.

Me and Jackie was out one night and I was on LSD and Jackie wasn't so we were in two worlds entirely, and we'd been to this big club down in King's Cross and in the early hours of the morning I couldn't face me mum so there used to be a café down Bethnal Green, Lou's café, and we went there this particular morning. Years ago you used to get the scooter boys in there. There was these two fellas sitting in there, Ronnie and Jimmy. She liked Jimmy and I liked Ronnie, so this particular morning we sat there for a while and Ronnie had this old red van and he said I'll take you for a ride until you feel better and he looked after me like my dad looked after me and I started going out with him. He lived down King Edward Road, it was so posh his house, everything in its place, and he had a scrap metal yard down Totley Street, along from the Aberdeen pub. I thought the world of Ronnie. His mum was this manageress of a Turkish factory up in Stoke Newington, and she got me this job machining and I was only there for a half a morning, I couldn't stand it. He had a brother, Kenny, too, and Georgia went out with him for a while. Me and Ronnie was on and off for quite a while then he met someone and went out with them proper.

In 1972 Georgia had Charmaine and we'd take her out in the pram to Victoria Park and we'd argue about who was pushing her, and all the boys used to drive around tooting, we'd have our hot pants on pushing our pram, looking a million dollars. Georgia didn't really want a child but my mum said, 'Don't worry, I'll take care of her', something her own mum had never done, and that's what my mum done, she brought Charmaine up and so did I.

Me and Georgia used to do bar work together and Georgia did the topless dancing, the little things she used to wear you could see through them, so then she decided she may as well strip. She used to go out and buy a plain bra and knickers and buy lace, little pearl buttons, fringes, and she used to sit there for hours making little costumes. She used to dance in the Arabian Arms in Cambridge Heath Road. I used to go to work with her sometimes and when I saw those men gawping at her I'd have a row with them even though that was what they were there for.

There used to be a shop over Mare Street, and she'd let you pay a deposit for a little top. Me and Georgia bought tracksuits from there. I had a purple one and she had a black one and we'd go out in them. We used to dress the same quite a lot. The boys would be driving round and the cars would all be tooting and you wouldn't have to pay in the pubs because you'd be treated all night long. We'd come out with £1.50 between us and we could each have two or three lagers and enough money for chips or a cab home. We used to love the old chips in newspaper, walking home, all the vinegar dropping down your sleeve.

From the mid seventies onwards Christine works in a series of East End pubs. 'The governors were governors then and they'd have about eight of their friends working and the atmosphere was so nice,' she recalls. 'I worked at the Empress of India near Victoria Park on a Saturday night and they'd have eight barmaids and we'd all look the part. Freddie used to DJ and he used to give Georgia a load of records.'

It is at the Empress of India that Christine meets Gavin.*

The night he asked me out a milkman, Steve, asked me out too and I picked Gav. He was a handsome bloke and he'd had so many girlfriends. He had this little book up his place and sometimes I might try to have a little spy in it and he'd score these girls. I think he give me about 5 out of 10 but I kept going over to his place. I didn't want him coming in my home because it was poor. One time coming home late from work though he was there, they'd asked him in, and I went mad. They asked him how much he

* Not his real name.

earned, where he worked. He told me that he'd asked me out when I was about sixteen and I come out of the Green Gate pub but I had long hair, platform shoes on and he was a hippy and he said I told him to eff off.

A flat come up in Lefevre Walk [in Old Ford]. In them days they used to have a thing for engaged couples, you could put your name down, it was like a ballot. Me and Gav was only courting at the time and we went on holiday to Minehead and we heard we'd got picked out and we was going to get a flat but you had to be married to get this flat. Maybe if this flat hadn't come up we wouldn't have got married.

But something in the marriage isn't right. 'I stayed because I didn't want to be on my own,' Christine says. Before too long she finds herself pregnant and gives birth to a son, who she names after his dad. 'I'd take him to the park but I hated it, I couldn't wait to get away. It was all so quick. Your life changed dramatically, then you're having a child, then you're breaking up and you don't know where you are. I was only twenty-four. I used to stay with my mum or round Georgia's most of the time. It wasn't much fun at me mum's but I didn't want to be on my own.' And then catastrophe! When the baby is seven months old his father leaves and Christine is all on her own. 'After that all I done was work while Mum and Georgia looked after my son. I was busy, busy. I couldn't settle in Lefevre Walk. I'd met this girl Marian when we were both pregnant, and we'd meet up and we'd drink.'

And so here's the thing about the sixties. For Christine and Georgia and all the women like them, the freedom and good music, the pill, the promise of a life different from their mothers', meant nothing the moment a baby came along, and they found themselves hard up, unsupported and lonely, stuck in some flat in the sky bereft of the comforts of family and neighbourhood.

'Men went to work and it was their money to spend on drink, their money to spend on having a good time,' says Linda Plenty.

She's working at Randolfi's a few doors from Kelly's pie and mash, another lone mother, like Christine, looking after her four children and barely scraping by.

I got a separation order [from my husband] in seventy-three but he used to keep coming back and there was nothing I could do because his name was on the rent book. I went to the council – one day late at night he got up the drainpipe and smashed the window, the neighbours heard, I told them to call the police, so they came and arrested him and I went back to the council and asked to be moved. They said you'd got to get him to sign the lease over. They thought I was lying that my husband left me. I said, he's not going to do that. And they wouldn't do anything, so what I done, I took [the kids] to the children's department at Bow and I said I can't afford them, I've sold all my bits of gold and I can't pay me rent, so you'll have to take them. And then they found me somewhere all right.

33

Things changed because they had to . . .

Bet Lewis

Sitting at one of the tables in Kelly's on a Saturday afternoon at any time during the seventies, you can be forgiven for thinking that nothing much has changed in the Roman since the war. The eels are as fresh and juicy as they ever were, the pies and mash taste the same, the view from the window of the Needle Gun pub, the school, the public conveniences where Marian Old once worked all the same, the market stalls are run by Harry Da Costa and the Old family, and the stalls are still supplied by Brian Baker. A couple of doors up the road, Randolfi's is still churning vanilla ice cream and lemon sorbet to Esterina's Italian recipes. On the surface, all is as it ever was.

But this comfortable familiarity masks a deeper reality – that of change not merely physical, the transformation of grids of terraces, rubble heaps and the windowless shells of bombed-out houses into tower blocks and labyrinths of low-rise housing, but cultural, some might even say spiritual. The fabric of the East End – its values of solidarity, community, a feeling of shared destiny – is beginning to wear thin. The stains, which were always there, are suddenly more obvious, perhaps because the colour is just starting to fade now too. The seams are looking strained. Patches are appearing, and there are raised grids where someone or something has done some darning, but these will only hold for so long. If the East End were a garment, by the end of the sixties you'd be saving up for a trip down the Roman to look for a replacement.

And while there's no obvious sense of this yet in Kelly's pie and mash shop at 526 Roman Road, the first intimations are, in fact, already there. Since the death of Bill Kingdon, Theresa Kelly's brother, in 1969, his widow Bea has taken over the running of the shop with her daughter Sue. They're also helping at the branch at number 600 Roman Road. The market is almost as busy as it ever was, and there's an undimmed appetite for pies and mash. On Saturdays especially there are always queues, '[but] because they knew they were going to get served quickly people were quite prepared to stand and wait. They didn't seem to mind queuing. I think it was the wartime mentality, they still had it in them,' Sue says. The little girl, who passed her most formative years in a pram at the back of the shop, is now a young woman with ambitions and a keen desire to expand her horizons. 'So I went to college.' But after a couple of years the pies call and she returns to the shop at 526.

'In the seventies it was so, so busy: three people working behind the counter, three continually making pies, two people baking and four people washing up.' And there's yet more to do at the branch at number 600. Even with extra staff, Bea is worked off her feet. Both Bea and Sue feel a need to continue Bill's work. For decades the pie shop had been Bill's life. Now it is his legacy. To keep it going is to pay tribute to his memory. It's why Bea and Sue like to keep the old shop looking more or less unchanged. A few updates are unavoidable: some cracked tiles need replacing, the mirror above the counter is swapped for something more modern, and, eventually, the engineer who'd been keeping the old coke oven in working order retires to Essex, necessitating the purchase of a new electric oven.

Bea and Sue continue to mourn Bill but the shop keeps them occupied, and for Sue the pleasures and pressures of marriage and young children soon take over and she finds herself less able to help out. In the busyness of their days and weeks and months they scarcely notice how much the East End is changing.

There has been a population of Sylhettis and Gujaratis or 'lascars' in London since the seventeenth century, when the East India Company began employing men from the Sylhet and Gujarat as stokers on their ships. Men from the Sylhet, which became part of Bangladesh, began arriving in larger numbers in Britain after the Second World War, mostly making their way to the steel and textile mills of the north and north-west. By the end of the fifties some had drifted down to London, settling for the most part in Whitechapel, Aldgate and around Spitalfields, and working in the rag trade. After a few years of hard graft and thrift they began to bring over their families, who for the most part settled in small privately rented flats in and around Brick Lane. Unlike their menfolk, who had by then been in Britain for years, the newcomers often didn't speak English and found it hard to integrate.

In 1971 the trickle becomes a flow as Bengalis flee the civil war in Bangladesh in favour, predominantly, of London. As Jews move to the outer boroughs and began to assimilate, formerly Jewish bakeries around Brick Lane become curry houses, and in 1976 the synagogue on the corner of Fournier Street and Brick Lane, which had itself been converted from a French Protestant church in 1898, is transformed into the Brick Lane Mosque Jamme Masjid. Back in Bangladesh the new immigrants become known as Londonis. They work in the rag trade and in increasingly popular curry houses catering for the newly fashionable taste of 'Indian' food. According to families, friends and neighbours left behind, the Londonis appear to be living an enchanted existence, though in reality many are living in scrubby rooms and dingy subdivided flats which other East Enders have long since rejected.

The new arrivals precipitate a change in housing policy. Since council house building began in earnest after the end of the First World War, the sons and daughters of existing tenants have been given priority on housing waiting lists, a policy designed to keep extended families together. Now all that has changed. The new criterion for housing waiting lists relies solely on assessing deepest need. In the mid seventies, with immigrants arriving in increasing numbers from Bangladesh for the first time, the new policy means newly arrived families are often housed first. The policy makers, themselves most often middle class and comfortably housed, either fail to think the new rules through or are so hampered by both financial constraints and urgent need that they continue to push the poorest families to the top of the lists (never mind that many are housed in sub-standard accommodation) – what some of those who consider themselves dyed-in-the-wool East Enders see as new immigrants leapfrogging their own children in housing allocation. And even when their families are offered council accommodation, it's often on the outskirts of the city or in one of the newly developing Essex suburbs. Understandable resentment quickly spills over into overt racism. Gangs of skinheads begin to roam the streets of the East End with 'Paki-bashing' in mind. The atmosphere grows dark and ugly. Phil Price, whose ancestors fled the pogroms, remembers seeing Bengali youths 'run[ning] squealing from groups of white youths.' Chris Chistadoulou, another son of immigrants escaping civil war, recalls football games in which all-white teams competed against teams comprised of Bengali, Caribbean and other players on makeshift grounds patrolled by menacing dogs. It sometimes seems that the darkest days of the 1930s, when Moseley's Blackshirts goose-stepped their way across the East End, have returned in another guise. But as the Jews had before them, at the Battle of Cable Streets and elsewhere, Bangladeshis begin to fight back. In 1976 the Anti-racist Committee of Asians in East London is formed to combat racism and what would now be called 'hate crime', and the following year 3,000 people march through Bethnal Green in protest at racist attacks.

The street parties held throughout the East End in 1977 to mark the Queen's Jubilee hark back to a tighter, friendlier time, but as families sit down in the old terraces and turnings to eat pie and mash and jellied eels and fish paste sandwiches and drink sarsaparilla, gangs of skins patrol the thoroughfares staking out Bengali youth. It all comes to a head after the murder, in May 1978, of Altab Ali, a twenty-five-year-old Bengali textile worker, by three teenagers in St Mary's churchyard in Whitechapel. Seven thousand protestors march from Brick Lane to Downing Street to demand action.

Bow and Old Ford are never at the centre either of the violence or of the protests, which go on a mile or two to the west, not least because the Bangladeshi population around the Roman has remained small, but in April 1978 all that changes when a Rock Against Racism concert takes place in Vicky Park featuring, among others, X-Ray Spex and Steel Pulse. Organisers expecting 20,000 participants are quickly overwhelmed by the numbers – a crowd of about 80,000 turn out to hear the Clash play 'White Riot'.

As the decade draws to a close, a BBC camera crew arrives in the Roman to film a documentary about the market. To listen to the stallholders and the customers, you wouldn't sense anything was amiss. The market is packed. There's Harry Da Costa and the Old brothers talking up their business. There's a tidy line outside Kelly's. There are Brian Baker's barrows heaped with cauliflowers. There are Bangladeshi Britons among the stallholders, and British Asians and black Britons among the crowds. There is Joe Bugner* the boxer shouting out to raise funds for charity. But a single shot, no more than a few frames, tells another story. In an interview with Harry Da Costa, the camera closes in on a railway arch behind his stall and there, daubed in white paint, is the insignia of the National Front. Harry makes no mention of it, nor does anyone else, and that, surely, tells its own story. Later, Harry claims he never had much trouble from anti-Semites, 'a few idiots is all', but trouble was out there all the same. Perhaps Ann Simmons puts her

* Born József Kreul in Hungary, himself an immigrant.

finger on it when she says, '[Skins] were always around, always showing their "heavy heads" as they used to call them . . . letting [immigrants] know they were here. And they were wrong. All the time. But what can you say? If you said anything you got beaten up yourself. So you didn't say nothing.'*

And this is what's changed on that day in Vicky Park. The concert sends a message to minority groups they are not alone. And if that does little to change the lived experience of people on the ground, it at least gives them cause for hope. The truth is, the old East End is dying and everyone who lives there and loves it, of whatever background or ethnicity, knows it will take something more than a rock concert to fix what ails it. The factories have gone or are going, the old streets and neighbourhoods have been torn up and replaced by soulless high-rises and warren-like estates, and bombed-out lots sit idle behind screens daubed with swastikas. At Millwall and West Ham, gangs of youths kick the shit out of one another. Down in the docks, which had, as recently as 1968, been part of the largest port system in the world, strike action against closures only serves to hasten the end. First to close are the inner docks at St Katherine's at Wapping, then East and West India at Poplar, and finally the Royals at Canning Town and Silvertown. Everything in the East End at the end of the decade seems to be diminished and turned in on itself.

Rafi Chowdhury† watches all this happen from his sewing bench in a factory off the Roman, making clothes for Marks & Spencer, and from the balcony of his family's council flat in Aldgate. His journey to work every day takes him past the market in the Commercial Road, and he takes note as stalls set up selling okra and bitter gourd, then methi and tamarind and, as the decade goes on and the number of stalls grows, fruit and vegetables and spices his mother had cooked with back in Bangladesh appear, laid out

* Ann Simmons, Mapping the Change.
† Not his real name.

like jewels on the sides of the street all the way from Whitechapel to Stepney. He is young now, but he has ambitions, and in a part of the capital where it often seems that doors are closing, Rafi begins to see the possibility of throwing off his dreary, trudging existence at the sewing bench and opening a door to a new life for himself and his family.

34

The whole area had a sad look about it and people began to think about moving away out to Essex.

Margaret Bradley

By the late seventies the London docks have been in decline for a decade, doomed not only by containerisation but also by the loss of manufacturing and distribution around the capital. In the ten years leading up to the first closure, of the East India Dock in 1967, Greater London had lost half a million jobs in manufacturing and distribution, many in the East End. One by one throughout the seventies, the closed docks to the east of Tower Bridge shut down to shipping. In 1981, the last ship leaves the largest and newest of the enclosed docks, the King George V in Silvertown, bringing to an end over a thousand years of marine trade in the upper Thames. By the early eighties, 60 per cent of the land and enclosed water in what would become the docks urban development area, later 'Docklands', is standing vacant, and, for the most part, derelict.

The closures are devastating to the economy of the East End, the speed and scale of job losses completely unprecedented. Between 1978 and 1983, 12,000 dock-related jobs in the East End disappears. Just as they had during wartime, those who could got out. In the decade between 1971 and 1981 the population of the area around the London docks declines by nearly 20 per cent.

Governments of all stripes are shockingly slow to respond to the crisis. It's not until the early eighties that the London Docklands Development Corporation begins drawing up plans for regenerating the area. The new 'Docklands' which begins to rise from the ashes of the old docks is unrecognisable to those who live around it. From their flat on the fourteenth floor, Tel and Rita watch as most of the old warehouses, refrigerated units, railway yards and dockside factories are bulldozed and a forest of high-rise office buildings, 'luxury waterside apartments' and skyscrapers begins to hug the sky. In this shiny new world the draw is no longer the push and pull of trade. In 'Docklands' the magnet is money.

It takes a while for the impact of all this change to be felt in the Roman. The market has always been where East Enders went for knockdowns and bargains and the kind of prices not even the new supermarkets could match. Those who are feeling the pinch gravitate to the market so, on the surface at least, the Roman appears to be booming, but from the early eighties onwards a lot of the talk on market day is about who is getting out and how. For those with enough savings to buy their council homes under Margaret Thatcher's Right to Buy scheme, an escape route presents itself. Thousands buy their properties then promptly flip them, sometimes through dodgy or third-party arrangements, and use the profit to propel themselves out and away, to Essex, Kent or the Costas. Some of these flats find their way into private ownership, but many more are bought in bulk by landlords and then rented to tenants who might well have qualified for council housing if only the supply of council housing were not in the process of being sold off. Now these same neighbourhoods which have weathered overcrowding, disease and poverty – not to mention the might of the Luftwaffe – are falling apart through a policy which, however well-intentioned, has a divisive effect. Most people remain because the East End is where they belong, even though to stay often requires sacrifice, but those who want to leave and haven't the money to buy their properties are left with the sense that they've been written off, washed up on what seems increasingly to be a forgotten corner of the capital. Instead of creating neighbourhoods of homeowners with stakes in their community, Right to Buy has the opposite effect in the East End, cutting a swathe through communities whose values have for generations been measured not by homeownership but by solidarity, neighbourliness and family loyalty.

The scale of construction is dizzying. For a while the development does create some jobs for locals, but everyone is acutely aware that these will be temporary. Like thousands of others who witness the glittering towers going up and are daily inconvenienced by the noise and chaos, Tel and Rita sense, rightly, that nothing that is happening on the Isle of Dogs will be likely to play out positively in their own lives. At least not in the long term. To Rita, bringing up the kids and working evenings in the teabag factory, and Tel working all day painting and decorating for the council and taking over the childcare in the evenings, the new Docklands is more mirage than anything real. *They* will never live in one of the new luxury waterside apartments, they won't shop in the pricey new boutiques. The new financial services jobs are ones for which they will never be qualified.

With councils strapped for cash and all this focus on private development, Tel's job as a council employee is soon in jeopardy, and by the mid eighties he is facing redundancy. But Tel is well known and liked around the Roman and it isn't long before 'I bumped into a friend who said Freddie Whistler might have something, so I rang Cyril and he said come up and meet me outside the Ritz.'

Cyril was working for Hare and Humphries, all specialist decorating then. So up I went into the West End and there was Cyril outside the Ritz and he said, 'Come with me', and he took me round to Spencer House.* We worked there for three years in the state rooms at Spencer House and Buck Palace, Clarence House, the Royal Launch. I did all the painting and gilding except for in Buck House because of that criminal record I got when I was a Ted. We done the Reform Club, me and Cyril, and the guvnor come up and says, 'Nice job boys', but when he come to take all the photos for the magazine we was sent out. When I was in Lady Di's [rooms at Spencer House] I painted a door sixteen times. I even did Lady Di's toilet. The foreman used to come up with an Arc light [to inspect the finish]. I was on one set of doors in the library at Spencer House for 15 weeks. It got so I went and bought a plastic ball and chain and fixed it to me leg. They used to call me Radar because I had to have eyes in the back of me head.

It's a good job, decently paid, and Tel is proud to be working on such magnificent buildings. This is quality work, no expense spared, for people who can pay for sixteen coats of paint on a door and barely notice the dent in their pockets. Even if the clients *are* too toffee-nosed to acknowledge you or include you in the magazine spread of the finished work, it beats emulsioning council flats for a living.

But then disaster hits. 'I was down a very famous bank in Fleet Street and I was out in the hallway on my own and Cyril said afterwards you out there on your own is wrong.' Cyril hears the crash from the room next door and rushes out to see Tel lying on the floor with the steps on top of him. 'Cyril picked the steps off me, which was wrong and all.' At first it seems Tel hasn't been badly hurt. He's crawling around on the floor and shouting blue murder, but it rapidly becomes apparent to Cyril that he's only crawling about because he's unable to stand. Soon after that, he blacks out,

---

* Built between 1756 and 1766, Spencer House, St James's Place, is considered to be the finest surviving eighteenth-century mansion in London. It now serves predominantly as offices.

and Cyril does what anyone would have done – he goes to the nearest phone and dials 999.

'I was sedated for about a week at the Royal London Hopsital in Whitechapel. I had a fractured skull, broke me arm,' Tel recalls. But the real impact is from the head injury. No one is able to say if Tel will make a full recovery. '[The accident] wiped my brain. Rita would say, "Fancy a ride to Stratford?" and we'd get on the 276 and I couldn't handle it, having to remember so many things. I was off work for a year.' The council moves the family out of the fourteenth-floor flat into more suitable low-rise accommodation. All the same, the financial and emotional strain on everyone is immense. 'The firm wanted to loan me some money but we wouldn't take it,' Tel says now.

In many ways, the story seems like a metaphor for the eighties. Tel, sharp as a tack, amiable, hard-working, spending his days gilding the homes of those already living gilded lives. Tel, fifteen weeks painting a single door to a glass finish, then hustled away so as not to spoil a picture of his work in a magazine. Tel falling from someone else's ivory tower. But one of the many very remarkable things about Tel and Rita is that neither of them is bitter. They're not even angry.

Christine is, though. Christine is quietly very angry. And with reason. As the skyscrapers on the Isle of Dogs go up, Christine's life comes tumbling down. Through the eighties she is working in the pubs and clubs and at odd jobs here and there, raising her boy, looking after her mother after her father died and spending what little spare time and money she has down the Roman or with her sister Georgia and their kids in Vicky Park. It is a life, though, for reasons Christine can't pin down, that's not quite enough. Not for Christine and not for Georgia. 'I thought I was a happy-go-lucky person but there is a photo of me when I was about thirty and I look so sad. I thought I was just down in the dumps but there was something gone in me.' With her marriage over, her mother increasingly withdrawn and her half-siblings scattered, Christine looks to Georgia for solace and what remains of fun.

Even now, so many decades later, Christine can hardly bear to speak about the day her sister died, except to say it was in a traffic accident and Georgia was a passenger. In a way, how it happened matters less than the fact that that it did. Georgia was thirty-six. 'Something went in me and never come back.'

After Georgia's death, Christine turns to her half-brother, Robert. They've always been close, not Christine and Georgia close, but loving and companionable. 'When I was about five or six he took me to Southend with Georgia and I remember singing "It's Been a Hard Day's Night" and he bought us both a little silver necklace each.' It took a while longer for the penny to drop. 'I didn't really know about being gay, but when I first found out about my brother I remember thinking I don't want my friends to find out at school.'

A strange double standard about gay people has long existed in the East End. While the music halls of the Victorian and Edwardian periods were dominated by gay men, drag acts were routine in the pubs during the fifties and sixties, the activities of sailors in the parks and back alleys and urinals of the East End were an open secret, Nancy-boys paraded the streets dressed as women and it was commonplace for young men, whether gay or otherwise, to raise a bit of extra cash by 'rorting' either with incoming mariners or with men coming in to the East End from wealthier parts of the capital. There were rules unspoken but clear: so long as homo-sexuality was only publicly acknowledged under the guise of 'permanent bachelorhood' and gay men made no attempt to seduce 'straights', homosexuality was generally tolerated in the East End long before it was in most other parts of the capital. The Port of London Authority police in particular grew used to turning a blind eye.

Despite this, in the mid eighties Robert felt the need to escape, and went to live in what was then Britain's 'gay capital', Brighton. His new-found happiness is infectious. As Christine remembers it now, 'He used to come up to London and he'd always come to me first and say, "Get the kettle on, I'll have a bit of bread and jam", and you'd feel lifted by his presence.'

Then HIV/AIDS happened and things changed. 'My mum would say, "Don't sit on the toilet seat, I won't eat no food they've handled", and it was so sad because I'm sure my brother loved his mum.' And Beatrice had already lost so many of her children, to lose another to prejudice seemed unnecessarily cruel. Yet, it's hard to judge Beatrice, who had, during her lifetime, received so little kindness herself.

Christine can't recall quite when her brother began to look ill. No one really spoke about it. She does, however, remember precisely when he died, because it was almost exactly sixteen months after Georgia. 'He loved opera and classical music and the day of his funeral they played his favourite and one of his ex partners, Ivan, you should have heard his cry.' Then they put on "The Sun has Got His Hat On" and everyone was laughing.'

Christine did a lot of crying then, for long-departed George, her father, and for Bea, her mother, so locked inside herself as to be almost unreachable. She cried for her half-sister, Ann, who she'd never met and who was now living somewhere in Australia, and for the death of her sister Shirley, and for the all-too-short lives of Sheila and Robert and Georgia. Christine cried for her marriage and for her sense that life had somehow dimmed. She cried for the good times, memories of heading up West with Georgia, in the fancy car of some admirer, the two of them dressed to the nines and off their heads, and for the fact that even then, in the midst of all the revelry, she sees now, there was a certain kind of desperate melancholy, a sadness which none of the dark glamour of the new architectural developments with their promises of renewal would ever be able to shift.

As the Isle of Dogs continued to fill with bright new buildings, a slow but steady decline set in on the Roman. For a long time it seemed that the old driftway had been forgotten by the planners. As it had centuries before, the district began to feel cut off and remote. The new Docklands Light Railway skirted along to the south, with a station at Bow Road, but it did not serve the Roman directly. The nearest Tube station, at Mile End, remained a good fifteen-minute walk away, and a series of new low-rise housing developments seemed to make no impact on the falling numbers using the market. Now that the branch railway at Coborn Road had closed, the only really local transport remained the number 8 bus.

It's this bus that Christine takes to her cleaning job. In 1979 Bryant & May's, once the largest factory in London, where match-women had staged the first all-women's strike and where six-year-old Martha Robertson and the young Ann Simmons, Bet Lewis and Rita Willetts had all toiled, ceased manufacturing matches. For a long time the site sat abandoned and in a state of disrepair, but in 1988 the developer Kentish Homes began an ambitious redevelopment of the site into one of London's first 'gated communities'. The old factory buildings were converted into 733 'apartments', a gym, bar and restaurant were built, and the grounds landscaped and separated from the surrounding houses by fencing and a large gate. 'Parisians have the Latin Quarter, New Yorkers have Greenwich Village. Now, in East London, a stone's throw from the City, there's a New Quarter,' proclaimed the sales brochure.* It's here in the newly named 'Bow Quarter' that Christine lands a cleaning job. 'It was dead quiet. I hated the long corridors. To me the place felt haunted.'

This is what the whole district feels like in the eighties, a place where the ghosts of past and present are fighting for survival, in a world in which, as yet, there is no clear future.

* Patrick Wright, *A Journey Through Ruins, The Last Days of London* (Oxford University Press, 2009), Chapter 16.

35

They don't want anything changed . . . they want everything the same.

Leanne Black

It's a Saturday morning in the spring of 2017. In the Roman, Rafi Chowdhury is setting up his stall selling cut-price clothes. Dresses £10, jackets £15. He travels all round the markets these days, not just in the capital but on the periphery. He knows all the wholesalers in Aldgate and Whitechapel. Like Rafi himself, they are mostly of Bangladeshi origin. The hours are long and the margins are tight, and he has to spend a lot of time travelling and more still standing out in the cold and wet, but it's a decent living. As he does every Saturday morning, he's picked up a takeaway coffee in the café on the corner, which is owned by Turks. The prices there are more reasonable than in the art cafés selling sourdough bread and smashed avocado. While he waits for customers Rafi makes conversation with one of a number of Bangladeshi shop owners in the Roman now. This one sells vegetables and fruit. In the last few years the selection has expanded four- or fivefold. If Rafi's mother were still alive she'd be in heaven. There's almost nothing you can't get now. It's odd, Rafi thinks, because if you ask some of the elderly white people, or even the elderly black people in the Roman where they do their shopping, they'll tell you that there aren't any greengrocers in the Roman these days. They'll say you used to be able to get absolutely anything in the Roman, but now

236

you have to go elsewhere if you want decent fruit and veg. In Rafi's experience, the opposite is true.

What Rafi and his elders can agree on is that the new Saturday market in the car park on the corner of St Stephen's Road and the Roman doesn't seem to have much to offer any of them. A mobile food van is setting out the sign advertising its £6.50 toasted cheese sandwiches. There is a good smell of melted butter in the air. The sandwiches may be wonderful, but who's got £6.50? Beside the van a group of young women are laying out market trolleys selling crafts and artisan condiments. A local historian is standing under a London plane tree not far from Phil Price's minicab offices, rehearsing the guided history tour he will be leading later in the day. It's already lively, packed to the gunnels with young people, hipsters mostly, a few young families, mostly white, the area's new middle class. There's an art project going on with a local college, something to do with reminiscence. Someone's set up an old black cab and a few of the old-timers are protesting about how many of their beloved boozers have been converted into luxury apartments, but Rafi doesn't use cabs or drink so the project passes him by. If he's honest, this part of the market doesn't really speak to him at all. He's pleased to see it so busy, but he doesn't reckon he'll be splashing out £6.50 on a toastie or £5 on a jar of the kind of green tomato chutney his wife whips up for almost nothing.

A few steps away from the new market, past Kelly's Pie and Mash shop, Brian Baker is at work in his yard, customising a stall for a regular customer. Business isn't what it was. These days so many of the sellers come from outside London and travel from market to market, and they don't want the old-fashioned barrows, trolleys or even the frames Brian has for rent. A few old-timers remain, the diehards, mostly from the Bangladeshi community, among them Rafi. For one or two of his most loyal customers, Brian has created bespoke stalls with built-in shelves and tiers. It keeps him busy. Since his wife died he prefers to spend his days in the yard rather than at home. There's always some metal tyre to refit, some wheel spoke to repair. The creation of the new market up in the car park has brought a welcome uplift in business. The stallholders are using some of the traditional old trolleys made by his grandfather, say they add a special nostalgic atmosphere to that part of the market. Brian's son is in the business too, though who knows how much longer either of them will be able to carry on. 'It's all wossname,' Brian says. He's not wrong.

It remains to be seen whether any of the shops will benefit from the new Saturday market. Kelly's pie and mash, George's Plaice the wet fish shop, Percy Ingle's bakery, Abbott's carpets and Dennington's the florists are all still getting by. Back in 2012 there was a great deal of talk about regeneration but nothing quite caught and the moment the Olympics was over, business went back to how it had been before, only with tighter parking restrictions and higher rents. A couple of years later a retail consultant called Mary Portas turned up with a camera crew, took one of the shopkeepers to Paris to see how it was done there, and encouraged the others to think in terms of retail 'stories'. On the whole, retailers thought better parking might be have been more useful.

After the buzz of the Olympics died down, a few independent retailers decided it was time to take retirement. Among the closures was W. F. Arber, Printers. It was a sad day for the Roman when Arber's closed in 2014, after 117 years. Gary Arber was eighty by then, and tired. The new parking restrictions had made it almost impossible for his customers – many of them artists from the newly opened studios on Fish Island – to pick up and drop off their work. Since selling up, he and Ruby have stayed close to home in Romford, where Gary spends his days pottering in his shed, constructing ever more elaborate feeders for the garden birds. The back garden of the same house where once he watched a Nazi plane as a boy is full of half-finished projects, which keep Gary perennially busy. He says he doesn't miss the old days. He's not given to nostalgia.

The creative community in particular has been sorry to see Gary go. He has become something of a legend among them. They like what he represents: the value of craft, authenticity, an independence of spirit. The Island is now home to the largest concentration of visual artists in Europe, though that's likely to change. Property developers stalk the ramshackle yards and graffiti-covered streets, looking for old buildings they can turn into million-pound industrial chic lofts. Bow and Old Ford is currently caught in a kind of hipster creep pincer movement: on the eastern side of the Bow flyover are the artists' studios, and beside them, a population of creatives and counterculturals eking out a living on houseboats and barges in the canal; on the western side, hipsters and young creatives have begun spreading in from Shoreditch and Bethnal Green on the hunt for affordable accommodation. Mother Kelly's under the arches at 251 Paradise Row, near where Samuel and Matilda Kelly opened their first eel, pie and mash shop a hundred years ago, is now an 'industrial' bar. Young creatives queue outside Pellici's, hoping to absorb a little of the café's old gangster vibe. Many of the old-time boozers where Christine pumped beer while Georgia danced, have transformed into gastropubs or else been converted into luxury apartments. A new kind of retailer has moved in, selling posh coffee, single estate olive oil, whimsical bunting and craft beer.

The old East End survives in patches. Back in the Roman, a hop, skip and a jump from the new market, the Randolfi brothers, Gino, Raymond and Michael, are cutting ham and salad rolls and stocking the display with pieces of millionaire's shortbread. 'Business is hard,' says Michael. For now the trio survive on the loyalty of regulars, among whom are Ted and Bet Lewis, who will probably drop by for a sandwich later. Linda Plenty might come in for a mug of tea. Terri will likely say hello on her way to work at the branch of Kelly's in Bethnal Green. Ann Simmons may bring her daughter. There will be a bit of to and fro. Gino will ask after relatives. Michael might start up some banter about a song on the radio. There will be teasing and enquiries after relatives. Raymond, the straight man in the Randolfi comedy trio, will set down the sandwiches with a pleasant 'Hope you enjoy that.'

The café will last the brothers out to retirement. There won't be anyone to take over. None of the Randolfis has children. Their mother Esterina died in 2016 and her loss has hit them all hard, though if asked anything requiring an emotional response, they will tend to pull up the drawbridge and send arrows flying at the questioner, while Gino readies himself with barrels of boiling oil. The three brothers are miraculous in many ways. Someone should write a book or a play or a film about them.

By the time the new market in the Roman gets going properly, the old market will have been geared up and selling for a few hours already. Customers still arrive from all over London and the Kent and Essex suburbs looking for bargains, but the new Westfield shopping centre just a mile or so away in Stratford has taken much of the younger or more moneyed custom. The shops on either side of the market stalls now mostly cater to elderly cockneys, not so elderly British Asians, black Britons and young hipsters, which leads to an interesting mix: there's Percy Ingles bakers, selling eclairs and bread puddings; a sweet shop displaying great jars of loose pear drops; a self-styled *enoteca* offering Italian charcuterie; several Bengali greengrocers hawking okra, amaranth and snake gourds; and art cafés offering artisan coffee and smashed avocado. The Albert pub on the corner is already busy. It is popular in particular with London Irish. A couple of doors down, opposite Randolfi's, the Needle Gun pub is now the City View Hotel, catering mostly to construction workers brought in to work first on the Olympic Park and Westfield shopping centre and now on a variety of regeneration projects. Beside the hotel, the Bow mosque and Muslim centre is scaffolded up in preparation for expansion work. Next to that is the Roman Road School, though, this being Saturday, it is locked.

At Kelly's at number 526, Bill and Bea Kingdon's daughter Sue and her son Neil are in the kitchen at the back, making pastry and stewing eels. Sue has been working here on and off for more than half a century. Like his mother, Neil grew up on pies and mash, but he's only recently started co-managing the shop with his mother. After four decades as manageress, Meg 'Pie Name' Bradley has recently retired and with her husband moved to the Med, a dream awakened on that trip to Italy with Aunty Chris half a century ago. Leanne Black is now at the counter filling salt and pepper pots. Like Meg before her, Leanne is a woman with a velvety smile and warm cheeks and the kind of voice people pay to hear. 'We're one of the only shops left where people can bump into their friends,' she says. That includes Leanne herself. 'There are faces you see all the time, and when you don't see them you worry. You do get attached.' Leanne's job is part server, part performer, part social worker and part counsellor. 'Seventy per cent is your work, thirty per cent is a bit of a show. You have to push yourself a bit. I'm a bit of an agony aunt, really.'

And like Meg, Leanne has had to oversee one or two changes. Neil, a graduate with a degree in environmental science from Leeds University, swept into the shop a year or two ago with quite a few new ideas. Out went the saveloys and fruit pies and in came the chicken and leek and vegetarian pies and the fruit crumbles. Leanne worried that it would all be too much. So did a few of the old customers, but Leanne did her best to calm a few frayed nerves. 'I'm partly there to reassure people,' she says. The regulars need to know that nothing will change. 'A lot of people even feel put out if "their" table is occupied. There can be loads of other tables empty but if "their" table is taken there are lots of looks and raised eyebrows, as if to say, "Who do *they* think they are?"'

Among the stalwarts these days is Les, who lives in the care home at the top of the road and comes in every afternoon at 2.30 for a pie. Les is a collector of badges. 'His jackets are always covered in badges, Costa Coffee, whatever, he's not proud. At the moment Les is an Arsenal supporter, but it's really whatever badge he can get hold of,' Leanne says.

Joan comes in four days a week for a one-two, one pie and half a portion of mash with liquor and a cup of tea. She likes me to take it over with her condiments. She's always giving me scratch cards for the car park even though I don't drive. I say to her, 'Don't waste them on me' but she insists, so I've now got about twenty parking scratch cards. Then there's Michael, but I use the term 'customer' loosely because he comes in and stands at the counter and doesn't buy anything. In all the time I've been here he's only ever bought, like, one pie, and he wanted it burnt, with half a pot of liquor. Every Saturday morning Elaine comes in. I think she has some learning disability. Only I really know what she's saying. You take over her pie and mash and cut it up and take the salt and vinegar to her. She gets upset if I'm not there.

Tel remains a regular. Sometimes he'll go with Rita or he'll bring back a takeaway. When their son Stephen visits from Oxford, where he works in IT, the first thing he always wants to do is to go down to Kelly's for pie and mash.

Tourists are making their way to Kelly's in increasing numbers. 'They come in for one pie or sometimes for one and one,' Leanne says. They often leave bemused. Eels, pie and mash is really something you have to grow up with. And even then . . . The old-timers like to claim the pies are not the same as they used to be. Marian Old, Aunty Ginger, says the pastry's harder these days, though it's more likely to be that her dental plate doesn't fit quite so well. A couple of years ago, at the age of ninety-one, she moved into a nursing home in Bethnal Green. 'The world I lived in, I can't grumble. I could die any day, I'm not worried, so long as I go peacefully.' At ninety-three and 'still rabbiting', she's teaching herself to read. There's a book in her bedside cabinet, a biography of Cilla Black. She'd like to be able to make her way through that before she leaves this world. Always loved Cilla, did Aunty Ginger. Before she went into the home she'd be in Kelly's most days. These days a carer will go out and fetch her back a pot of eels and mash every so often. 'I miss my eels,' she says, 'But don't worry, I'm not lonely.' Every day she watches the pigeons that gather on the roof beside her room and asks herself, 'Who put their hearts in there? I look at the spider on the curtains and I think, "Who put your heart in there?" Our Lord is who.'

For some, eating pie and mash is not unlike communing with God, or, at least, with some higher power. Customers come from all over the world for a taste of a past that still lives vividly inside them, or that they may hardly recall or only know from older relatives but to which they nevertheless feel viscerally connected. Julie Wassmer, who grew up in Lefevre Road in Old Ford, has a theory about this. 'In the same way that an immune system develops according to the environment to which it's exposed, so does a love of pie and mash,' she says. 'Fortunately, I found a man, who, though of Armenian heritage, loved it at first taste: liquor, pepper, chilli vinegar, spoon and fork – so I married him.'

There are only a handful of pie, mash and eel shops left in London now, but new shops do open up to cater to the cockney diaspora: Franks, on Canvey Island, Coles in Worksop, Manze's in Braintree, T. & J. Kelly's at Debden. By the time this book is published there will be another in Whitstable. Members of pie and mash clubs travel round the country sampling their favourite meal and leaving long and considered reviews of the pie crust on social media.

In 2017 Kelly's Noted Eel and Pie Shop at 526 Roman Road closed, though only for restorations. Neil and Sue plan to strip away the eighties tiles and use the original fittings from the shop at 600 Roman Road to restore number 526 to something like its former glory. There will be marble table tops and chrome fittings and milk glass lamps. The beautiful glass screen etched with eels swimming in a kelp forest will be returned to take pride of place. The photographs of George and Theresa Kelly, Bob and Bea Kingdon, of Meg Bradley and her Aunty Chris, and George

Burdett will be rehung. It's a great deal of work, and no small investment. The shop will be closed for months and there will doubtless be debts to be repaid when it opens once more. Neil could almost certainly make a better living by following his training in environmental science, but he'd rather follow his heart and try and make a go of it here, on the Roman in Bow, at Kelly's, because if there's one thing Neil knows, feels in his blood, in his genes, his DNA, it is that everything needs to change so everything can stay the same.

Acknowledgements

This book would not have been possible without the support of those who generously gave of their time and stories. I am particularly grateful to Bill and Iris Allen, Gary and Ruby Arber, Pauline Ausling, Brian Baker, George Beech, Leanne Black, Margaret Bradley, Alfie and Carol Burns, Chris Christadoulou, Terri Cook, Harry and Joel Da Costa, Tom Disson, Ray Gipson, Kim Green, David Hoffman, Bet and Ted Lewis and the Lewis family, Peter Liversidge, Bonnie McLaughlin, Ron Moss, Marian Old, Linda Plenty, Phil Price, Gino, Edmund and Michael Randolfi, Ann Simmons, Sue and Neil Vening, Terry and Rita Willets and Christine Yeend.

Excerpts from Mapping the Change used with kind permission of Tower Hamlets Local History Archives. I thank the following for their contributions: Elsie Hobart, Alfred Pater, Rose Rawlings, Hazel White, Brenda Wood.

To avoid too much confusion I have tried to be consistent with names. This occasionally means using a woman's married name before she was actually married or, conversely, referring to her by her maiden name after her marriage. Apologies if this causes any offence.

One or two of my interviewees asked not to be named. You know who you are. Thank you. For those who were kind enough to talk to me but whose stories, for reasons of space, I could not use, I apologise. I am very grateful to you, and your contributions helped to shape the whole.

For permission to quote from copyright material, I am grateful to the following: Helen Pankhurst, for kind permission to quote from Sylvia Pankhurst, *The Suffragette Movement: An Intimate Account of Persons and Ideals* (Longmans, Green & Co., 1931). C.S. Lewis Company Ltd for kind permission to quote from *The Last Battle* by C.S. Lewis © C.S. Lewis Pte Ltd 1956.

Every reasonable effort has been made to trace copyright holders, but if there are any errors or omissions, John Murray Press will be pleased to insert the appropriate acknowledgement in any subsequent printings or editions.

This book is based upon recollections. Wherever possible I have sought to confirm facts and dates using other sources. I hope I have kept inaccuracies and factual errors to a minimum though I am wholly responsible for any that remain.

For help with contacts and research, I am grateful to The Bow Belles, The Bow Geezers, Malcolm Barr-Hamilton and the staff at the Tower Hamlets Local History Library and Archives, Katie Dove at Age Concern, Carolyn Clark, Christine Hevey at Circle Housing, Torange Khonsari and the Public Works Group, Liza McCarthy and the staff of the Bow Ideas Store, Carlotta Novella, Sheila Rawlins, Lucy Schofield and Nadia Valman.

Thank you to Nick Davies at John Murray Press and to Kate Hewson at Two Roads who cooked up the idea to write about a pie and mash shop in the East End and thought I might be a good person to do it, and to Caroline Westmore, Hilary Hammond and the team at John Murray who have steered the book towards publication. Thanks, as ever, to Peter Robinson and Matthew Marland at Rogers, Coleridge & White for support, hand-holding and pictures of monkeys.

Simon Booker saw me through life while I was writing this book and forced himself to sample jellied eels at my request. There can be no greater love.